WHO WILL BE SAVED?

·WHO· WILL BE SAVED?

DEFENDING THE
BIBLICAL UNDERSTANDING OF
GOD, SALVATION, & EVANGELISM

PAUL R. HOUSE & GREGORY A. THORNBURY

EDITORS

CROSSWAY BOOKS • WHEATON, ILLINOIS
A DIVISION OF GOOD NEWS PUBLISHERS

Cover design: David LaPlaca

First printing, 2000

Printed in the United States of America

ISBN 1-58134-143-1

Library of Congress Cataloging-in-Publication Data

Who will be saved? : defending the biblical understanding of God, salvation, and evangelism / Paul House and Greg Thornbury, editors.
    p.   cm.
Includes bibliographical references.
ISBN 1-58134-143-1 (tpb. : alk. paper)
    1. God. 2. Salvation. 3. Evangelistic work. I. House, Paul R., 1958- II. Thornbury, Greg, 1970-
BT102.W495 2000
234—dc21   99-047920
                                       CIP

15	14	13	12	11	10	09	08	07	06	05	04	03	02	01	00
15	14	13	12	11	10	9	8	7	6	5	4	3	2	1	

To
Carl F. H. Henry
(1 Corinthians 4:15)

CONTENTS

The Contributors   9
Preface *Paul R. House and Gregory A. Thornbury*   11

PART ONE: WHO SAVES?

Introduction *Paul R. House*   15
1 The Living God of the Bible *Carl F. H. Henry*   19
2 The Eclipse of God at Century's End: 43
  Evangelicals Attempt Theology Without Theism
  R. Albert Mohler, Jr.
3 The Never-Changing Christ for an Ever-Changing   59
  Culture *Daniel L. Akin*

PART TWO: WHO WILL BE SAVED?

Introduction *Paul R. House*   77
4 Are All Doomed to Be Saved? The Rise of Modern   83
  Universalism *Timothy K. Beougher*
5 "Misgivings" and "Openness": A Dialogue on   111
  Inclusivism Between R. Douglas Geivett and
  Clark Pinnock
6 Buddha, Shiva, and Muhammad: Theistic Faith in   129
  Other Religions? *Winfried Corduan*
7 Forum Discussion on Inclusivism *Paul R. House,*   145
  Timothy George, Carl F. H. Henry, D. A. Carson,
  Scott Hafemann, C. Ben Mitchell

PART THREE: HOW SHALL THE LOST HEAR THE GOSPEL?

Introduction *Paul R. House*   163
8 The Gospel Truth: A Sermon on Ephesians 2:1-10   167
  Timothy A. McCoy
9 No Other Gospel *George Martin*   179
10 The Great Commission to Reach a New Generation   193
   Thom Rainer
11 "The Proper Subject of Theology": Giving Voice to   209
   the Doctrine of Salvation in a New Century
   Gregory A. Thornbury
Afterword: The Need for Vigilance and Vision *Paul R. House*   225
Scripture Index   231
Name Index   237

THE CONTRIBUTORS

Daniel L. Akin, Dean of the School of Theology, The Southern Baptist Theological Seminary, Louisville, Kentucky.

Timothy Beougher, Billy Graham Associate Professor of Evangelism and Church Growth, The Southern Baptist Theological Seminary, Louisville, Kentucky.

D. A. Carson, Research Professor of New Testament, Trinity Evangelical Divinity School, Deerfield, Illinois.

Winfried Corduan, Professor of Philosophy of Religion, Taylor University, Upland, Indiana.

R. Douglas Geivett, Associate Professor of Philosophy, Talbot School of Theology, Biola University, La Mirada, California.

Timothy George, Dean of Beeson Divinity School, Samford University, Birmingham, Alabama.

Scott Hafemann, Hawthorne Professor of New Testament Greek, Wheaton College, Wheaton, Illinois.

Carl F. H. Henry, author and theologian. Founding editor of *Christianity Today*. Senior Research Professor, The Southern Baptist Theological Seminary, Louisville, Kentucky.

Paul R. House, Professor of Old Testament, Trinity Episcopal School for Ministry, Ambridge, Pennsylvania.

George Martin, Associate Professor of Missions, The Southern Baptist Theological Seminary, Louisville, Kentucky.

Timothy A. McCoy, Pastor, Ingleside Baptist Church, Macon, Georgia.

C. Ben Mitchell, Assistant Professor of Bioethics and Contemporary Culture, Trinity Evangelical Divinity School, Deerfield, Illinois.

R. Albert Mohler, Jr., President, Professor of Christian Theology, The Southern Baptist Theological Seminary, Louisville, Kentucky.

Clark Pinnock, Professor of Theology, McMaster Divinity College, Ontario, Canada.

Thom Rainer, Dean of The Billy Graham School for Evangelism, Missions and Church Growth, The Southern Baptist Theological Seminary, Louisville, Kentucky.

Gregory A. Thornbury, Instructor of Christian Studies, Union University, Jackson, Tennessee.

PREFACE

PAUL R. HOUSE AND
GREGORY A. THORNBURY

Every generation of Christians must face challenges to the faith once delivered to the saints. Most times these threats come from without. Those who do not believe in Christ or the accuracy of the Scriptures have always opposed what Christianity confesses and teaches. Other times the threat comes from within as those who profess to know Christ advocate ideas and doctrines that are not in keeping with the Scriptures or the church's historic creeds and confessions of faith. Still other times orthodox Christianity faces opposition from both within and without its ranks. Though we do not want to overstate the difficulties of our times or to be alarmists, today's church faces doctrinal challenges from a variety of places on a variety of issues. No doubt the most critical challenge faced today is opposition to the traditional, biblical view of God and the connection between God's character and the doctrine of salvation. This book seeks to address these challenges by examining the biblical definition of God, salvation, and the Gospel and its propagation.

All the articles in this volume except for Gregory A. Thornbury's were first published in *The Southern Baptist Journal of Theology*, the faculty journal of The Southern Baptist Theological Seminary in Louisville, Kentucky. That journal was founded to advance orthodox theological thinking in a pluralistic age. We were honored to have several excellent evangelical authors help us in the first two years of publication, the time period from which these essays are drawn. These particular pieces were chosen for inclusion in this volume because together they present a unified, theologically sound view of God and salvation.

Several persons deserve special thanks for their help in this project. Heather D. Oldfield, associate editor of *The Southern Baptist*

Journal of Theology, edited and proofread many of the articles in their original form. Christi Sanders-Huskison, Kyle D. McClellan, and Richard A. Bailey, assistant editors of *The Southern Baptist Journal of Theology*, also worked on the articles in earlier stages. These persons made Paul House's job as the journal's first editor enjoyable and interesting. It was great to share the common cause of launching a new publication. Marvin Padgett and the Crossway Books staff offered invaluable editorial guidance for this book, while Molly House and Kimberly Thornbury gave familial support. We are also grateful to the authors of these articles for their commitment to sound scholarship and their reverence to the Lord.

For these and other kindnesses we are extremely grateful.

Paul R. House
Trinity Episcopal School for Ministry
Ambridge, Pennsylvania

Gregory A. Thornbury
Union University
Jackson, Tennessee

PART ONE

WHO SAVES?

INTRODUCTION

PAUL R. HOUSE

American Christianity is currently engaged in a crucial debate over the doctrine of God. This discussion includes and affects academicians, pastors, and laypersons. Virtually every denomination in the United States has been or will be affected by this struggle, and no group that ignores this theological discussion will likely survive with its ecclesiastical integrity and doctrinal purity unscathed. Nothing less than the biblical, orthodox doctrines of God and of salvation are at stake.

CHALLENGES TO THE
TRADITIONAL DEFINITION OF GOD

For centuries Christians have agreed that God is sovereign, omnipotent, omniscient, omnipresent, and good. They have believed that his power and his kindness mesh perfectly. Christians have thought that his omniscience includes specific knowledge of contingent future events and that this knowledge does not eliminate human freedom or responsibility. They have agreed that God does not change because God is inherently perfect and therefore not in need of alteration, evolution, or improvement. Arminians, Calvinists, and Wesleyans have disagreed over the implications of these convictions, of course; yet they have assumed that members of other faith traditions shared their beliefs about God's nature.

To be sure, scholars who propounded scriptural definitions of God addressed contrary theological views in the past. J. Gresham Machen's *Christianity and Liberalism* (1923) argued that early twentieth-century liberalism is not biblical Christianity and is therefore in reality a new religion. Though in a quite different way, obviously, Karl Barth agreed in his *Romans* (first edition 1921) and in his monumental *Church Dogmatics* (1936-1953). Since World War II evangelical writers such as Carl F. H. Henry, George Eldon Ladd, David Wells,

Millard Erickson, and Walter C. Kaiser, Jr. have attempted to keep
American Christianity grounded in a biblical definition of God. John
R. W. Stott, J. I. Packer, Alister McGrath, and others have done a sim-
ilar work in the United Kingdom and Canada.

Such efforts have become increasingly necessary. For at least three
decades process theologians have regularly depicted God as a constantly evolving, ever-greater deity. In the past fifteen years postmod-
ernists of various types have deemed it appropriate, even biblical, to
define God in diverse, even contradictory ways. These scholars often
deny that God knows all that will happen in the future, arguing that
divine foreknowledge of contingent events would make human freedom impossible. They also tend to conclude that it is not necessary to
have a conscious personal relationship with Jesus Christ to have eternal life, for salvation may come through other religions. In other
words, they do not consider texts such as Numbers 23:19 and Psalm
90 accurate summaries of the Bible's teaching about God's immutability, nor passages such as Acts 4:12 or John 14:6 correct summaries of
the indispensability of a specific, conscious personal commitment to
the risen Christ for salvation.

Surprisingly, some recent adherents of variations on these viewpoints have evangelical roots and affiliations. Clark Pinnock, a member of the Evangelical Theological Society and the author of several
works that promote a high view of biblical authority, advocates the
possibility of God's limited omniscience and an openness to salvation
through other religions. Richard Rice, John Sanders, and David
Basinger, all of whom either teach at traditionally evangelical institu-
tions or write for evangelical publishers, have helped Pinnock provide
a philosophical and biblical apology for what these scholars call
freewill theism. Clearly, their conclusions about the doctrine of God
drive their notions about salvation and the work of the church.

EVANGELICALISM AND THE
CURRENT CHALLENGE

Given the internal and external challenges to the doctrine of God,
evangelical Christianity must reassert the inerrantly revealed biblical

definition of God. Trinitarian interpretations of Scripture must state afresh the immutability, eternal goodness, and absolute sovereignty of God the Father, Maker of heaven and earth. Evangelicals must likewise stress the uniqueness of Jesus Christ, the eternal *logos*, the Son of God, through whom alone salvation may be gained. They must also celebrate anew the Holy Spirit, the one who inspires Scripture, convinces of sin, teaches righteousness, and gives ministry gifts to believers. Certainly these truths must be presented in a manner suitable for convincing today's readers and hearers of their truth. Hard issues such as the existence of evil and suffering must be addressed honestly. But these core objective truths must never be compromised or obscured. Upon these beliefs the Church and its academicians must stand, and it is upon these convictions that the writers in this section build their case for the doctrine of God.

ONE

THE LIVING GOD OF THE BIBLE

CARL F. H. HENRY

That God lives is at once the simplest and profoundest statement to be made about him, for his life embraces the full reality of his sovereign being and activity. Both the Old and New Testaments speak of "the living God" (2 Kings 19:16; Acts 14:15; unless otherwise indicated, Bible quotations in this chapter are taken from the *Revised Standard Version*). That the Father "has life in himself" (John 5:26) is no figure of speech but a declaration of God's essential being. Pagan gods and idols simply have "no breath in them" (Jer. 10:14). There is no other God but the one living God (Deut. 4:35; 2 Kings 19:15). God alone is God, and there is none like him (Exod. 8:10; 15:11; 1 Chron. 17:20; Ps. 86:8; 89:8).

For this very reason the formula for an oath in Old Testament times was "as the Lord lives," "as God lives," or "as the God of Israel lives." When Hebrews were menaced, they used this phrase to present Yahweh as the living One who, in contrast to the lifeless, nonexisting heathen gods, evidences his existence and presence in absolute supremacy. Only rebels dispute God's active sovereignty (Jer. 5:12); only fools deny that God exists (Ps. 14:1; 53:2; Job 2:10). By a self-affirming oath, Yahweh himself confirms the dependability of his promises and warnings: "As surely as I live, declares the Sovereign LORD" (Ezek. 17:16; 33:11, NIV).

What God's life is cannot be determined by analyzing creaturely life and then projecting upon deity a vitality that characterizes intricate living creatures. The Bible never depicts God's life as an observable phenomenon, something known by empirical investigation that enables us to comprehend transcendent divine existence. God's life is not a unique configuration of impersonal processes and cosmic events. Nor is it merely a more durable form of the vitality imparted to lifeless man when God breathed into him "the breath of life, and man became a living being" (Gen. 2:7, NIV) and the bearer of God's image (Gen. 1:26). All conjectural attempts to refine the being of the world and of man into some generalized concept that can be projected upon an imagined deity are more hindrance than help for comprehending the One who through his own self-revelation makes himself known as the living God.

God is "the fountain of living waters" (Jer. 2:13; 17:13), "the fountain of life" (Ps. 36:9). The Father "has life in himself" (John 5:26)— that is, originally and absolutely. Christ is "the Author of life" (Acts 3:15), or, in magnificent brevity, "the life" (John 14:6; Phil. 1:21; Col. 3:4; 1 John 1:2). The agent in the creation of all the forms and structures of the universe was the divine *Logos* (John 1:3); as the incarnate *Logos* or God-man he additionally received from the Father the divine prerogative to bestow redemptive life upon the penitent, and resurrection life in the age to come (John 5:26).

God is the incomparable "I AM WHO I AM" (Exod. 3:14). "There is no plainer description of the divinity of God," Barth remarks, "than the phrase which occurs so frequently in the Pentateuch and again in the Book of Ezekiel: 'I am the Lord your (or thy) God,' and it has its exact New Testament parallel in the 'I am' of the Johannine Jesus. . . . In this biblical 'I am' the Subject posits itself and in that way posits itself as the living and loving Lord. . . . He who does this is the God of the Bible."[1]

The Bible has no twilight zone of demigods and semi-gods; it knows only the living *theos* and inert and false *theoi*. Unlike much conjectural philosophy, the Bible is not concerned merely with divinity or being in general; its hallmark is the highly particular self-revealed God. It is no happenstance that the definite article is used (*'o theos*) to designate the God of Israel. The Old Testament is well aware that outside Israel both *El*, the generic term for God, and *elohim*, the plural polytheistic term, were in common use throughout the ancient world. In biblical theology, however, the living God as the one and only God wholly fulfills the species El, and except when referring pejoratively to the pagan gods, the biblical writers use *Elohim* with a singular verb for the one living God. Elohim concretely and fully manifests divine reality ("Know therefore that Yahweh thy Elohim, he is Elohim, the faithful Elohim, who keepeth covenant and mercy with them that love him and keep his commandments to a thousand generations," Deut. 7:9; "If Yahweh be Elohim, follow him," 1 Kings 18:21; "that this people may know that thou art Yahweh Elohim," 1 Kings 18:37). In these passages Elohim is called God absolutely, the one who alone is essentially divine ("Unto thee it was shown, that thou mightest know Yahweh; he is Elohim; there is none else besides him," Deut. 4:35). The living God claims not only exclusive validity among the Hebrews (Exod. 20:2ff.) but declares himself to be also the only God of the Gentile world and in fact of the entire created universe (Isa. 45:18-23).

Greek, Roman, and other ancient civilizations used the term *theos* even of outstanding rulers or emperors whom they worshiped as essentially divine. Homeric mythology postulated living gods that lack eternality but nonetheless outlast man's mortality; the Epicureans ascribed to their gods not nontemporal eternity but unending duration in time. But the Bible provokes debate not only over the authentic nature of divine life, but over that of human life as well. It affirms that God makes known his *vita* on his own initiative and that the *imago Dei* imparted at creation confers upon mankind a creaturely life superior to that of animal existence; in no case, however, has man or any creature a latent potential for divinity. Ancient religious philosophers applied the term *theos* to impersonal cosmic powers; by the easy device of capitalization they then conferred metaphysical status upon the Divine, the Good, the One, and so on. (Modern counterparts are similarly dignified as Space-Time or Being or Ground.) By such postulations God and the cosmos, in part or whole, become identical; certain elements of the world—its supposed intrinsic necessity, irrevocable laws, or evolutionary powers—are considered divine. Instead of acknowledging God as living and transcendent, Greek philosophers—notably Heraclitus and the Stoics—tended to equate

God simply with the living essence of the world. But Scripture sanctions neither this ancient Stoic conception of the universe as a psychophysical divine organism, nor the modern Hegelian regard for man and nature as evolutionary manifestations of the life of the Absolute, nor deity misdefined by process philosophy as the immanent ground of the universe and an aspect of all experience. The biblical God is a transcendent reality who preexisted both the world and man.

Process philosophy professes to overcome a Greek "static" God that obscures the deity's ever-active relation to man and the world. But it also restructures the biblical revelation of the living God and opposes central emphases of scriptural theism. This it does by substituting a necessary divine creation of the universe for voluntary supernatural creation and by excluding the once-for-all miraculous as a misreading of natural processes. Process theology also considers the universe as God's body, obscuring both the incarnation of God in Jesus Christ and the Church as the regenerate body over which the risen Christ reigns, and strips the grace of God of such decisive historical acts as Jesus' substitutionary atonement and his bodily resurrection from the dead. Process philosophy further dilutes the biblical revelation by excluding propositional, conceptual content from God's self-revelation and by correlating God's salvific activity not primarily with historical redemptive acts but rather with man's inner faith response to an interpersonal divine human encounter. Whatever process philosophers may presume to gain by such alternatives to a "static" deity, their projected reconstitution of God's nature actually deprives deity of major perfections and activities characteristic of the living God of the Bible and results in a view of the divine that is inadequate philosophically, scripturally, and experientially. The theory that created reality is necessary to God and is in some respects divine departs in crucial ways from the biblical revelation of God. On the basis of God's own self-revelation, biblical theists reject notions that make the universe God's body and essential to his life; they disavow views that replace the scriptural doctrine of God's primordial creation of graded orders of life, like that of Schubert Ogden, for whom God himself changes as "the ever-present primordial ground" of an evolving universe.[2] Ogden's insistence that God exists necessarily, but that his essence is in part dependent upon the universe, is self-defeating, for if God exists necessarily, he cannot be essentially dependent; on the other hand, if God is essentially dependent, he does not exist necessarily.

Far less does the Bible approve such naturalistic notions as that food and water or material factors fully account for man's survival; such nourishment does indeed nurture human life, but it is God who gives (Luke 12:15) and sustains it (Matt. 4:4). However much the twenty-first century pursues a higher quality of human life—one that the Bible commends in its own way—the quality of divine life will always transcend the human, unique as it is, and even at its best. Redemption can indeed lift the creaturely life of fallen man to the incomparable human joys of "eternal life" (John 3:16) by providing an imperishable human life fit for time and eternity. But God lives his own distinctive life; an immense ontological chasm separates man who "became a living being" (Gen. 2:7) and bears the divine image (Gen. 1:26) from the living God who created man and endowed him thus.

The God of the Bible eternally has life in himself. As theologians have sometimes put it, he has aseity, or life from and by himself in independent freedom. His essential life does not correspond merely to his personal relations to the cosmos and to human beings. Nor should the life God has in himself be contrasted with the life of creatures by asserting merely that creaturely life exists through his will and purposes. The fact is that though heaven and earth, the work of his hands, shall perish (Ps. 102:25ff.), God himself "endures." He neither became the living God by his creation of the universe, nor did he become the living God at some point in eternity past; he is the one living God, and is so eternally. He lives in eternal self-affirmation. His life is all that he thinks, decides, and wills in creative freedom. God perpetually wills and purposes his own being; this being depends upon nothing external to himself, yet is not internally necessitated as if he exists forever whether he wills to do so or not. He wills eternally to be himself in the fullness of his independent vitality, and he never ceases to be himself. God exists in absolute plenitude and power. He is wholly free to be himself and removes the mystery of his own being by making known his inner nature by voluntary self-disclosure.

The pagan gods cannot help others; they cannot even help themselves. They are mere zeds or zeros: "There is no breath in them. They are worth nothing, mere mockeries" (Jer. 10:14, NEB). The idols are "useless" (Ps. 31:6, NEB). Samuel pleads: "Give up the worship of false gods which can neither help nor save, because they are false" (1 Sam. 12:21, NEB). Jeremiah adds: "Our forefathers inherited only a sham, an idol vain and useless" (Jer. 16:19, NEB). The living God is to be obeyed because in self-disclosure he has declared his commanding and directive will. The false gods have neither mind nor will; they issue no summons to obedience, nor can they direct human action. "The Lord alone led him [Israel], no alien god at his side," declared Moses (Deut. 32:12, NEB). Jeremiah speaks of the pagan gods that are "no gods" (2:11); he rebukes Israel's rebellion and apostasy through Yahweh's pointed question: "How can I forgive you for all this? Your sons have forsaken me and sworn by gods that are not gods" (Jer. 5:7, NEB). Isaiah speaks by contrast of the whole earth as full of the glory of the living God (6:3).

While false gods are not authentic divine powers, the Old Testament indicates that through fallen man's imagination they gain a power of attraction in human experience, captivate the will, and elicit religious response. Such a response not only victimizes adherents, but it also evokes Yahweh's displeasure, for Yahweh is a jealous God: "You shall fear the Lord your God, serve him alone and take your oaths in his name. You must not follow other gods, gods of the nations that are around you; if you do, the Lord your God who is in your midst will be angry with you, and he will sweep you away off the face of the earth, for the Lord your God is a jealous god" (Deut. 6:13-15, NEB). Here one must cite especially the Decalogue: "You shall have no other god to set against me. You shall not make a carved image for yourself nor the likeness of anything in the heavens above, or on the earth below, or in the waters under the earth. You shall not bow down to them or worship them; for I, the Lord your God, am a jealous God" (Exod. 20:3-5, NEB; cf. Deut. 5:7-9). The living God is jealous not of false gods as real entities but of the power they exert over those who imaginatively invest idols with ontological existence and volition (cf. Deut. 4:23ff.).

The God of the Old Testament is indeed a God of social justice,

as many expositors today stress above all else, but he is no less promi-
nently the living God who challenges the false gods that lure away
man's attention and preempt his energies. This indictment of evil powers gives biblical religion great force in Asia and Africa where invisible spirits wield extensive influence over daily life. It is no less
significant for European and American life, however, where secular
man despite his intellectual dismissal of a transcendent world places
himself in idolatrous relationships to material things and natural processes. Harvey Cox reminds us that "from the perspective of Biblical
thought, neither the garden nor the machine can save man. . . .
Yahweh creates man to enjoy and attend the garden, but not to sacrifice to it; to make things for his own use, but not to pray to them."[3]
The passion for things and lust for money have become such a hallmark of materialistic Western culture that tangible realities hold priority among life's values.

✓ The pseudo-divine and the demonic inspirit much of twentieth-
century life in both the Occident and the Orient. Non-Christian
Formosan workers have a god of the living room, of the dining room,
of the kitchen, of the bedroom, of the bathroom. Besides worshiping
ancestors and numerous household gods, workers also revere the
gods of their profession; farmers, for example, fishermen, merchants,
even beggars and prostitutes worship their own special god. The
more miserable one's situation, the more gods one will implore. The
farmer lacking scientific techniques will worship the sun god, the
rain god, the river god. Even rural road workers using modern
machinery sometimes refuse to work until or unless they first pray
to the local gods.

Surviving in this invocation of invisible spirits is the blurred conviction that the living God is concerned with all human activity. But
while subdividing the deity into multiple divinities with a supersti-
tious kind of reverence may preserve regard for the transcendent, this
course is ridiculed by the younger generation under the pressures of
modern learning. Some students say they have no use for the Church
simply because they are students; they do not believe in God because
disciplines like computer science can solve all problems accurately
and quickly. The scientific desacralization of nature helps breed the

presumption that science dissolves the supernatural. Only the biblical revelation that banishes false gods and at the same time challenges the myths of modernity such as materialism, scientism, and eroticism avoids human capitulation to naturalism, be it Marxian, secular capitalist, or scientistic.

Some expositors ground the Old Testament case for Yahweh's exclusive divinity in man's internal response rather than in cognitive considerations. Instead of giving an unbiased statement of the Hebrew view, their explanation reflects the influence of the decision-oriented dialectical and existential theology of recent decades or involves lingering concessions to evolutionary theories of religious development. Obviously the Old Testament account of the living God is not a metaphysical discourse interested only in intellectual delineation; while its proximate interest is knowledge of God, its call to obedient faith in the living and active God stands everywhere in the forefront. But the revelation of the God of the Bible is not subcognitive. Hence we are not reduced to the alternatives of conjectural argumentation on the one hand or personal trust on the other. Of itself the latter would not be decisive for knowing the truth of the one God (even rebellious demons are said to share this, cf. Jas. 2:19).

Only decision-oriented theology can supply a basis for Gottfried Quell's protest that "there is perhaps an excess of rational argument in the complaints of the prophets" and for his disparagement of supposedly "arid, theoretical statements in the later literature."[4] Quell has in mind specially Daniel 11:36, with its prophetic reference to the willful king who speaks against "the God of gods"; Malachi 2:10 ("Have we not all one father? Has not one God created us?"); and the statement in Psalm 82:1 (KJV) that "God . . . judgeth among the gods," that is, among magistrates who rule as his representatives. But these passages are hardly as arid as Quell implies, and they surely do not exhaust the cognitive elements through which Old Testament revelation exhibits the one living God.

Kenneth Hamilton thinks that the Hebrew conviction that no God exists other than Yahweh arose as the end-product of a history of spiritual obedience to Yahweh and emerged "through a long process of education of Israel's imagination rather than a direct appeal to the intellect."[5] It is of course the case that an insistent divine demand for faith and obedience accompanies the biblical revelation of Yahweh. But to suggest as Hamilton does that as an intellectual commitment ethical monotheism has no Hebrew roots earlier than the eighth-century prophet Isaiah[6] grounds earlier monotheistic faith extrarationally in volitional response, if not in religious imagination, which Hamilton elsewhere depicts as the special domain of the pseudo-divinities. The Decalogue does indeed set the affirmation of Yahweh against other gods (Exod. 20:3; Deut. 5:7), in the context of a call to obedient love; but one hardly does justice to Mosaic representations to say that "it did not matter greatly whether the people believed that the gods of the nations had some kind of independent existence or whether they were pure fictions, empty 'wind.'"[7] Elijah demanded a clear choice between Baal and Yahweh (1 Kings 18:21), a choice that required trust and obedience to be sure, but hardly on that account, as Hamilton would have us believe, a choice that involved no "illumination of the mind by knowledge."[8]

Hamilton extends his "volition-centered" interpretation of biblical data to the New Testament as well. He thinks that, discouraged at Mars Hill by "little response from the philosophically minded . . . to Paul's apologetic efforts," the apostle thereafter preached Christ crucified "without regard to the Greek search for intellectual truth"[9] and followed what Hamilton supposes to be the Old Testament precedent of witnessing to God's acts instead of insisting on the intelligibility and reasonableness of faith.[10] Hamilton even deplores any attempt to state religious truth in "cool reason"—that is, in objectively valid terms— as an effort to demythologize and insists that only "through personal encounter" can we justify a personalized view of the universe.[11] So too when he expounds Paul's comments on eating food devoted to idols as turning on obedience rather than on knowledge,[12] Hamilton seems to confuse knowledge that is translated into obedient love with love in the absence of knowledge.

At the very opening of the Bible the Hebrew creation account leaves no room intellectually for other gods, nor does the Decalogue. Although in the Bible, as Hamilton says, "the 'nothingness' of idols is never asserted as a general truth to be known by itself," that is, apart from a summons to worship the living God alone,[13] it hardly follows that the Hebrews did not intellectually know the nothingness and powerlessness of the pagan deities.

In certain important respects the Hebrew monotheistic revelation strikingly differs from Greek philosophical monotheism, one crucial difference being the Hebrew emphasis on worship of Yahweh in the forefront over against the rather secondary and subordinate role that Greek philosophy assigns to worship. We need not on that account, however, subscribe to Hamilton's thesis that "monotheism as an intellectual system may be said to have been invented by the Greek mind."[14] Greek philosophers indeed presented their views more rigidly in an orderly philosophical scheme, independent of progressive divine revelation and premised on creative rational analysis that led to many rival expositions. But the Hebrews were not indifferent to concerns of logic and consistency. They did not, however, present their teaching about the one true and living God as a conclusion derived as an inference from the character of the cosmos or nature of man. They traced monotheism, both intellectually and volitionally, not ultimately to the invention of any human mind, Greek or Hebrew, but to the living God's self-revelation.

Some Greek philosophers conceived the cosmic elements and powers as "abstract and inexorable"; whether because of recalcitrance (Plato) or because of pure potentiality (Aristotle), matter itself was thought to be evil and resistant to the divine will. Even ancient Near-Eastern astrology and the divinization of cosmic as well as astral powers had anticipated some of these features. Near-Eastern religions connected cosmic forces with benevolent and malevolent divinities. Zoroastrianism ranged light and darkness against each other as good and evil principles, whereas Platonic philosophy connected matter with evil as an impersonal force.

The biblical writers, on the other hand, speak of superhuman powers as rebellious personal agents hostile to God's good governance of the world, yet ultimately subject to the Creator. Insofar as pagan polytheism had any ontological basis, it came about through the corrupt elevation and idolatrous worship of such spirits, worship that sacrificed the unity of the living God and exalted rebellious creaturely agents or mere cosmic forces to an absolute divine role.

But when Hamilton suggests that the Hebrews "personalized" the cosmic powers and that Hebrew monotheism was experiential rather than intellectual, he obscures the doctrines of satanology and angelology as well as underestimates the rational, revelational basis for biblical monotheism. In a universe that Near-Eastern religions populated with gods and intermediary beings, the Hebrews assign a remarkably subordinate role to angelology, one that nowhere reflects polytheism. While it remained for Christianity to give full expression to the fact that "no angel, no prince, nothing that exists, nothing still to come, not any power, or height or depth, nor any created thing, can ever come between us and the love of God made visible in Christ Jesus our Lord" (Rom. 8:38-39, JB), the Old Testament call for exclusive trust in the one Creator and Lord already implies this. By emphasizing that the whole realm of "principalities and powers"—or elemental spirits and energies—is subordinate to the Creator's agency and that nothing can permanently frustrate the personal action and purpose of the Lord of the universe, Paul stripped cosmic elements and forces of any paralyzing power over mankind and removed the temptation to divinize their elusive mysterious nature. As Hamilton well says, "the antidote to fear of the abstract powers was the concrete revelation in Christ of the living God, the Creator still personally active in his world."[15]

Writing of "the ambivalence of the being and nonbeing of the gods, of the power and folly of idolatry," Helmut Thielicke says: "The Old Testament attack on pagan gods and idolatry brings out the ambivalence that is their characteristic. They can win power and yet they are empty. Yahweh is the first and the last, and besides him is no god (Isaiah 44:6). Yet in a way that accepts the existence of the gods he can be compared with them and extolled as incomparably superior (Exodus 15:11; 18:11; Psalm 72:18 ff.; 86:8; 93:3; 96:4)."[16] "In comparison with the one true God the gods are impotent, vain and unprofitable (cf. Isaiah 44:8; 2 Kings 18:33 ff.; Jeremiah 16:19 f.)."[17]

In relation to the created universe, they are "entangled" in creation and implicated in "what is created and perishable." In relation to man, if God is my only Lord, the gods are disarmed and . . . nonexistent. If God is not my Lord, either because I do not yet know him and am outside the covenant, or because, as a weaker brother, I accept him only partially, and my spiritual life is still immature, then there are ethically unredeemed spheres to which God's lordship has not yet extended, and here the beaten gods can fight a rearguard action and set up pockets of resistance where nothingness can win power over me and come to existence.[18]

This ambivalent status of divinities other than Yahweh is not a result of evolutionary development from polytheism or henotheism to monotheism, but reflects rather the ambiguous ontology of the world of rival powers and spirits. The gods initially gain their standing merely as human conceptions, as products of human thought and imagination (Isa. 44:9-20). As Thielicke says, "this origin of the gods, this feature that they are creature rather than Creator, is the reason for their impotence, their nondeity. . . . As products of men's hands or minds the gods can have no reality independent of man."[19] When man fashions gods, they are empty and useless (Jer. 16:19ff.; 2 Kings 18:33ff.; Ps. 106:19ff.; Jer. 2:24), for they cannot respond to man's need (Jer. 2:19). Unlike Feuerbach, the Bible nowhere gives the impression that the gods, as postulations of hope and projections of fears, remain sheer fantasy with no power. These gods somehow do get men in their clutches. In biblical theism, Satan and other fallen angels have an objective existence. Although false gods are only products of idolatrous imagination, they nonetheless accumulate a coercive power that lends them demonic force.

The apostle Paul writes on the one hand of so-called gods (1 Cor. 10:19ff.) and on the other of "many 'gods' and many 'lords'" (1 Cor. 8:5). Nowhere does he compromise the fact that the Christian knows that there is only one God, the Father of Jesus Christ (1 Cor. 8:4ff.) and that faith in the self-revealing living God alone effectively disarms false gods by exposing them as mythical constructs. He unqualifiedly rejects the thesis that the idol "really amounts to anything" (1 Cor. 10:19ff., TEV), "itself is real" (JB), or "really exists" (*Phillips*) or that idols "are really alive and are real gods"(TLB). The Christian must nonetheless be careful not to regard idols as realities or to assign them an actual captivating power, for pagan practice, when properly seen, is nothing less than surrender to demons (1 Cor. 10:18-22). Theological truth must not be sacrificed. But moral sensitivity to weak brethren is nonetheless an issue. Yet the Christian must leave no doubt that those who regard false gods as powers and beings having majestic predicates and attributes pervert and reject the truth of the one living God.

Thielicke, therefore, seems to overexistentialize the Christian response to false gods when he relies on faith alone to cancel their latent power: "Within God's sphere of power, i. e., faith, in which God is the only one for us (1 Cor. 8:6, Col. 1:16 f.), the gods are disarmed and cast into the nothingness of nonbeing. They have no more being or significance for us."[20] It is true that vital commitment to the alternative, that is, to the God of the Bible, precludes merely adding Jesus Christ to one's household or shelf gods. But atheistic movements also appeal to ideological faith to demythologize not only the false gods, but the one living God as well. And nonbiblical religions often appeal to sheer commitment to exclude the God of the Bible as an alternative.

Yet the Bible, in proffering its revelationally reasonable case for the divine self-disclosure of the living God, strips the false gods of ontological status and leaves no doubt that because of fallen man's perversity it is God only who can now win the battle over the false god (Rom. 1:21ff.; 1 Cor. 1:21). By disregarding God in his revelation, fallen man in a catastrophic repudiation of the created orders changed the truth into a lie; Enlightenment rationalism, in turn, discarded the biblical God along with false gods.

The most radical modern cults of self-realization sponsor a contemporary kind of idolatry under the guise of humanistic self-esteem. Selfism elevates the subjective ego as the only god; here the living God becomes the self-exalting ego. Paul C. Vitz alerts us: "To worship one's own self (in self-realization) or to worship all humanity is, in Christian terms, simply idolatry operating from the usual motive of unconscious egotism."[21]

Even Erich Fromm's rather moderate work, *The Art of Loving*,[22] declares the God of Christian theology to be an illusion. And in *The*

Dogma of Christ[23] he dismisses Christianity as a fantasy compensation for human frustrations and debunks Christian doctrines as childish medieval beliefs. The concept of God, Fromm elsewhere informs us, has developed to the point that man is God; whatever realm of sacredness there is centers in the human self.[24]

Summarizing the philosophy of one of the recent self-assertion and self-deification cults, Carl Frederick writes: "You are the Supreme being. . . . You are IT. Choose . . . Choose to BE what you know you are."[25] This mood, as Paul Vitz points out,[26] is highly reminiscent of the existential atheism of Jean-Paul Sartre. "Life is nothing; it's up to you to give it a meaning, and value is nothing else but the meaning that you choose."[27] Here by asserting self-divinity, the renegade human spirit in a mighty counterstroke of rebellion against the living Lord seeks to escape the doom that awaits man as sinner, and the death and nonbeing that must climax human destiny in a world without God.

Otto Baab notes that many biblical passages distinguish the "pure worship of Israel's superhuman and transcendent God" from idolatry by emphasizing that idols are mere personifications and objectifications of the human will. "When the idol is worshipped, man is worshipping himself, his desires, his purposes and his will."[28] It tells something about man's spiritual deterioration that the Creator who images himself distinctively in man later enjoins the death of any man who murders his like (Gen. 9:6) and explicitly prohibits man from imaging God in created things (Exod. 20:4); fallen humanity, in turn, supremely exhibits its foolishness and futility by exchanging "the glory of the immortal God for images made to look like mortal man and birds and animals and reptiles" (Rom. 1:22, NIV). In ancient times, pagan Gentiles looked upon their earthly rulers as divine; in modern secular circles, a misguided cluster of intellectuals consider themselves divine.

Kenneth Hamilton comments that although supernatural polytheism and graven images have long been intellectually and culturally unfashionable, Western culture has not by any means discouraged idolatrous imagination nor excluded subtler manifestations of polytheism. "As happened in Israel," he remarks, "conscious profession of faith in the one God does not prevent the imagination of men's hearts turning them back to worship 'strange gods.'"[29] The idolatrous imagination that in past centuries shaped graven images in our time projects equally corrupt and corrupting alternatives to faith in the living God.

Like the fascination that pinups of a bikini-clad beauty hold for the single male, even if she be only an artist's conception with no life in the real world, the conscious and subconscious projections of a renegade humanity acquire artificial magical compulsion and imagined power. Conferring realism upon the merely imaginary at the expense of objective truth seems more and more to become a deliberate ambition of modern commercialism, a force that routinely commends its products through symbols of status and sex. Imagination elevates creaturely entities into superhuman influences that then take control of human experience. As Hamilton suggests, imagination is an "interior workshop"; here man fashions idolatrous images of God formed internally of concepts and ideas no less than externally of wood and stone.[30]

Hamilton observes that "the imagination of men's hearts," as the *King James Version* translates the original language of Scripture (Gen. 8:21; Deut. 29:19; 1 Chron. 29:18; Prov. 6:18; Jer. 23:17; Luke 1:51), reflects the seventeenth-century connection of the term *imagination* with unreality—that is, "the imaginary rather than the imaginative."[31] Seventeenth-century writers assigned to imagination a constructive as well as illusory role.

Hamilton even credits imagination with a superrational capacity to resolve some questions of truth and error and suggests that in the Christian life "personal decisions must go beyond 'knowledge' and rest on 'love.'"[32] Contending that "every philosophical or religious doctrine presupposes" an imaginative picture and images of the real world,[33] he nonetheless emphasizes that we should "labor to make our imaginatively conceived convictions look intellectually respectable."[34] Quite apart from this somewhat ambiguous image-dependent epistemology that demotes the cognitive elements basic to Christian commitment, Hamilton nonetheless offers incisive insights into the forms of idolatry that currently preempt the devotion of secular Western

man and, for that matter, all too often powerfully confront even professing Christians. The modern emphasis on imagination—the human
mind's power to call up images—gives new force to the biblical contrast between Christ, the express image of God, and the idols or false
images of God. The Old Testament and New Testament alike associate graven images with faithlessness toward God. Throughout the
entire biblical era, idol-worship was the most characteristic phenomenon of Gentile religion. Nothing so precisely sharpens the contrast between the pagan and Christian concepts of God as the pagan
charge that the early Christians were atheists because they neither
venerated prescribed images nor had images of their own.

━ As indicated, idolatry in the Bible involves far more than the worship of man-made images of wood and stone; it includes also the imaginative deification of powers and concepts to elicit supreme allegiance
and absolute respect. Unlike ancient Babylonian astrologers, Moses
and the ancient Hebrew prophets deplored sun-worship, moon-wor-
ship, star-worship, and worship of other created elements (Deut.
4:19; Jer. 10:2; Ezek. 8:16ff.). But as Donald J. Wiseman comments,
although the astrologers yielded the cosmos and life to the control of
impersonal mechanical fate and drew signs from "the relations of the
moon to the sun, eclipses, or, less extensively, from . . . planetary
movements . . . their observations were never applied to individuals."
Israel, he adds, knew that "direct Divine revelation . . . rendered div-
inatory techniques unnecessary"; because of their fidelity to monotheism the Hebrews avoided "the polytheistic practices of their neighbors
who worshipped planets and stars."[35] In Paul's time, observes G. B.
Caird, the polytheistic gods of the Greco-Roman world had been
largely displaced by impersonal law or superhuman elemental spirits;
these were thought to control the universe and consequently sapped
individual life of meaning and hope.[36] Augustine argued against
pagans who applied astrology to individuals.

The Pauline protest against "vain . . . imaginations" (Rom. 1:21,
KJV; cf. JB: "they made nonsense out of logic and their empty minds
were darkened") thus gains force against the secular priorities of the
modern civilized world no less than against the crude spiritual aberrations of remote primitive tribes. When loosed from the constraints

of rational divine revelation, religious imagination plunges man readily into spiritual idolatry; creative imagination confers an imagined reality and dynamic power upon the nonexistent to shape and direct cosmic and human affairs; it becomes the playground of imaginary idolatrous divinities, those sham-gods of both primitive and literate cultures.

Hamilton identifies "relevance," "change," and "liberation" as specially influential contemporary cultic images. These catchwords gain added authority through the modern communications media and the slogans and clichés of Madison Avenue. The notion of inevitable progress, still somewhat current in contemporary philosophy, and the premium placed on change both work against inherited and traditional conceptions of God, truth, and the good. If progress and change are the very stuff of reality, then even deity, as Hamilton observes, must "conform to the idea of progress."[37] Setting the mood for all things both human and divine, the "perennial new" nurtures the idea that supernatural Christianity must yield before novel views of God and Christ; the Bible, it is said, must decrease in value for modern man. "Anything labeled relevant is above criticism, anything labeled irrelevant is beneath contempt. The affirmation of the supreme worth of relevance becomes an article of faith, and the pursuit of relevance a cult."[38] Relevance or immediate appeal thus displaces even worth and goodness, and tradition is deplored as the very essence of irrelevance. When the spirit of the age dictates which beliefs are acceptable or unacceptable, their relevance has become "an absolute power."

Thomas J. J. Altizer pontificates that "nothing delights the enemy of faith so much as the idea that faith is ever the same yesterday, today, and forever, with the obvious corollary that faith is hopelessly archaic and irrelevant today."[39] The equally obvious corollary—which Altizer seems blithely to ignore—is that even Altizer's alternative cannot be permanently relevant. The cult of the perennially new must anticipate the sudden death of its own mental offspring. On close reexamination such offspring often gain a measure of staying power by adopting preferred fragments of inherited views and parading them in contemporary dress.

Hamilton's protest against relevance sometimes seems overdrawn.

After all, among the virtues of divine revelation and divine redemption is their relevance for all men in all generations. By contrast many items promoted as indispensably pertinent to human welfare soon reveal their irrelevance to human good and destiny. Hamilton himself argues for the permanent validity of the divine commandment against graven images, a command that on first thought may seem irrelevant for our day. Basic to the argument of his book *To Turn from Idols*, says Hamilton, is "the contention . . . that the warning against worship of idols given in the Second Commandment remains very pertinent to our own culture."[40] Just as early Christianity recognized the first commandment "to be as pertinent as ever in the context of contemporary culture,"[41] so, too, nothing is more urgent for mankind today than to hear Yahweh's call "to turn from the idols that exercise power over contemporary imaginations" and to resist "conformity to the pattern of the present age."[42] What Hamilton protests, in other words, is the absolutizing of relevance in the process of demoting all other concerns. "If relevance is absolutized," he says, "the wholeness of truth is . . . completely inconceivable. . . . All that anyone needs to know is what is declared to be relevant for contemporary man . . . and all that is relevant is given in the Perennial New. Relevance is asserted by repeating slogans and catchwords, thus arbitrarily ruling out any rational discussion of truth and falsehood, and by-passing by dogmatic pronouncement the delicate, exacting task of trying to examine an issue comprehensively and in its proper context."[43] What Hamilton does is shift emphasis from the perennially new to living tradition, from catchword-dogmatism to reverence for truth. But unless living tradition is itself subject to a permanently valid norm, it, too, will not escape impermanence. And reverence for truth, important as it is, cannot of itself establish the truth of revelation. Indeed, if personal trust is more decisive for monotheism than are rational considerations, as Hamilton elsewhere indicates, then truth does not seem to matter all that much.

While idols are truly nothing, as Paul stresses (1 Cor. 8:4; 10:19), idolatry is something, and a very serious something; indeed, it is a terrible sin (1 Cor. 10:7; cf. Acts 7:40ff.; 1 John 5:21). Not only does idolatry eclipse worship of the living God, but it also entails bondage to demonic powers that intimidate and dominate the human spirit (cf. Rom. 1:23, 25; Gal. 4:8; Eph. 2:2). "What gives Paul's battle against idolatry its seriousness and what distinguishes it from the rationalistic arguments of Hellenism," Ethelbert Stauffer observes, is the fact that idolatry involves not merely so-called gods that are in themselves nothing, but also a real world of demonic powers.[44]

Early Christianity rejoiced that those enlightened by divine revelation and by the Holy Spirit have the "ability to distinguish true spirits from false" (1 Cor. 12:10, NEB). The apostle John affirms that human beings need to assess spirits abroad in the world on the basis of their witness or nonwitness to Jesus Christ (1 John 4:1-3). Just as in his Gospel John emphasizes that the Holy Spirit witnesses to Jesus Christ (John 15:26; 16:4-9ff.), so in his first epistle he stresses that in view of God's self-disclosure in Jesus Christ his Son, we must be on guard against idols (1 John 4:4-6). Corrupt religious imagination fashions notions of deity that have no basis in divine disclosure and scriptural testimony.

Only in daily experience can the creedal confession of monotheism be put to constant test. Service of the living God requires repudiating all idols—be they the philosopher's deifying of elemental forces of the cosmos (Gal. 4:8ff.), the political tyrant's imposition of obligations that God disallows (Acts 4:19; 5:29), the secularist's idolatry of mammon ("You cannot serve both God and Money," Matt. 6:24, NIV; cf. Luke 12:19), the glutton's capitulation to appetite ("whose god is their belly," Phil. 3:19, KJV), or even Western tourists' tolerant curiosity about ancient temple idols (2 Cor. 6:16; 1 Thess. 1:9).

The living God calls us from worship of false gods to the permanent responsibilities entrusted to us at creation. The living God is himself the God of life and death (Num. 27:16; Deut. 32:39; Job 12:10; Luke 12:20; 2 Cor. 1:19; Jas. 4:15). Death does not belong to life but contradicts it as its opposite. God governs the book of life, in which he inscribes the names of his people (Isa. 4:3) and assures their heavenly felicity (Exod. 32:32; Ps. 69:28; Mal. 3:16) in view of their obedient response to his Word that calls for life-or-death decisions (Deut. 30:15-20; 32:46-47). God reveals himself as the absolute and exclusive God of human existence—as man's creator, preserver, judge, redeemer, and companion even in and beyond death (Ps. 23:4, 6; 73:23ff.). He is judge of both the living and the dead (1 Pet. 4:5). Since life is a gift of God, the Bible does not view death as natural or necessary but as a consequence of sin. Life in God is indestructible, whereas creaturely life is conditional. God can declare human beings dead ("in your transgressions and sins," Eph. 2:1, NIV; cf. Col. 2:13) while they are still physically alive (Matt. 8:22; Luke 15:24), or he can declare them eternally alive even in the face of physical death (John 11:25ff.; Phil. 1:23).

Eschatological life is of course not wholly new in all respects; in it God contravenes the vulnerabilities of man's earthly existence by arresting and reversing the power of sin. While eschatological life remains somatic, it involves also the indestructible life that God confers in association with the resurrection body. Natural immortality of the soul is not a biblical tenet. Christian belief in the soul's ongoing divine preservation (Mark 1:27) and in bodily resurrection should remind us that the living God alone is the real life-giver.

The resurrection of the crucified Jesus becomes in New Testament context the central historical reality upon which resurrection faith focuses. Christ's triumph over death strips death of its sting (1 Cor. 15:56)—that is, of its "power to hurt" the believer (TEV).

The difference between the biblical revelation of bodily resurrection and pagan theories of spirit-immortality involves more than simply realistically rejecting idealistic notions that man's psyche is inherently divine and therefore indestructible. Scripture teaches that sin involves a violent rupture in the created relationship between God and man and requires a radical negation by divine redemption. The New Testament portrays the resurrection of the crucified Jesus as a threshold event, one that inaugurates the new eschatological age and guarantees the future resurrection of mankind. But the regeneration conferred even now by faith in Christ the Redeemer already involves participation in eternal life (John 5:24-25; 1 Tim. 6:12, 19). Life, whether creation life, redemption life, or resurrection life, is not a vitality inherent in man or something that he can develop. It is a supernatural gift. Even now, on the authority of the revealed Word of God and by faith in the substitutionary death of the Savior for his sins, the alienated sinner may enjoy this gift of eternal life (Eph. 2:5ff.). Cancellation of spiritual death already now in the present frees redeemed man for new daily possibilities of life in the Spirit. The force of physical death is experientially neutralized since the believer identifies himself with the historical death and resurrection of Christ who in his coming final victory will completely abolish physical death. The apostle Paul pinpoints the believer's perspective by the words, "dying, and, behold, we live" (2 Cor. 6:9). That the redeemed sinner may in virtue of divine preservation and grace live eternally in God's intimate presence gains its wonder not only from the fact that myriads of creatures are intended by creation to have only brief temporal existence, but also from the fact that the redeemed will forever enjoy the company of the supernatural bestower of creation, redemption, and resurrection life and that God will even express his own proper life in unobstructed spiritual and moral union with all who love him. In other words, the very real facts of day-to-day existence occur within the dynamic relationship the believer already bears to the risen Christ; from the eternal order Christ the Lord is mediating to him love, joy, peace, and other virtues distinctive of the age to come.

But God's personal relationships to his creatures, and particularly to human beings, do not exhaust his interpersonal activity, nor do these divine-human relationships take divine priority. Throughout eternity the living God is active within himself, active in unending interpersonal relationships in the Godhead. This fact we discern only on the basis of his self-revelation. What we know of God's attributes and activities is not arrived at through conjecturing some abstract being-in-general, a being that is first contrasted with all finite beings and then dignified as divine and glorified with all the appropriate perfections. The dipolar deity projected by process philosophy is much more abstract than the self-revealed triune God presented in the Bible. Process thinkers, like some rationalistic philosophers before them, thrust an identity upon God that they infer from the functions of the cosmos, the cosmos being gratuitously viewed as his body. All the attributes or characteristics that appropriately belong to his being, the God of the Bible makes known in living self-disclosure. Any distinction that we properly make in God we make only if we acknowledge one or another perfection that he, the living, self-revealing Lord, has revealed to man. For Jesus, faith in God is first and foremost faith in the true and living God self-disclosed as holy, loving, and merciful, but also as the God of wrath and judgment. The Gospels consequently remind us that God is true (John 3:33), good (Mark 10:18), holy (John 17:11), loving (John 3:16), merciful (Luke 6:36), righteous (John 17:25), wrathful (John 3:36), and so on. These and other emphases recur in the epistles. Numerous statements bearing on the nature of the living God speak of the unlimited and unrivaled fullness of his perfections: he is "God only wise" (Rom. 16:27, KJV), "who only hath immortality" (1 Tim 6:16, KJV), and who in brief is the "only wise God" (1 Tim. 1:17, KJV; Jude 25). Only because the living God by cognitive disclosure lifts the veil, as it were, on the inner life of the Godhead do we know that from all eternity he decreed to create the temporal universe, proposed the incarnation of the *Logos*, freely elected fallen sinners to salvation, and much else.

God publishes his holy will to the human race; the living God relates himself to the forces of the cosmos and the experiences of mankind, hears the prayers of his creatures, providentially governs the fortunes of the redeemed (Rom. 8:28), and sovereignly influences the direction of human history toward the sure and final triumph of righteousness (Rom. 8:29ff.).

In its affirmations about him the Bible does not set before us simply the fact of God's personality and stop there; it implements that fact by maintaining centrality for the living God's personal revelatory disclosure. When John boldly declares, "God is love" (1 John 4:8), he is not equating God with some impersonal power; rather, he is characterizing the personal God who is the source and norm of all love (1 John 4:16). When he declares that "God is light" (1 John 1:5), he is not reducing deity to some impersonal aspect of the natural universe; rather, he is presenting the self-revealing, personal God as the source and norm of all light—natural, rational, moral, and spiritual.

In attesting the personal self-disclosure of the living God, Jesus frequently used the term *theos* in correlation with *pater* ("Father"), or the name *Father* instead of the term *God*. Yet few turns in the history of thought are stranger than the fact that almost from the beginnings of Western secular philosophy, worldly-wise scholars have insisted that one must choose between divine personality and divine sovereignty; God is sovereign but not personal and living, they have argued, or conversely, God is personal and living but not sovereign. All the more ironic is the fact that even Judaism, not because of disbelief but because of excessive reverence, came to avoid the name of Yahweh, so that, as Karl Georg Kuhn remarks, "this name for God continued to exist only as a written symbol, not as a living word."[45] No less ironic is the fact that in the mid-1800s Hegelian modernism disputed God's personality. The living God of the Bible became a conjectural abstraction to be freely manipulated by elitist philosophers.

CHAPTER 1

1. Karl Barth, *Church Dogmatics II/1*, eds. G. W. Bromiley and T. F. Torrance (Edinburgh: T. and T. Clark, 1936-1969), 301ff.
2. Schubert Ogden, *The Reality of God and Other Essays* (London: SCM, 1967), 210.
3. Harvey Cox, *The Seduction of the Spirit* (New York: Simon & Schuster, 1973), 300.
4. Gottfried Quell, "*Theos: El* and *Elohim* in the Old Testament," *The Theological Dictionary of the New Testament (TDNT)*, Vol. 3, eds. Gerhard Kittel and Gerhard Friedrich (Grand Rapids, Mich.: Eerdmans, 1965), 89.
5. Kenneth Hamilton, *To Turn from Idols* (Grand Rapids, Mich.: Eerdmans, 1973), 18.
6. Ibid., 18ff.
7. Ibid., 21.
8. Ibid., 20.
9. Ibid., 27ff.
10. Ibid., 28.
11. Ibid., 33-34.
12. Ibid., 14ff.
13. Ibid., 20.
14. Ibid., 23.
15. Ibid., 29.
16. Helmut Thielicke, *The Evangelical Faith*, trans. Geoffrey W. Bromiley (Grand Rapids, Mich.: Eerdmans, 1974), 93.
17. Ibid., 98.
18. Ibid., 98ff.
19. Ibid., 94.
20. Ibid., 97.
21. Paul C. Vitz, *Psychology as Religion: The Cult of Self-Worship* (Grand Rapids, Mich.: Eerdmans, 1977), 93.
22. Erich Fromm, *The Art of Loving* (New York: Harper & Row, 1956).
23. Erich Fromm, *The Dogma of Christ* (New York: Holt, Rinehart and Winston, 1963).
24. Erich Fromm, *You Shall Be As Gods* (New York: Holt, Rinehart and Winston, 1966).
25. Carl Frederick, *Playing the Game the New Way* (New York: Dell, 1974; New York: Delta, 1976), 168ff.
26. Vitz, *Psychology as Religion: The Cult of Self-Worship*, 33.

27. Jean-Paul Sartre, *Existentialism and Human Emotions* (New York: Philosophical Library, 1957), 58.
28. Otto Baab, *The Theology of the Old Testament* (New York: Abingdon-Cokesbury, 1949), 105ff.
29. Hamilton, *To Turn from Idols*, 40.
30. Ibid., 54ff.
31. Ibid., 29.
32. Ibid., 31-32.
33. Ibid., 32.
34. Ibid., 39.
35. Donald J. Wiseman, "Astrology," *Baker's Dictionary of Christian Ethics*, ed. Carl F. H. Henry (Grand Rapids, Mich.: Baker, 1973), 42.
36. G. B. Caird, *Principalities and Powers* (Oxford: Clarendon Press, 1950), 51.
37. Hamilton, *To Turn from Idols*, 82.
38. Ibid., 67.
39. Thomas J. J. Altizer, "Commentary," *The Religious Situation: 1968*, ed. Donald R. Cutler (Boston: Beacon Press, 1968), 242ff.
40. Hamilton, *To Turn from Idols*, 12.
41. Ibid., 27.
42. Ibid., 228.
43. Ibid., 134.
44. Ethelbert Stauffer, "*Theos*," *The Theological Dictionary of the New Testament (TDNT)*, Vol. 3, 100.
45. Karl Georg Kuhn, ibid., 93.

TWO

THE ECLIPSE OF GOD AT CENTURY'S END

Evangelicals Attempt Theology Without Theism

R. ALBERT MOHLER, JR.

The sense of an ending is not a fact of nature, observed Frank Kermode; it is a feature of human consciousness.[1] We ascribe meaning to the turn of a new century and felt a sense of ending as the twentieth century came to a close. If a sense of ending is not a fact of nature, it is certainly a fact of our experience.

As the nineteenth century closed, Friedrich Nietzsche proclaimed that God was dead and that we had killed him. The twentieth century was not an era of great theological achievements. The romantic liberalism of the early decades gave way to the unstable halfway house of neoorthodoxy, which in turn surrendered to a host of radical and revisionist theologies, united only in their denial of classical orthodoxy. That century also saw the development of a resurgent evangelicalism in English-speaking Protestantism. Matured and chastened by the theological controversies of the century's first fifty years, evangelicals coalesced into a formidable intellectual, evangelistic, and cultural movement. If the radical and revisionist theologians were united in their rejection of classical orthodoxy, evangelicals were defined and recognized by their fervent commitment to the classical, evangelical, orthodox, and biblical convictions of historic Christianity.

As the century concluded, the radical theologians became even further radicalized, and the revisionists continued their program of eviscerating the historic claims of Christianity. The declining precincts of "mainline" Protestantism were not safe territory for the supernatural claims of Scripture or for the doctrinal foundations of classical orthodoxy.

What about the evangelicals? The second half of the twentieth century began with great promise. The newly resurgent evangelical movement quickly produced a credible body of theological literature in the defense of Christianity's historic doctrines. Alarmed by the massive theological accommodation of the age, the evangelicals contended for biblical truth and claimed an intentional continuity with the classical Christian tradition of orthodox doctrine.

The closing years of the century demonstrated a very different pattern, however. The ideological acids of modernity, the theological accommodationism of the age, and the temptations of the larger academic culture infected evangelicalism to the point that the theological integrity of the movement was clearly at stake. Having debated issues ranging from biblical inerrancy to the reality of hell, evangelicals are now openly debating the traditional doctrine of God represented by classical theism.

My argument is that the integrity of evangelicalism as a theological movement, indeed the very coherence of evangelical theology, is threatened by the rise of the various new "theisms" of the evangelical revisionists. Unless these trends are reversed and evangelicals return to an unapologetic embrace of biblical theism, evangelical theology will represent nothing less than the eclipse of God in the new century.

THE DOCTRINE OF GOD IN CRISIS

The very concept of God is among the most contested issues in contemporary thought and culture. To some, the notion of God in this postmodern culture is an oppressive concept. To others, the concept of God is merely a matter of emotivism and sentiment. Clearly, to suggest that the doctrine of God is in crisis is not to suggest a fading interest in spirituality. To the contrary, few cultures could exceed the sheer variety of spiritualities found in modern America.

God, in fact, seems to have become a commercially popular topic of interest. In just the past few years God has been the subject of a full-length biography that reached the best-sellers lists. The volume, *God: A Biography*, treated God as a narrative character who, though not the God of the Bible, was a significant literary figure.[2] In addition, God is the subject of a recent 400-page history. Karen Armstrong, whose various writings on spiritual issues have catapulted her to fame, recently released *A History of God*.[3] Nevertheless, Armstrong is not concerned with the Creator God who is sovereign and transcendent, but only with God as a cultural artifact, a literary character, or a religious symbol. Armstrong claims as her warrant the decline of the classical and biblical doctrine of God as a culturally binding symbol. As she states, "When one conception of God has ceased to have meaning or relevance, it has been quietly discarded and replaced by a new theology."[4] Thus, according to Armstrong, a doctrine of God reveals very little about God and very much about those who formulate the doctrine.

Indeed, Armstrong seems to have little confidence that we can know much about God himself. She explains, "it becomes clear that there is no objective view of 'God': each generation has to create the image of God that works for it."[5] If this be true, we should shudder to think of what doctrine of God would "work" for this generation.

We have seen the eclipse of the God of the Bible at century's end and on into the new century. In the wake of the Enlightenment, the prophets of extremity and the high priests of suspicion (Freud, Nietzsche, and Marx) and those who followed them have led the onward march of secularism and protest atheism. Modern culture commonly denies God as God, as well as the very notion of God as an objective referent. Furthermore, discussion of God, at least the God of the Bible, has been evacuated from the public square. This official atheism, often masked by banal spirituality, is the result of a century of increased secularism and secularization.

Inside the Church, atheism has been played out in a myriad of forms. Modernism reduced God to a kindly, if incompetent, cosmic grandfather. Stripped of supernaturalism, God has been rendered a mere concept in most liberal theology. A myriad of secularizing theologies, ranging from modern to postmodern, have made the doctrine of God a matter of ideological controversy. Analytical philosophy reduced God to a symbol, and other philosophical trends have reduced deity to a linguistic referent. Process theology reduced God to a force within a pantheistic cosmos, struggling with creation. Liberation theology presented God as the Great Emancipator, yet clearly with much work to do. Revisionist theologies of various forms present God as a concept to be molded and transformed at will. Feminist theology has treated God as a patriarchal oppressor or transformed the concept of God to include the feminine. In the wake of modern feminism, the title *Lord* has been rejected as oppressive and masculine, and the Trinity has been reconstituted on egalitarian terms.

The God of classical theism is out. What Vanderbilt Divinity School theologian Edward Farley calls "the classical, catholic theology of God" must be surrendered, he argues. As John A. T. Robinson said during the 1960s, "Our image of God must go."

Various forms of protest atheism have become commonplace. Karen Armstrong rejects the classical doctrine of God as abhorrent: "An omnipresent, all-knowing tyrant is not so different from earthly dictators who made everything and everybody mere cogs in the machine which they control. An atheism that rejects such a God is amply justified."[6] Yet, protest atheism is not a force exclusively external to the Church. To the contrary, the temptation of protest atheism has been the driving force in much mainline Protestant theology. The God of the Bible has been abandoned by many of the Church's theologians.

What about evangelicalism? Surely we can be assured that within evangelicalism the God of the Bible is worshiped, recognized, and confessed. But a look at popular evangelicalism reveals a God of sentimentality not unlike the God of the early modernists. The "user-friendly" God of market-driven evangelicalism bears little resemblance to the God of the Bible. This God is often presented as nothing more than a domesticated deity or, as R. C. Sproul has lamented, "a cosmic bell-hop."

Years ago A. W. Tozer warned, "The God of the modern evangelical rarely astonishes anybody. He manages to stay pretty much within the constitution. Never breaks our by-laws. He's a very well-behaved God and very denominational and very much one of us, and we ask Him to help us when we're in trouble and look to Him to watch over us when we're asleep. The God of the modern evangelical isn't a God I could have much respect for."[7]

Though certainly true decades ago, Tozer's statement is even more clearly warranted today. In popular evangelical piety we find a confusion of anthropomorphisms and feel-good conceptions of God. In many circles God is merely a therapeutic category. Many evangelicals are now mostly concerned about what good this God will do for us, how well this God may make us feel, and how much self-esteem this God may give us as His gift.

GOD IN THE HANDS OF EVANGELICAL THEOLOGIANS

The bankruptcy of modern evangelical piety is both a symptom and a reflection of the breakdown of the classical doctrine of God among many evangelical theologians. This doctrinal shift reveals deep fissures in the evangelical movement.

The new developments among those who call themselves evangelicals are strikingly similar to the pattern of the early modernists and liberals. Some evangelicals have adopted the language and the categories of the liberalism that began the twentieth century. The evangelical movement was driven by an explicit commitment to stand for biblical truth, even as that truth was under assault by the modern, secular, and anti-supernaturalistic worldview. That is to say, evangelicalism grew out of an explicit rejection of liberalism and modernism. To some extent, evangelicals knew who they were not only by the positive substance of what they confessed, but also by the negative measure of what others denied. Yet, over the final thirty years of the last century, evangelicalism became itself marked by an increasing theological pluralism. Doctrinal diversity is no longer merely an issue extraneous to evangelicalism. The evangelical movement is now marked by theological pluralism and diversity, even concerning the doctrine of God.

To some extent, many evangelicals appear to believe that the health of evangelicalism is established by how many different positions, convictions, and confessions can be drawn within the tent. Early evangelicals were willing to stand together, even while acknowledging differences on baptism, church government, and other issues of denominational distinction. This early diversity pales in significance to the pluralism now urged upon evangelicalism by many of its theologians. The doctrine of God is the central organizing principle of Christian theology and establishes the foundation for all other theological concerns. Evangelicals believe in the unity of truth. Therefore, a shift in one doctrine—much less the central doctrine—necessarily implies and involves shifts and transformations in all other doctrines.

My concern in the face of an evangelical crisis of theism does not relate to simple belief in God. Rather, the crisis is focused on the classical Christian doctrine of God as revealed in Holy Scripture and developed by the believing church through centuries of theological development. That is, the crisis of evangelical theism is seen in the denial of the God of classical theism as sovereign, transcendent, omnipotent, and omniscient.

The God of classical theism is self-existent, self-sufficient, simple in his being, and immutable. His moral character is revealed in attributes of love, holiness, and mercy. His power is evident as omnipotence, omniscience, and omnipresence. The doctrine of the Trinity affirms that this God is one in three and three in one—one God in three persons. This God is the sovereign Lord over all his creation, who rules, decrees, and reigns, and whose creation of the cosmos was *ex nihilo*. The God of the Bible is the sovereign Lord over all beings, all objects, and all time.

Needless to say, this is a God far removed from popular spirituality. This is not the God referenced in popular, cultural conversation, nor the God of much evangelical worship and piety. A study of religious belief conducted in the 1970s reveals just how radically our culture has compromised the doctrine of God. Sociologists asked the question, "Do you believe in a God who can change the course of events on earth?" One answer, which became the title of the study, was "No, just the ordinary one."[8] That is to say, modern men and women need no longer believe in a God who can change the course of events on earth, just the "ordinary" God who is an innocent bystander. Measured against the biblical revelation, however, this is not God at all.

The crisis of belief in the biblical doctrine of God is deeply rooted in modern culture. In his Bampton Lectures, philosopher Alasdair MacIntyre identified modernity as the root problem. The modern worldview, he acknowledged, is inherently hostile to the traditional doctrine of God. Indeed, the worldview of modernity rejects any claim of transcendence or the supernatural. Thus, MacIntyre suggests, "theology must choose between the orthodox path—which many modern persons will find incomprehensible—or the path of adaptation, which will lead away from orthodoxy."[9]

MacIntyre sets the issue clearly. These are the only two paths available to modern theology. Those who continue to confess and worship the God of classical theism will be increasingly marginalized in secular society. More to the point, the classical doctrine of God is now increasingly marginalized even within the Church.

We evangelicals who confess biblical theism must recognize that we will become increasingly incomprehensible to a secular culture. Our theological witness will grow increasingly foreign and antiquarian to a culture opposed to authority and dismissive of truth. To hold to the classical doctrine of God is, in some quarters, to be socially as well as theologically and ideologically displaced. To speak of God in terms of classical Christian theism is to employ a language and to reference a worldview unknown to many evangelicals.

As MacIntyre indicates, the only other path is some form of adaptation. This is the path taken by mainstream Protestantism and those who seek to negotiate a truce with the modern worldview. The result is, of course, a surrender of transcendence and the loss of the coherence of biblical theism.

Long ago those committed to liberalism chose the road of radical adaptation. Divine transcendence and sovereignty were forfeited, and God became merely symbolic—impotent but nevertheless intellectu-

ally interesting and culturally useful. The God of modern liberalism
may at best be consulted. He certainly is not feared. A generalized theological confusion now marks the church. As Lutheran theologian
Robert Jenson has suggested, "Plainly, western Christenism is now
baffled by its God."[10] Evidently many Christians are baffled by their
God—that is, the God of classical theism as confessed by the believing church. This God is out of place in our modern world, surrounded
by the theological immaturity of the contemporary church. The coming evangelical generation appears largely defenseless against the
modern worldview.[11]

Jenson argues that this bafflement is the inevitable consequence
of modernity. Current ideologies rule out the supernatural, the transcendent, and the very notion of God himself. God, suggests Jenson,
suffers three great disabilities in the modern age:

> God is useless in the context of a community that interprets
> itself and its world mechanically; God is offensive in the con-
> text of our pragmatism of historical liberation; and God is par-
> ticular in the context of universal acquaintance.[12]

Jenson's list of God's three apparent disabilities in our age is
instructive but not exhaustive. Postmodern culture has clearly
rejected the God of the Bible and has replaced the self-revealing God
of Holy Scripture with a deity cut down to size in order to fit modern
ideological conceptions. The secular worldview is so thoroughly committed to scientific naturalism that no concept of God is now necessary to explain the cosmos. For many, any concept of God is now
useless or irrelevant. What is at stake for the believing church? As I
stated above, the doctrine of God is the central axiom of Christian theology. Or as J. I. Packer has argued, theism is the paradigm of Christian
theology. That is to say, theism is "the basic conceptual structure in
terms of which all particular views of doctrine should be formed and
focused."[13] Packer continues, "Views that reflect a different paradigm
may be interesting, but they cannot be fully Christian."[14] Packer is
precisely correct. Classical Christian theism is the paradigm of
Christian theology and thus is the form, morphology, and structure of

Christian thinking. No other paradigm, no matter how interesting and fascinating, can be considered authentically Christian.

Where does evangelicalism stand on this account? Ominous signs of evangelical compromise are already apparent. In 1990 the evangelical news magazine *Christianity Today* trumpeted what some have called "The Evangelical Megashift." Robert Brow argued that evangelical theology has shifted from an Augustinian and Reformation foundation to a doctrine of God far more congenial to modernity. Brow declared and championed this theological revolution. What will this revolution reject? Rendered obsolete and out of step are such central doctrines as substitutionary atonement, any penal understanding of the cross, forensic justification, imputed righteousness, and eventually the notion of hell. This revolution has declared out-of-date a notion of God as omnipotent, omniscient, and sovereign. Brow is quite confident of the eventual victory of this theological revolution. As he stated, "A whole generation of young people has breathed this air."[15]

Clearly, Brow is correct in his assessment that an entire generation has breathed deeply the fumes of modernity.[16] Research indicates that the hegemony of the modern worldview is leading to theological transformation and compromise in evangelical ranks. As James Davison Hunter states:

> This overall course—of tradition conforming to the cognitive and normative assumptions of the modern worldview—is relatively new to Evangelicalism, but not to the theological enterprise generally. It has gone furthest in liberal theological traditions. And though the Evangelical pattern has not gone as far as theological liberalism, the two share the central process.[17]

Young evangelicals are not alone in following this process of cultural accommodationism. Older evangelicals have largely paved the way for this pattern of theological acquiescence. The pattern has played out sufficiently for Brow to be confident of the eventual triumph of a new theism within evangelicalism. Brow understands that behind this shift in doctrine is a larger and more fundamental shift in consciousness. As he observed:

Many readers of *Christianity Today* will recognize that they have moved in some of these directions without being conscious of a model shift. And the old model can be modified and given qualifications for a time. But once three or four of these changes have occurred, our thinking is already organized around the new model. We may still use old-language and assume we believe as before, but our hearts are changing our minds.[18]

Brow is not alone in urging evangelicalism toward this theological revolution. He is joined by such figures as Richard Rice, John Sanders, William Hasker, David Basinger, and Clark Pinnock. These, joined by a few others, are the current molders of the theological "megashift."

Of these, Clark Pinnock deserves special attention. If any single character in modern evangelicalism represents this doctrinal revolution, it is Pinnock. More than any other evangelical theologian, Pinnock has intentionally represented and championed this megashift and the redirection of evangelical theology. In *The Openness of God*, Pinnock sets forth his justification for revising classical theism: "I believe that unless the portrait of God is compelling, the credibility of belief in God is bound to decline."[19]

Setting two rival conceptions of God in tension, Pinnock distinguishes between the classical doctrine of God and the new "open" doctrine of God. He criticizes the classical doctrine of God as too Augustinian and too dependent upon formal philosophical categories. This classical conception, he argues, presents God as an aloof monarch who is unchangeable, all-determining, and irresistible. Over against this doctrine of God, Pinnock presents his new model, with God conceived as a caring parent, characterized by love and responsiveness and attitudes of generosity, sincerity, openness, and vulnerability. God the aloof monarch is here set against God the caring parent.

Clearly, Pinnock can claim some biblical foundation for his notion of God as a caring parent. The Bible presents God as Father, a loving parent whose reign over creation is not dictatorial but is the expression of omnipotent love. But this parental conception of God urged upon us by Pinnock also suggests that the qualities he identifies as openness and vulnerability are inherent in the biblical notion of God as parent.

When applied to the doctrine of God, the very notions of openness and vulnerability demand explanation and clarification. To whom or to what is God understood to be open? How are we to conceive God's vulnerability?

First, we must recognize the false dichotomy presented by Pinnock and the other exponents of the new theism. Their pattern is to present the traditional doctrine of God in terms that are so impersonal, remote, and static that the doctrine is seen to violate the texture of Scripture. But Pinnock is neither fair nor accurate in his presentation of the traditional doctrine of God.

Pinnock claims to have retained a notion of God's sovereignty. Nevertheless, he admits that the mode of God's sovereignty presented by his new conception is radically different from sovereignty as conceived in classical orthodoxy. Essentially Pinnock argues that the doctrine of God developed by the early church was overly influenced by Hellenistic philosophy and a "tilt toward transcendence." He blames Augustine and the early churches' use of Greek philosophy as the fountainheads of a distorted doctrine of God that, he charges, continued its development through the medieval synthesis and the Reformation and continues even today in popular piety. At base, Pinnock argues that the classical doctrine of God is overly dependent upon Greek philosophy and insufficiently established in Scripture.

The static and transcendent doctrine of God championed by classical orthodoxy is, Pinnock charges, no longer culturally compelling. It is a doctrine that fails to fit congenially within the modern worldview and contemporary intellectual culture. Rather than fight the trend, Pinnock suggests that evangelicalism will do well to adopt modernity's thought forms. He states:

> Modern culture can actually assist us in this task because the contemporary horizon is more congenial to dynamic thinking about God than is the Greek portrait. Today it is easier to invite people to find fulfillment in a dynamic, personal God than it would be to ask them to find it in a deity who is immutable and self-enclosed. Modern thinking has more room for a God who

is personal (even tri-personal) than it does for a God as absolute substance. We ought to be grateful for those features of modern culture which make it easier to recover the biblical witness.[20]

Pinnock sets clearly the most important issue faced by evangelical theology. But is it our task to force the biblical doctrine of God to answer to modern culture, or to address modern culture with the biblical doctrine of God? If modern culture—or any culture—establishes the baseline for the doctrine of God, such a doctrine will certainly bear little resemblance to the God of the Bible.

Pinnock's revisionism does not extend only to the general conception of a doctrine of God, but to the particulars as well. The doctrine of the Trinity is reconceived as a community of persons rather than as modes of being, and Pinnock urges a social understanding of the Trinity as a replacement for the historic affirmation of an ontological trinitarianism. Providence is redefined, for the God of freewill theism is stripped of the traditional understandings of omniscience and omnipotence. Instead, Pinnock defines providence in these terms: "At great cost, God is leading the world forward to the place where it will reflect the goodness that God himself enjoys."[21]

Though Pinnock denies that his new doctrine of God is a form of process theology, the pantheistic structure of process philosophy is evident in Pinnock's system. He claims to hold to a doctrine of creation *ex nihilo*, but God appears to have collapsed into the cosmic system after the act of creation. Pinnock fails to demonstrate how his new theism avoids the admitted biblical failures of process theism.

In the new evangelical theism, God's power is redefined in terms of partnership with his people. In language that would fit well within modern political discourse, God's partnership is exercised through his empowerment of creation. This empowerment is essentially relational and limits God's own sovereign power, or at least his exercise of power. As Pinnock explains:

Condescension is involved in God's decision to make this kind of world. By willing the existence of significant beings with independence status alongside of himself, God accepts limitations not imposed from without. In other words, in ruling over the world God is not all-determining but may will to achieve his goals through other agents, accepting the limitations of this decision. Yet this does not make God "weak," for it requires more power to rule over an undetermined world than it would over a determined one. Creating free creatures and working with them does not contradict God's omnipotence but requires it. Only Omnipotence has the requisite degree and quality of power to be (in Henry Boer's words) an "ad hoc" God. One who responds and adapts to surprises and to the unexpected, God sets goals for creation and redemption and realizes them "ad hoc" in history. If Plan A fails, God is ready with Plan B.[22]

This extended statement must be taken in one piece in order to see the full effect. By these words the theological revolutionaries set forth the case clearly. God's rulership over all creation is reduced to an "ad hoc" sovereignty. In creation, Pinnock argues, God necessarily took a great risk and refused to be an all-determining deity. This notion of "ad hoc" sovereignty shakes our theological foundations. The God of the Bible, whom Pinnock claims to present more faithfully than classical theism, is not a God who exercises an "ad hoc" sovereignty. His sovereignty is absolute and unconditional and, though presented in intimate and personal terms, does not compromise God's essential character or power. The theism Pinnock presents understands God to be ready with Plan B when his Plan A fails. But the God of the Bible is not a God whose plans ever fail.

If God's providence and power are radically redefined, God's omniscience is basically eviscerated. The relationship between human freedom and divine foreknowledge has been argued since the earliest centuries of the Church. Origen and Celsus argued the issue, and in a modern context Pinnock now raises the issue as a necessary redefinition of the doctrine of God. As he argues, "Philosophically speaking, if choices are real and freedom significant, future decisions cannot be exhaustively foreknown."[23] He continues, "It would seriously undermine the reality of our decisions if they were known in advance."[24] Without embarrassment, Pinnock claims modern libertarian notions of human freedom and autonomy as adequate justification for limiting the knowledge of God. He continues his argument, "I would contend that the Bible does not represent God in possession of exhaustive knowledge of all future contingents. On the contrary, it presents God as a dynamic agent who deals with the future as an open question."[25] This radical revision of the traditional doctrine, he admits, is "a faintly heretical possibility."[26]

God's sovereignty is further redefined in terms of his "ad hoc" conception. God does the best he can do under the circumstances, argues Pinnock. In taking the risk of creation, God accepted the vulnerability that was inherent in creating a universe of free creatures and contingent objects. This was necessary, he argues, in order to ensure genuine human freedom and the meaningfulness of human existence.

God, as presented by Pinnock, is always ready with Plan B when Plan A fails. We must presume that Pinnock would allow for Plans A, B, C, D, E, etc. as necessitated by subsequent world events that are unexpected and unknown by God.

Clearly, this requires a thorough redefinition of divine sovereignty. As Pinnock defines God's sovereignty, it means:

> God is sovereign according to the Bible in the sense of having the power to exist in himself and the power to call forth the universe out of nothing by his Word. But God's sovereignty does not have to mean what some theists and atheists claim, namely, the power to determine each detail in the history of the world.[27]

God, according this system, is "the ground of the world's existence and the source of all its possibilities."[28]

God brings his will to effect by his power "to anticipate the obstructions the creatures can throw in his way and respond to each new challenge in an effective manner."[29] The God presented by those who advocate this "creative love theism" is responsive and clever, but not sovereign in any legitimate sense. This God is resourceful but does not insist on having his way. He allows his creatures to frustrate his plans and obstruct his design. Human freedom is set against divine sovereignty in such a way that one claim limits the other.

In Pinnock's argument, divine sovereignty and foreknowledge are limited by a very straightforward assertion of human freedom. As Pinnock acknowledges, "I stand against classical theism which has tried to argue that God can control and foresee all things in a world where humans are free."[30]

THE THEOLOGICAL CHALLENGE:
THE RECOVERY OF THEISM

This brief review of current theological revisionism among evangelicals hardly begins to raise the full scope of issues at stake. My concern is directed at the heart of these issues—the call for a revised doctrine of God.

Those who demand the transformation of the classical Christian doctrine of God claim the radical shift of thought in modern culture as sufficient cause for their doctrinal modification. In response, while theology must always take modern thought forms into consideration, the biblical doctrine of God must not be surrendered. Our task is not to ensure that our doctrine of God is culturally compelling, but that it is biblically faithful.

The "creative love theism" advocated by an increasing number of evangelicals represents a clear and present challenge to the doctrinal integrity of the evangelical movement. This finite theism fails the test of biblical fidelity and presents a God hardly recognizable in the light of Scripture and more than 2,000 years of Christian theology.

B. B. Warfield once remarked that God could be removed altogether from some systematic theologies without any material impact on the other doctrines in the system.[31] My fear is that this indictment can be generalized to much contemporary evangelical theology. Evangelicals are not arguing over the denominational issues that marked the debate of the twentieth century's early years. Sadly, evangelicals now debate the central doctrine of Christian theism. The question is whether evangelicals will affirm and worship the sovereign and purposeful God of the Bible or shift their allegiance to the limited God of the modern megashift.

CHAPTER 2

1. Frank Kermode, *The Sense of an Ending: Studies in the Theory of Fiction* (Oxford: Oxford University Press, 1967).
2. Jack Miles, *God: A Biography* (New York: Alfred A. Knopf, 1995).
3. Karen Armstrong, *A History of God* (New York: Alfred A. Knopf, 1993).
4. Ibid., xx.
5. Ibid.
6. Ibid., 383.
7. A. W. Tozer, *The Quotable Tozer*, Vol. 2 (Camp Hill, Penn.: Christian Publications, 1994), 78.
8. Grace Davie, "An Ordinary God: The Paradox of Religion in Contemporary Britain," *The British Journal of Sociology*, 41 (1990), 395-422.
9. Cited in David Wells, "Modernity and Theology: The Doctrine of God," in *Faith and Modernity*, eds. Philip Sampson, Vinay Samuel, and Chris Sugden (Oxford: Regnum Books, 1994), 125-126.
10. Robert W. Jenson, "The Christian Doctrine of God," in *Keeping the Faith: Essays to Mark the Centenary of Lux Mundi*, ed. Geoffrey Wainwright (Philadelphia: Fortress Press, 1988), 25.
11. James Davison Hunter, *Evangelicalism: The Coming Generation* (Chicago: University of Chicago Press, 1987).
12. Jenson, "The Christian Doctrine of God," 27.
13. James Packer, "Taking Stock in Theology," in *Evangelicals Today*, ed. John King (London: Lutterworth Press, 1973), 25.
14. Ibid.
15. Robert Brow, "The Evangelical Megashift," *Christianity Today*, February 19, 1990, 12.
16. James Davison Hunter identifies this process as "Cognitive Bargaining."
17. Hunter, *Evangelicalism*, 48.
18. Robert Brow, "The Evangelical Megashift," 12.
19. Clark Pinnock, *The Openness of God* (Downers Grove, Ill.: InterVarsity Press, 1994), 101.
20. Ibid., 107.
21. Ibid., 111.
22. Ibid., 113.
23. Ibid., 123.
24. Ibid.
25. David Basinger and Randall Basinger, eds., *Predestination and Freewill: Four Views of Divine Sovereignty and Human Freedom* (Downers Grove, Ill.: InterVarsity Press, 1986), 139. Contributors to the volume included John Feinberg, Norman Geisler, Bruce Reichenbach, and Clark Pinnock.
26. Ibid.
27. Ibid., 145.
28. Ibid.
29. Ibid., 146.
30. Ibid., 151.
31. His specific concern was Charles G. Finney's *Systematic Theology*.

THREE

THE NEVER-CHANGING CHRIST FOR AN EVER-CHANGING CULTURE

DANIEL L. AKIN

From the first century to the present, Christians have declared that "Jesus Christ is Lord" (Phil. 2:11; cf. 1 Cor. 12:3; Rev. 19:16) and that he is "the same yesterday and today and forever" (Heb. 13:8). His followers have proclaimed by faith what will one day be evident to all. Every earthly and temporal power will recognize and be subject to the majesty and sovereign lordship of Jesus. James D. G. Dunn addresses the significance of Jesus for first-century believers and the decisive nature of his impact on their lives when he asserts:

> Some movements have no dominant figure in the beginning; but Christianity began with Jesus. And it was the meaning of Jesus, of what he had said and done, together with what the first Christians understood him to be and to have been, to be doing and to have done, which was the most significant factor in the new sect's own developing self-understanding and developing sense of distinctiveness over against the other religions, sects and philosophies of the time.[1]

As the community of faith, the Church remains the herald of the meaning of Jesus, proclaiming who he is and what he has done. In the midst of an ever-changing world, the Church must be faithful in its witness to Jesus and his Gospel. Throughout history the Bride of

Christ has affirmed its faith through simple confessions such as that found in Romans 10:9 and through more developed creedal statements such as the Nicene Creed (A.D. 325), where the Church confessed its belief in

> one Lord Jesus Christ, the only-begotten Son of God, begotten of the Father before all worlds, God of God, Light of Light, Very God of Very God, begotten, not made, being of one substance with the Father by whom all things were made; who for us men, and for our salvation, came down from heaven, and was incarnate by the Holy Spirit of the Virgin Mary, and was made man, and was crucified also for us under Pontius Pilate. He suffered and was buried, and the third day he rose again according to the Scriptures, and ascended into heaven, and sitteth on the right hand of the Father. And he shall come again with glory to judge both the quick and the dead, whose kingdom shall have no end. . . .

In the Chalcedonian Creed (A.D. 451), the Church affirmed that the Lord Jesus is

> at once complete in Godhead and complete in manhood, truly God and truly man, consisting also of a reasonable soul and body; of one substance [homoousios] with the Father as regards his Godhead, and at the same time of one substance [homoousios] with us as regards his manhood; like us in all respects, apart from sin; as regards his Godhead, begotten of the Father before the ages, but yet as regards his manhood begotten, for us men and for our salvation, of Mary the Virgin . . . one and the same Christ, Son, Lord, Only-begotten, recognized in two natures, without confusion, without change, without division, without separation; the distinction of natures being in no way annulled by the union, but rather the characteristics of each nature preserved and coming together to form one person and subsistence [hupostasis], not as parted or separated into two persons, but one and the same Son and Only-begotten God the Word, Lord Jesus Christ; even as the prophets from earliest times spoke of him, and our Lord Jesus Christ himself taught us. . . .

It has been the conviction of faithful Christians from the inception of the Church that to neglect or compromise such orthodox confessions is tantamount to the betrayal of the Lord. Indeed, there is no genuine Christianity other than that based upon the absolute truth of Jesus Christ as the incarnate Son of God. The Body of Christ, if it is to be the true Church of its Lord, must proclaim and embody the Gospel of Christ and the Christ of the Gospel to all people. It is called to evangelize men and women "from every tribe and language and people and nation" (Rev. 5:9), embracing them in a loving community of faith and discipleship under the lordship of Jesus Christ. In obedience to this Christ-centered mandate, the Church extends itself to all who are in need, especially the disenfranchised, the poor, the oppressed, the despised, the abused, and the hurting. Because its Savior is the Savior of the world (1 Tim. 4:10; 1 John 4:14), the Church is called to be a family of diversity that includes people of every race, color, class, and nation. We affirm that we are stronger and better together than we can ever be apart.

Unfortunately, something has gone terribly amiss. We live in a culture that has gone mad in its rebellion against God. Today the Church itself appears on the verge of insanity, having forsaken the exclusive claims of its Christ and the instruction of His Word. We have lost our way and abandoned our moorings. Tragically, the deadly virus of modernity has even infected evangelicalism. R. Albert Mohler correctly asserts:

> The theological unity that once marked the movement has given way to a theological pluralism. . . . Indeed, by the late 1970's it was clear that basic theological fissures were forming. . . . Though the division originated in debates over the formal principle of Scripture, it soon spread to material doctrines including Christology, the Atonement, justification, and virtually every other major doctrine.[2]

My main concern is how Christology (the person and work of Jesus Christ) will be understood in the future. George Barna has noted that while most Americans believe good and positive things about Jesus, almost half believe that he sinned. Furthermore, pseudo-scholars continue to conjure up bizarre concoctions and fantasies about the historical Jesus that are popularized by a naive and sensationalist media, unfortunately resulting in significant confusion for the majority of Americans, most of whom are biblically and theologically illiterate. Such reinterpretations of Jesus fail to recognize his historical significance. Jaroslav Pelikan has said, "Regardless of what anyone may personally think or believe about him, Jesus of Nazareth has been the dominant figure in the history of Western culture for almost twenty centuries. . . . It is from his birth that most of the human race dates its calendars, it is by his name that millions curse and in his name that millions pray."[3]

Christians believe that Jesus will continue to be the dominant figure in the twenty-first century, and in every future century. If the Church is to maintain fidelity to "the faith that God has once for all entrusted to the saints" (Jude 3), however, the twenty-first-century Jesus must be the Jesus of the first century. Our ever-changing culture needs the never-changing Christ who alone can provide both the foundation and direction for Christian faith and practice as the Church faces the challenges of a new era. Four pillars from the New Testament can provide stability for the Church in the new millennium, a time when the Church needs to be recalled to biblical authority and when it needs to define and defend its faith clearly and fully. Drawn from the comprehensive revelation of the New Testament, these four key Christological texts show how to know and worship the One whom Augustine described as "beauty ever ancient, ever new."[4]

PILLAR ONE:
LOGOS CHRISTOLOGY (JOHN 1:1-18)

Logos Christology is founded upon the prologue to John's Gospel (1:1-18), which has been a bulwark for reflection on a number of crucial theological themes by several significant thinkers. For example, Millard Erickson identifies five attributes and activities ascribed to the *Logos*: (1) preexistence, (2) deity, (3) creative work, (4) incarnation, and (5) revelatory work.[5] Bernard Ramm has written, "It has been standard teaching in historic Christology that the *Logos*, the Son, existed before the incarnation . . . pre-existence is part of the protology ('first things') or the theology of beginning."[6] D. A. Carson addressed the significance of the title *Logos* when he explained that "John's summarizing title for Jesus is the 'Word.' It is a brilliant choice. In the beginning was the Word; in the beginning God expressed himself, if you will. And that Self-Expression, God's own Word, identified with God yet distinguishable from him, has now become flesh, the culmination of the prophetic hope."[7]

By using *Logos*, John takes a familiar first-century term and fills it with new meaning. The *Logos* existed in the beginning and is in some sense distinct from the Father. Yet the *Logos* is God. He is the member of the trinitarian Godhead who is the agent of creation and the source of both life and light. He is the "only begotten" (*monogenes*) of God (1:14, 18; 3:16, 18; 1 John 4:9)[8] who took on flesh (*sarx*), human nature apart from sin, and entered history to reveal, literally to exegete (*exegesato*, v. 18), the invisible God. John's use of *Logos* "seems to imply that the word he is speaking of is that prophetic word which goes forth from God's mouth to accomplish creation, judgment, redemption and renewal. John uses *Logos* because it is the natural word for expressing the meaning of the Hebrew word *dabar* when the word was used in the context of God's revelation."[9] Yet this Word is more than verbal expression. He is a person, and that person is the very Son of God. C. K. Barrett clarifies the issue when he remarks, "The deeds and words of Jesus are the deeds and words of God; if this be not true the book [John's Gospel] is blasphemous."[10]

Logos Christology is ontologically focused, for it addresses the *person* of Jesus Christ rather than his work. *Logos* Christology emphasizes how the Son of God is *different* from us. A focus on the Incarnation, on the other hand, reveals how He has become like us. Both truths must be maintained in delicate balance.

The importance of the doctrine of the Incarnation cannot be overstated. It is the vital and nonnegotiable expression of historic orthodox Christianity. B. B. Warfield asserted the central character of this essential formula even as theological compromise was sweeping the late nineteenth century:

One of the most portentous symptoms of the decay of vital
sympathy with historical Christianity which is observable in
present-day academic circles is the widespread tendency in
recent Christological discussion to revolt from the doctrine of
the Two Natures in the Person of Christ. The significance of
this revolt becomes at once apparent, when we reflect that the
doctrine of the Two Natures is only another way of stating the
doctrine of the Incarnation; and the doctrine of the Incarnation
is the hinge on which the Christian system turns. No Two
Natures, no Incarnation; no Incarnation; no Christianity in any
distinctive sense.[11]

Warfield knew what was at stake. He realized that the doctrine of
the incarnation of the Son of God permeated the New Testament and
could not be rejected without devastating results. Thus he concluded
that

the doctrine of the Two Natures of Christ is not merely the synthesis of the teaching of the New Testament, but the conception which underlies every one of the New Testament writings
. . . it is not only the teaching of the New Testament as a whole
but of the whole of the New Testament, part by part.
Historically, this means that not only has the doctrine of the
Two Natures been the invariable presupposition of the whole
teaching of the church from the apostolic age down, but all the
teaching of the apostolic age rests on it as its universal
presupposition.[12]

James D. G. Dunn is led by the historical evidence to argue:

There was no question in my mind that the doctrine of incarnation comes to clear expression within the New Testament—
certainly at least in a sense which clearly foreshadows the
further growth or evolution to the full blown doctrine of the
historic Christian creedal statements. On almost any reckon-
ing, John 1:14 ranks as a classic formulation of the Christian
belief in Jesus as incarnate God.[13]

To profess that Jesus of Nazareth was God become man is a staggering claim. Yet, the Church's experience of Jesus drove a band of first-century Jews to this startling confession. Some modern critics deny this fundamental tenet of orthodox Christianity. The authors of *The Myth of God Incarnate*[14] and the participants in the "Jesus Seminar" are just a few proponents of a movement that is already on the way to the fringe of Christian scholarship. Other experts may seek to redefine *Logos* and the Incarnation. Those now enamored with "Spirit Christology"[15] fit this description. Surely Carl F. H. Henry is correct when he claims that "more than any other century since Christian beginnings, our century seems confused over the identity of Jesus and unsure even of what the Nazarene thought of himself and of his role in the world. . . . [But] for an orthodox Christian, the most important phrase in all intellectual history is that 'the Word became flesh' (John 1:14)."[16] The identification of Jesus as the God-man must be affirmed in this new century.

PILLAR TWO:
SERVANT CHRISTOLOGY (PHILIPPIANS 2:6-11)

The Christ-hymn of Philippians 2:6-11 has been called "a christological gem unparalleled in the New Testament."[17] With language akin to the Servant Song of Isaiah 52:13—53:12 and the washing of the disciples' feet in John 13:3-17, Paul presents Jesus "as the supreme example of humble, self-sacrificing, self-denying, self-giving service. . . ."[18] The hymn is rooted in ethical concern but branches out to address Christology and soteriology as well. It is the ethical focus, however, that is the focal point in "servant Christology."

Verse 5 commands[19] believers to have the mind of Christ. This mind is characterized by unity (v. 2), humility (v. 3), and sensitivity to others (v. 4). The idea of humility is developed in the hymn as God's willingness to be involved with humanity unfolds. Jesus is described in verse 6 as continually existing in the form (*morphe*) of God. Gerald Hawthorne points out that *morphe* expresses the manner in which a thing appears to human senses and always identifies the form that completely expresses that thing's underlying being. Therefore, when applied to God the word refers to his essential being, to the actual nature and character of God.[20]

Paul is clearly advancing the first-century church's understanding of Jesus in a unique and powerful manner. Dunn asserts that "there was little or no good evidence from the period prior to Christianity's beginning that the Ancient Near East seriously entertained the idea of a god or son of god descending from heaven to become a human being in order to bring men salvation, except perhaps at the level of popular pagan superstition."[21] Yet this is exactly what Paul is saying. Though himself brought up and trained in the strict monotheism of rabbinic Judaism, Paul is compelled by his own encounter with and personal reflection on the risen Lord to affirm the essential deity of Jesus.

And yet, "equality with God" (v. 6) was not a right Christ felt he had to seize or acquire, since it was his by nature. So he emptied himself and took the *morphe* of a *doulou* (v. 7). The parallel of *morphe theou* and *morphen doulou* is too striking to be accidental. Images of both an ambitious Satan and Adam certainly come to mind as each in his own way attempted, albeit unsuccessfully and tragically, to seize equality with God. A servant Christology shows a better way, and the text itself adequately addresses what is involved in self-emptying (*kenoo*): (1) He took the form (*morphe*, "essential nature") of a slave (*doulos*); (2) he was made in the likeness (*homoioma*) and fashion (*schema*) of a man; (3) he humbled himself (cf. 2:3); (4) he became obedient unto death; and (5) he died on the cross.

These verses reveal something about the very nature and being of our God. They demonstrate that it is of the very essence of this deity to give and to serve. The Son of God did not seize status. Rather, he served. He did not surrender his deity, but he did add humanity. As Erickson notes, "The incarnation was more a gaining of human attributes than a giving up of divine attributes."[22] Further, the type of humanity he added was not that of a sovereign, but that of a slave. He received not a crown, but a cross. Death is exactly what Christ endured. And it was not just any death, but death by means of an instrument that would move Cicero to write, "Let the very name of the cross be far away not only from the body of a Roman citizen, but even from his thoughts, his eyes, his ears" (*Pro Rabiro*, 5.10, 16).[23]

Verses 9-11 express the divine economy and ordering of status. Theologically, exaltation grows out of humility and service. This is a principle of the kingdom, one that is certainly neglected in American Christianity. Those who would be super-exalted (v. 9) must first be super-abased. Believers are called to make themselves very low in humble, sacrificial service to others. Such servants embody what God intended humanity to be. As William Hendricks has noted, Jesus models "what humanity ought to be and not what it has become."[24] Jesus is our ultimate example (1 Cor. 11:1). As Erickson argues, "Jesus is not only human as we are; he is more than human. Our humanity is not a standard by which we are to measure his. His humanity, true and unadulterated, is the standard by which we are to be measured."[25]

Christ humbled himself but was exalted by God. His acceptance of service unto death was his ultimate yes both to God and to a lost humanity. It was his ultimate act of obedience to his Father in self-giving, self-sacrificing, self-denying service to others.[26] Servant Christology calls us to serve others as our Lord has served us.

PILLAR THREE:
COSMIC CHRISTOLOGY (COLOSSIANS 1:15-20)

As God-man, Jesus Christ defies simplistic explanation. The incomparable Christ transcends human wisdom. As Ben Witherington has written, "No one descriptive term or title adequately encompasses the man who fits no one formula."[27] John calls him the *Logos*. Philippians 2 identifies him as the *morphe* of God. The hymn found in Colossians 1:15-20 introduces Cosmic Christianity through new but related concepts. Here Christ is the image (*eikon*) of God, the firstborn (*prototokos*) over the cosmos and the Church, the one in whom all the fullness (*pan pleroma*) of God dwells in a body (cf. 2:9-10). Of this text F. F. Bruce writes, "This is one of the great Christological passages of the New Testament, declaring as it does our Lord's divine essence, pre-existence, and creative agency."[28] Bruce links its themes to John 1:1-4, Hebrews 1:2-4, and the Divine Wisdom motif of Proverbs 8:22-

31. Cosmic Christianity is mentioned often in theological circles but is seldom defined adequately. Its biblical warrant originates in this text; so any developing theology along this path should be firmly rooted here.

Paul's thinking can be conceived as concentric circles of concern that begin with the cosmic and the universal but move progressively inward, first to the ecclesiastical and finally to the personal. As "the image of the invisible God," Christ makes visible the God no one has seen (cf. John 1:18). It could be said, "Christ is like God." It could also be said, "God is like Christ." That he is the visible manifestation of God is immediately and logically tied to his supremacy over three entities: (1) creation (vv. 15-17), (2) the Church (vv. 18-20), and (3) the Christian (vv. 21-23). Christ is the Lord, the preeminent One whom each of these is to serve. His lordship and supremacy is therefore cosmic, but it is equally personal. He is in no sense a part of creation, because he is its author in every detail. There is no room for pantheistic or panentheistic development. A finite theism is also clearly ruled out.

The all-encompassing nature of his cosmic rule is made clear through the word "all" or "everything," used eight times in verses 15-20. Nothing is outside or beyond his sovereign lordship. All reality has been created by him and for him. Furthermore, whether regarding creation, the Church, or the Christian, as Lord, Christ sustains and maintains the existence of each. Christ is origin and goal, principle of cohesion and center, Master of the visible and the invisible. Without Christ there would be no reality. Without Christ nothing would be, nor would anything exist.[29] Yet through the Son whom the Father loves (v. 13), the cosmos (material creation), the Church (spiritual creation), and the Christian (personal creation) have been brought under the sovereign rule of God. In the old creation and in the new creation, the one and all-sufficient "head" (a distinctively Pauline formulation), the Lord Jesus Christ, reigns supreme.

For the Church in a new millennium, the import of a Cosmic Christology is staggering. Christ is to have first place in all things. His theology is to be our theology. His ethic is to be our ethic. His mind is to be our mind. His heart is to be our heart. Christ is to have sovereign control over his Body, the Church, whether that Body is manifested universally or locally. Its members, each one uniquely gifted for service (Rom. 12; 1 Cor. 12; Eph. 4; 1 Pet. 4), are to be in absolute dependence upon and in complete surrender to him for life, power, and mission. In all things, and in each individual, he and he alone is to be supreme.[30]

PILLAR FOUR:
REVELATIONAL CHRISTOLOGY (HEBREWS 1:1-3)

Revelational Christology has usually been identified with Wolfhart Pannenberg and his *Jesus—God and Man*,[31] where he argues that all of history is under God's direction and is therefore a revelation of God.[32] It is important to examine Pannenberg's underlying methodology. His fundamental belief is that Jesus is at the center of every Christian theology, and that human knowledge of God is only made possible through God's revelation in Christ. Pannenberg asserts that "one can only speak about God himself in that at the same time one talks about Jesus."[33] This basic principle reflects the fact that God desires to reveal himself and has done so in the person of Jesus Christ. History, therefore, is best conceived as the stage upon which the divine actor has played his role. A Revelational Christology, while cognizant of God's mighty acts in history, focuses on the God who invaded history, the God who brought eternity into space/time reality, the God who is the Lord of history.

This emphasis on the God of history is the heart of Hebrews 1:1-3. Francis Schaeffer expresses the essence of this passage when he states, "He [God] is there and He is not silent."[34] William Lane writes that the author of Hebrews brings us "face-to-face with the God who speaks. He has repeatedly taken the initiative to disclose himself because he wants to be known."[35] But in these last days he has spoken and disclosed himself decisively, climatically, even finally and for all time in the person of his Son, our Lord Jesus Christ. Because of God's determination to be known, we can genuinely and "truly truthfully" know God. In our day many people stress the *absence* of God and the *silence* of God. Hebrews 1 is a much needed corrective for those obsessed with *deus absconditus* ("the hidden God").

Lane underscores the important fact "that it was necessary for God and the human family to be able to speak the same language." In the person of his Son, the Lord spoke through one who is:

1) "Appointed heir of all things" (v. 2).
2) The one "through whom he made the universe" (lit. "ages") (v. 2).
3) "The radiance of God's glory" (v. 3).
4) "The exact representation of his being" (v. 3).
5) "Sustaining all things by his powerful word" (v. 3).
6) The "purification for our sins" (v. 3).
7) The one who "sat down at the right hand of the Majesty in heaven" (v. 3).

God has met our need to know him "with our senses: to see him, listen to him, to touch him. . . . Like the alternating patterns of a kaleidoscope as it is turned in the hand, we are asked to consider Jesus who is eternal Son, Jesus who is the incarnate Son, Jesus who is the exalted Son."[36] This information is what Christians in the turbulent first century needed to know. This is also what Christians in our anxious century need to know. Lane concludes, "The word that the Son spoke to them yesterday is the word that he speaks today. And the word that he speaks today is the word that he pledges tomorrow and forever. . . . His abiding, unchanging quality lends stability to men and women in a period marked by instability."[37]

CONCLUSION

N. T. Wright has noted correctly, "The historian of the first century . . . cannot shrink from the question of Jesus."[38] Indeed, no one can shrink from the question of Jesus. What one thinks and believes about Jesus will impact any complete theological framework, any thoughtful worldview. As Wright comments, "If you see Jesus differently, everything changes."[39]

Melanchthon criticized speculative probing and reflection about God and Christ, arguing, "We do better to adore the mysteries of Deity than to investigate them . . . since to know Christ means to know his benefits, and not as they teach, to reflect upon his natures and the modes of his incarnation."[40] But surely those who would give exclusive attention to such a dictum are destined for theological error. Clearly, the Spirit of God moved the authors of Holy Scripture to reflect upon the mystery of the Incarnation. This fact is evident in the four pillars we have examined. They demonstrate that Jesus Christ is not only "God for us," he is also "God with us" (Matt. 1:23). Athanasius, and later Anselm, saw clearly that Jesus had to be both fully God and perfect humanity in order to redeem lost humanity.[41] Christology and soteriology are forever wed. Christological investigation is no mere exercise in metaphysical musings. There is no access to the work of Christ apart from his person. One must know Christ to have access to his work.

Furthermore, the Jesus we so often read about today, one who is only a wise teacher, religious sage, political revolutionary, Jewish peasant, Cynic spinner of proverbs, or inspiring guru, is a Jesus far removed from biblical revelation and one who is spiritually bankrupt and totally insufficient to meet the deepest needs of hurting humanity. Such is a vision of a Christ who is totally inadequate to energize and mobilize the Church to be salt and light (Matt. 5:13-16) in a world immersed in darkness. I. Howard Marshall gets to the heart of the matter when he argues, "The Christian faith has as its object the Jesus whose earthly life is a matter for historical investigation, but this investigation cannot be carried on in independence of faith . . . always [bear] in mind . . . that the Jesus of Christian belief is more than a merely historical figure."[42] Marshall also points out that the early church's theological reflection was in some sense the inevitable outworking of its encounter with the risen Christ. He contends that upon careful examination, the Jesus of history and the Christ of faith are one and the same. Marshall adds that

> the object of . . . faith is . . . the Jesus whose existence and ministry have been confirmed and illuminated by historical research, but whose significance is only fully seen in the light of that experience of the risen Lord which had coloured the interpretation of Jesus offered in the Gospels and the rest of the New Testament and which continues to illuminate the mind of

the believer. For as we have seen, ultimately the earthly Jesus is inadequate. Christian faith joyfully embraces the Jesus of the Bible, assured that the biblical accounts have a firm base in history, but knowing that "the Jesus of the historians" is not enough; only the biblical Jesus Christ, the earthly and the heavenly Lord, is adequate as the object of faith.[43]

This is the foundation of a Christology for the twenty-first century. This is the Lord who can provide the only truly satisfying solutions for the cries and pains of a world at the precipice of destruction. This is the Lord of whom Dietrich Bonhoeffer could write:

> They must come face to face with him. We may also have to come face to face with Goethe or Socrates. That is part of our culture and ethos. But far more depends upon our confronting Christ—life or death, salvation or damnation . . . it is seen that all rest upon the sentence, "And there is salvation in no one else" (Acts 4:12). The encounter with Jesus is fundamentally different from that with Goethe or Socrates. One cannot avoid encounter with the person of Jesus because he is alive. With some care Goethe can be avoided, because he is dead. A thousandfold are the ways that men have used to resist or evade an encounter with Christ.[44]

"Jesus Christ is the same yesterday, today, and forever" (Heb. 13:8, NKJV). This is the eternal, never-changing Christ for an ever-changing culture. Those who call Jesus "Lord" must be faithful to who he is, what he has done, and the task that he has assigned. Alister McGrath describes this relationship when he observes, "In its deepest sense, the love of God for man is that of a God who stoops down from heaven to enter into the world of men, with all of its agony and pain, culminating in the grim cross of Calvary."[45] Our great God and Savior has so loved us. Dare we love others any less? Dare we ignore the awesome responsibility that is ours? These four pillars—John 1:1-18, Philippians 2:6-11, Colossians 1:15-20, and Hebrews 1:1-3—form the solid foundation upon which any Christian orthodoxy must stand.

CHAPTER 3

1. James D. G. Dunn, *Christology in the Making* (Grand Rapids, Mich.: Eerdmans, 1980, 1989), ix.

2. R. Albert Mohler, Jr., "'Evangelical': What's in a Name?" in *The Coming Evangelical Crisis,* ed. John H. Armstrong (Chicago: Moody Press, 1996), 33.

3. Jaroslav Pelikan, *Jesus Through the Centuries* (New Haven, Conn.: Yale, 1985), 1.

4. Augustine, *Confessions,* as quoted in Pelikan, 223.

5. Millard Erickson, *The Word Became Flesh* (Grand Rapids, Mich.: Baker, 1991), 26-27.

6. Bernard L. Ramm, *An Evangelical Christology* (Nashville: Thomas Nelson, 1985), 47.

7. D. A. Carson, *The Gospel According to John* (Grand Rapids, Mich.: Eerdmans, 1991), 96.

8. In the New Testament *monogenes* only appears in these five texts.

9. D. H. Johnson, *"Logos,"* in *Dictionary of Jesus and the Gospels,* eds. Joel Green et al. (Downers Grove, Ill.: InterVarsity Press, 1992), 484.

10. C. K. Barrett, *The Gospel According to St. John: An Introduction with Commentary and Notes on the Greek Text,* 2nd ed. (London: SPCK, 1955, 1978), 156.

11. B. B. Warfield, *The Person and Work of Christ* (Philadelphia: Presbyterian & Reformed, 1950), 211.

12. Ibid., 237.

13. Dunn, *Christology in the Making,* xiii.

14. John Hick, ed., *The Myth of God Incarnate* (Philadelphia: Westminster, 1977).

15. This particular Christology has representatives both in the liberal and neoliberal tradition. For a representative of the former see Roger Haight, "The Case for Spirit Christology," *Theological Studies (TS)* 53 (1992), 257-287; and for the latter see Clark Pinnock, *Flame of Love* (Downers Grove, Ill.: InterVarsity Press, 1996), 79-111. While it is clearly the case that a biblical Spirit Christology would yield significant fruit, it is sadly the case that theological aberrations tend to be the result. Such defections may include: (1) a denial of Christ's deity wherein he is viewed more as a Spirit-intoxicated man; (2) an inadequate view of the atonement with a questioning of penal substitution; (3) promotion of soteriological inclusivism with the utter uniqueness of Christ being denied or compromised; (4) a rejection of the functional subordination of the Spirit to the Son; (5) a tendency toward finite theism and an unbiblical free-willism; (6) an unfounded attack on *Logos* Christology as promoting "abstract thinking," saying that it is guilty of "strip[ping] the self-emptying of the Son of its radicalness and even put[ting] his true humanity in jeopardy" (Pinnock, 91). Since Pinnock never identifies those who are guilty of this imbalance, we are left in the dark as to their identity.

16. Carl F. H. Henry, *The Identity of Jesus of Nazareth* (Nashville: Broadman, 1992), 63, 67.

17. Gerald Hawthorne, *Philippians,* WBC (Waco, Tex.: Word, 1983), 79.

18. Ibid.

19. The phrase is governed by a present imperative.

20. Ibid., 83-84.

21. Dunn, *Christology in the Making,* 251.

22. Millard Erickson, *Christian Theology* (Grand Rapids, Mich.: Baker, 1984), 734.

23. Quoted in Hawthorne, *Philippians,* 90.

24. William Hendricks, *Who Is Jesus Christ?* (Nashville: Broadman, 1985), 29.

25. Erickson, *The Word Became Flesh,* 721.

26. Hawthorne, *Philippians,* 89, 91.

27. Ben Witherington, *The Jesus Quest* (Downers Grove, Ill.: InterVarsity Press, 1995), 244.

28. F. F. Bruce, *Colossians,* NICNT (Grand Rapids, Mich.: Eerdmans, 1957), 192.

29. David Wells, *The Person of Christ* (Wheaton, Ill.: Crossway Books, 1984), 62.

30. Peter T. O'Brien, *Colossians, Philemon*, WBC (Waco, Tex.: Word, 1982), 50.

31. Wolfhart Pannenberg, *Jesus—God and Man*, trans. Lewis Wilkins and Duane Priebe, 2nd ed. (Philadelphia: Westminster, 1977).

32. Ramm, *An Evangelical Christology*, 189.

33. Ibid., 19-20.

34. Francis Schaeffer, *He Is There and He is Not Silent*, in *The Complete Works of Francis A. Schaeffer*, Vol. 1 (Wheaton, Ill.: Crossway Books, 1982).

35. William Lane, *Call to Commitment* (Nashville: Thomas Nelson, 1985), 29.

36. Ibid., 32.

37. Ibid., 36.

38. N. T. Wright, *Jesus and the Victory of God* (Minneapolis: Fortress, 1996), xiii.

39. Ibid., xiv.

40. *Loci Communes*, in W. Pauck, ed., *Melanchthon and Bucer*, LCC 19 (Philadelphia: Westminster, 1969), 21-22.

41. Athanasius, *On the Incarnation*; Anselm, *Cur Deus Homo*.

42. I. Howard Marshall, *I Believe in the Historical Jesus* (Grand Rapids, Mich.: Eerdmans, 1977), 106.

43. Ibid., 246.

44. Dietrich Bonhoeffer, *Christ the Center*, trans. Edwin H. Robertson (San Francisco: Harper & Row, 1960), 34.

45. Alister McGrath, *Understanding Jesus* (Grand Rapids, Mich.: Zondervan, 1987), 147.

PART TWO

WHO WILL BE SAVED?

INTRODUCTION

PAUL R. HOUSE

As the previous section indicates, not all challenges to orthodox belief come from outside evangelical circles. It is possible, after all, for individuals who confess a high view of Scripture to hold unbiblical theological ideas. The recent advocacy of inclusivism by some evangelicals is a significant example of this problem. To be sure, it is no secret that non-evangelicals have argued for decades that there may be a second chance after death for those who have never heard the Gospel, that salvation may be mediated through non-Christian religions, and that God's loving nature precludes the possibility that a majority of the human race is headed for an eternal hell. Interestingly, these thinkers have rarely disputed that the Bible teaches the notions they oppose. Rather, they have knowingly challenged the accuracy of the Scripture on these issues.

What is relatively new, and troubling, is that key thinkers from the evangelical tradition now agree with them in certain key respects. Though no one of goodwill can question the motives of individuals like Clark Pinnock, Richard Rice, and John Sanders, their arguments for inclusivism are faulty on methodological, theological, and practical grounds. It is clear that they believe their views will lead to more compassionate evangelism; but sadly, this goal in reality is undermined by their own theological position.

METHODOLOGY

Inclusivists employ a questionable eclectic methodology. Though it is impossible to critique them fully here, it is fair to say that inclusivists use biblical terminology to begin their arguments, then define those terms in non-biblical ways. For example, they routinely start discussions by asserting the biblical principle that God is love. Next, rather than defining this concept through contextual exegesis, they shift to a philosophical proposition: "A loving God will not give some persons opportunities to hear the Gospel that others will not have." Then they proceed to claim that this conclusion necessitates a further one, which is that salvation may reside in other religions, or even that saving faith may be exercised for the first time after death. Another example of this type of argumentation is the tendency to affirm that salvation comes only through Christ, which is certainly a biblical truth. Having stated the scriptural principle, however, they then argue that Jesus' death mediates salvation through other religions, a notion foreign to biblical theology. As Winfried Corduan argues in this section, inclusivists often gloss over the real differences between Christianity and other world religions. Through this sort of blended methodology the inclusivist sounds biblical without having to apply the whole of the Bible to his or her conclusions.

Further, inclusivist methodology sometimes includes emotional arguments that have little or no evidential basis. For instance, in this section Clark Pinnock asks why Doug Geivett cannot be more open to the possibility of more persons being saved. Of course, this question is not an argument. It is a less-than-subtle attempt to make those who disagree with inclusivism appear small-minded. Such questions are as inappropriate in organized discourse as a person committed to the exclusive nature of salvation in Christ asking inclusivists why they are so blind and liberal. The issue is not who loves people more; the issue is whose interpretation of Scripture is most accurate.

BIBLICAL THEOLOGY

Inclusivists also fail to take the whole of biblical theology into account. They are especially deficient in their analysis of the Old Testament's contribution to the debate, which in turn leads to an inadequate reading of relevant New Testament passages. Three issues deserve mention in this regard.

First, it is true that salvation comes to Jew and Gentile alike in the Old Testament, and it is true that not everyone who knows the living God in the Old Testament comes to this knowledge through direct commitment to the Sinai covenant. Abimelech, Melchizedek, Rahab,

Job, and others come to know God without the benefit of specific help
from the chosen people. Still, it must be emphasized that these biblical figures, however they enter into a relationship with God, know the
Lord in the same way that the Scriptures state that Israelites know
God. In other words, God does not reveal himself through Baalism or
some other ancient polytheistic religion. Thus, while it is true that the
Lord makes himself known through visions or other means, it is not
true that he is revealed as one who may be defined differently than the
one true God described in the rest of Scripture. Rather, these individuals receive knowledge of the creating, revealing, saving God known
by Abraham, Isaac, and Jacob.

Second, as their New Testament successors do in the book of Acts
and elsewhere, Old Testament figures urge non-Jewish audiences to
serve the living God. This tendency is not as prevalent as it is in the
New Testament, but it exists nonetheless. Jonah preaches to the
Assyrians, Daniel bears testimony to the Babylonians and to the Medes
and Persians, and several of the prophets denounce the nations' worship practices and promise a bright future for them if they come to
serve the Lord. There is no indication that the Lord mediates salvation
through any of the ancient religions known to the Old Testament writers. In fact, these religions are routinely criticized as mere imaginations of the human mind.

Third, the Old Testament does not indicate that the world is filled
with persons who would trust in the Lord if only they had the chance
to do so. In fact, quite the opposite is the case, for even the chosen people neglect the salvation revealed to them. Converts are won to the
Lord, but most who hear the truth reject it. It is also true that the Old
Testament offers no chance for salvation after death. Rather, the day
of the Lord is portrayed as providing a final destruction of the wicked.

The New Testament does not disagree with the Old Testament
in any of these matters. If anything, Jesus' preaching mission to his
fellow Jews, the early church's missionary efforts among Jews and
Gentiles alike, and the picture of final judgment offered in
Revelation and other books necessitate the doctrine of salvation
through specific faith in Christ alone during one's lifetime. Whether
ministering to polytheists or monotheists, the early church claimed

that committed, cognizant faith in Christ is the only way to eternal life. As for other religions, the New Testament uniformly considers continuing adherence to these faiths a serious barrier to a saving relationship with Christ.

EVANGELISM AND MISSIONS

Because of its methodological and theological weaknesses, inclusivism is also faulty on practical grounds. Again, the issue is not who loves lost people and who does not. There is not the slightest doubt that evangelicals who are inclusivists desire that millions of non-Christians will find eternal life. Nor is there any doubt that traditional evangelicals have the same desire. After all, evangelical missionaries have risked everything dear to them to take the Gospel to those who have never heard of Christ. They have used every conceivable legitimate means (and even some reprehensible illegitimate means) to make Christ known. At times they have found individuals who long to hear about Christ because of a vision or the influence of some other religion. It seems, though, that in every instance of this interest in the Gospel the seeker wishes a way out of a religion that does not honor Christ as the unique Son of God, and the visionary knows of Christ as the Scriptures reveal him, not as another religion portrays him. Missionaries have also found that many millions who hear about Christ do not respond to the Gospel by believing in Christ. Despite this latter fact, every effort must be made to encourage further attempts to preach the Gospel to the lost wherever they live.

The missionary record of traditional evangelicals is not perfect, but it is clearly on the side of doing everything possible to propagate the Gospel. It is too early to judge the missionary record of inclusivists, but it is likely that they will find it hard to preach their views zealously. Urgency will probably not mark their missionary efforts, nor will their reading of Scripture on the issue of evangelism likely prove compelling to non-Christians or Christians. These results will stem from faulty theology, not from a lack of zeal or the lack of an effective way to "market" the Gospel. Inclusivism may not prove as deadly to evangelism and missions as universalism, but there is little reason to think otherwise.

CONCLUSION

Inclusivism as defined in this section and in other publications bears the mark neither of full-orbed biblical theology nor of effective theological methodology. Clearly, inclusivism represents the thinking of caring, scholarly Christians who rely on extremely debatable philosophical reasoning for their position. At worst, inclusivism compromises the teachings of Scripture in a way that will undermine the effective propagation of the Gospel. Allowing the lost to take refuge in erroneous theology is not compassion; it is kindness gone awry. Thus, inclusivism is an unwilling yet culpable partner in the lost not taking responsibility for their adherence to idolatry and not confessing faith in Jesus Christ, the only name "under heaven given to men by which we must be saved" (Acts 4:12).

FOUR

ARE ALL DOOMED TO BE SAVED?

The Rise of Modern Universalism

TIMOTHY K. BEOUGHER

With none to heed their crying
For life, and love, and light
Unnumbered souls are dying
And pass into the night.[1]

Or do they? Do people who die without acknowledging Christ as their Savior really "pass into the night"? Or should that hymn, which embodies orthodox Christian thought about the fate of those who die without Christ, be abandoned along with other "outdated" beliefs? Should traditional Christian teaching concerning the final judgment and an eternal hell be "brought up to date," modified to fit the tolerant spirit of the times?

It has long been noted that there are three possible positions concerning the extent of the salvation of humankind: (1) *None* will be saved; (2) *some* will be saved; or (3) *all* will be saved. The traditional Christian teaching concerning the hereafter has been the second option: Only *some* will be saved. Within this position debates are ongoing as to exactly who will be saved (must one have explicit faith in Christ?) and what the final condition of the lost will be (will they suffer eternal, conscious torment?). Various *Southern Baptist Journal of Theology* articles have analyzed different challenges to traditional Christian teaching on these issues.[2]

This chapter seeks to explain and critique the third option—namely, *all* will be saved—the doctrine of universalism. Though it is presented in many forms, the basic teaching common to universalist systems is that God will eventually bring all people to salvation. The advocates of this position may disagree on the timing and the means of this final salvation, but they all claim (either hopefully or dogmatically) that it will take place.

We will begin by defining universalism and explaining its appeal. Then we will set forth a brief survey of the history of universalism. Next we will present the teachings of universalism (both in its "hope-so" and "dogmatic" forms), then give an evangelical critique. We will end with concluding remarks and suggestions about where to go from here.

N. T. Wright maintains universalism is "perhaps the greatest unspoken premise of modern thought within the Christian church."[3] While his sweeping assertion may be debatable, the importance of the issue is not. The doctrine of universalism involves more than a mere difference of opinion concerning eschatology. As Ronald Blue points out, this debate touches on several major doctrines of Christianity.[4]

DEFINING UNIVERSALISM:
"WIDE IS THE ROAD THAT LEADS TO LIFE"

Universalism may be defined as the teaching that though hell may exist, it will eventually empty, for God's will to save all persons individually will finally triumph.[5] All human beings ultimately will be saved. Hell thereby becomes a "means of grace" where God's love eventually wins everyone, even Judas (and some would say even Satan), back to himself.

The doctrine of universalism has been presented differently by those who have advocated it throughout the centuries. Some have claimed that no person is bad enough to be rejected ultimately. Recent universalism stresses that God's power and love is so great that it will eventually secure the salvation of the entire human race.[6] As Richard Bauckham notes, "Only the belief that ultimately all men will be saved is common to all universalists."[7]

How does the universalistic position work out in practice? While there are varying versions, universalists generally agree that those who leave this world in unbelief will enter hell. But having entered, they will sooner or later come out, having been brought to their senses and seeing their error in not acknowledging Christ. While in hell they will make a positive response to Christ because their suffering will have opened their eyes to the truth. Thus hell is real, but it is only temporary. All will be saved eventually, and God's universal salvific desire will have come to pass. No one will be finally lost. Hell will end up empty.

THE APPEAL OF UNIVERSALISM

Universalism has a strong appeal in cultures confronted by the pressures of pluralism. James Davison Hunter notes that in the face of intense religious and cultural pluralism during the past century, the pressures to deny Christianity's exclusive claims to truth have been "fantastic."[8] George Barna's 1993 survey of the beliefs of Americans (appropriately titled *Absolute Confusion*) found that nearly two out of three persons believe that all religions teach basically the same thing and that no one is superior to the others.[9]

Even evangelicals have not been immune to yielding to the pressure of pluralism. Using the results of his Evangelical Academy Project, Hunter notes that shifts in the evangelical theological view of salvation are discernible.[10] He reports that one of three "evangelicals" surveyed held the view that "the only hope for Heaven is through personal faith in Jesus Christ except for those who have not had the opportunity to hear of Jesus Christ."[11]

Hunter notes that these numbers signify a dramatic shift from the perspective of historical orthodoxy:

> The significance of all of this is plain. The introduction of these qualifications tempers the purity of the theological exclusivism traditionally held. Ultimate truth is not at issue here, only what people perceive to be ultimate truth. Thus, the existence of such a sizable minority of Evangelicals maintaining this stance represents a noteworthy shift away from the historical interpretations.[12]

This viewpoint is reflected in the comment made by former United States President and current Southern Baptist Sunday school teacher Jimmy Carter: "I cannot imagine an innocent person being deprived of God's eternal blessing because they don't have a chance to accept Christ."[13] Leighton Ford aptly illustrates this cultural pressure in his article entitled, "Do You Mean to Tell Me That in This Modern, Humanistic, Pluralistic, Tolerant Society You Still Believe in Hell?"[14]

Another appeal of universalism is that it appeases our feelings about persons being lost. When someone we know dies with his or her relationship to Christ in question, we begin to wonder if perhaps God might decide to save everyone in the end. I once talked with a pastor who had adopted universalism for this very reason. This man's father had never been interested in spiritual things, had never darkened the door of a church, and yet was, in this pastor's words, "a good man." This pastor told me, "The thought of my father being in hell was just too much for me to bear. The more I reflected on his situation, the more I became convinced that hell was a myth and that all would be saved." His theological shift came not from careful study of the Scriptures but from his own subjective experience and feelings.

A third appeal of universalism relates to the struggles of the missionary task. Bernard Ramm argues that belief in universalism is on the rise because the "task of world evangelism seems so hopeless."[15] With countless millions of people still unreached with the Gospel, the concept of universalism appeals to many people. In other words, if you think you are losing, then simply change the rules of the game.

But all sentiment aside, is the position of universalism a viable option for the Christian? Do the universalists present a convincing case? Before the arguments for universalism are presented in greater detail, I will offer a brief history of universalism.

THE HISTORY OF UNIVERSALISM[16]

Church historians generally agree that universalism first appeared in the Alexandrian School, especially with Origen (A.D. 185-254). Based on his belief that God's ultimate purpose is to restore the original unity in creation, Origen taught that all of the condemned and even the demons would eventually be brought, through a time of "purifying" punishment, into voluntary subjection to Christ.[17] Gregory of Nyssa, one of Origen's followers, taught salvation for all (including Satan!). Universalism was eventually condemned by the Synod of Constantinople in 543.

The condemnation of "Origenism" discredited universalism in the theological tradition of the East. In the West, the combined influence of Augustine's writings against universalism and Origen's heretical reputation insured that the Augustinian version of the doctrine of hell prevailed almost without question for many centuries.[18] During the Middle Ages universalism was propounded in the Platonic system of John Scotus Erigena (810-877).[19] During the Reformation period some of the radical Anabaptists and spiritualists, notably John Denck, were universalists.[20] Others espousing universalism prior to 1800 included some among the Cambridge Platonists and a few of the German Pietists.

F. E. D. Schleiermacher was the first prominent theologian of modern times to teach universalism.[21] In *The Christian Faith* Schleiermacher taught absolute predestination, rejecting any form of double predestination. All men are elected to salvation in Christ, he claimed, and God's desire to save all cannot fail. Schleiermacher argued against the traditional view of hell, claiming that the blessedness of the redeemed would be severely marred by their sympathy for the damned if the traditional teaching were true.

Nineteenth-century England saw a great deal of discussion on issues related to the future life. In 1853 F. D. Maurice was dismissed from his chair at King's College, London for teaching a theory of a "wider hope."[22] In 1862, for a tentative assertion of universalism in *Essays and Reviews* (1860), H. B. Wilson was condemned in the Court of Arches, being judged guilty of contradicting the Athanasian Creed.[23] F. W. Farrar denied eternal punishment in a series of sermons delivered in Westminster Abbey in 1877, which were subsequently published as *Eternal Hope* in 1878.[24] These sermons prompted a defense of the traditional doctrine of hell by E. B. Pusey.[25]

Bauckham notes that dogmatic universalism was less common in nineteenth-century England than "a general uneasiness with the traditional doctrine of hell."[26] Common to all these "wider hope" teachings was the assertion that death was not the decisive break that traditional orthodoxy had always taught:

> Repentance, conversion, moral progress are still possible after death. This widespread belief was certainly influenced by the common nineteenth-century faith in evolutionary progress. Hell—or a modified version of purgatory—could be understood in this context as the pain and suffering necessary to moral growth.[27]

The universalist thesis does not belong only to distant history, however. Twentieth-century advocates of some form of universalism include Karl Barth, John A. T. Robinson, Nels Ferré, and a host of lesser known theologians. Packer is right when he asserts that universalism "has come to stay" as a guest of Christianity.[28] And it is becoming more and more of a welcome guest in many circles. It has progressed from being "*the* heresy" to a commonly held position.[29] Richard Bauckham claims that since 1800 "no traditional Christian doctrine has been so widely abandoned as that of eternal punishment."[30]

"HOPE-SO" UNIVERSALISM

It is indeed a truism to note that the significance of Karl Barth's theology in the history of Christian thought has been tremendous. Concerning the topic under discussion, most concur that Barth neither affirmed nor denied the theory of universal salvation. Nevertheless, with his reconstruction of the doctrine of election, Barth has made many theologians suspicious about his opinion on the matter.[31] He appeared to teach the divine predestination of all human beings to salvation.

The Barthian doctrine of reconciliation too has led to the suspicion of universalism. Barth, speaking of Christ, says:

> His death [includes] the totality of all sinful men, those living, those long dead, and those still to be born, Christians who necessarily know and proclaim it, but also Jews and heathen,

whether they hear and receive the news or whether they tried and still try to escape it. His death was the death of all: quite independently of their attitude or response to this event.[32]

Bromiley detects in that doctrine "the trend toward an ultimate universalism."[33] Barthianism can also give the impression that the world is already redeemed and that evangelism consists simply in making known this fact.[34]

Barth perhaps can best be described as a "hope-so universalist" (as opposed to a dogmatic universalist).[35] He refused dogmatically to expect universal salvation because of his desire to protect the sovereignty of God's grace. Yet he still claimed that universal salvation "remains an open possibility for which we may hope."[36] He asserted that we have "no theological right to set any sort of limits to the loving-kindness of God which has appeared in Jesus Christ."[37]

Though Barth's influence seems to have waned in recent years, his teaching at this point continues to have adherents today. Carl Braaten, for example, asserts:

> We would teach a highly nuanced and qualified evangelical universalism. It is not a dogma, not a piece of knowledge, not something to which humans have a right and a claim. Yet, it is something for which we may cautiously and distinctly pray and hope, that in spite of everything that seems to point conclusively in the opposite direction, God's mercy will not cast off his world forever.[38]

Braaten concludes his essay by claiming:

> The scale is tilted decidedly [sic] toward the hope of universal reconciliation on account of Christ. We agree with Barth that it cannot be denied that eternal reprobation is a possibility, but in the light of God's verdict in the victory of Jesus Christ, it becomes an "impossible possibility."[39]

So "hope-so universalism," as I have defined it, argues that while one cannot proclaim dogmatically the certainty of universal salvation, it remains an open possibility for which one may hope.[40]

DOGMATIC UNIVERSALISM

Others go beyond Barth and Braaten and assert with full confidence that all will be saved. According to this viewpoint, we can not only hope for universal salvation—we can confidently expect it to happen! In this section I will set forth key arguments used by those who argue for dogmatic universalism by first looking at biblical arguments, then moving to philosophical/theological arguments.

Biblical Arguments

The biblical arguments for universalism can be grouped into three major divisions: (1) The saving desire of God; (2) the saving provision of God; and (3) the saving promise of God.[41] Due to space limitations, we cannot examine each separate verse used by those who espouse universalism, but the central issues raised by the various groupings of texts will be answered in my critique.[42]

The Saving Desire of God. Paul says that God "desires all men to be saved" (1 Tim. 2:4).[43] The apostle Peter also expresses the saving desire of God, writing that the Lord does not want "any to perish but for all to come to repentance" (2 Pet. 3:9). Thus Glasson states:

> And if God desires the salvation of every soul He has made, it is scarcely credible that the accident of death changes His attitude to His children. Does the Good Shepherd abandon His search for the lost sheep as soon as the border of earthly life is crossed, or will He ever cease to "go after that which is lost until he find it?"[44]

Universalists argue that if God desires it, then it will happen ultimately.

The Saving Provision of God. Included under this heading are the biblical passages that highlight the apparent universal value of the work of Christ, such as John 12:32 ("draw all men"), 2 Corinthians 5:19 ("reconciling the world"), Titus 2:11 ("the grace of God has appeared, bringing salvation to all men"), Hebrews 2:9 ("He might taste death for every one"), and 1 John 2:2 ("for those [sins] of the whole world"). Such texts, claim the universalists, speak of Christ dying for *all* mankind. If Christ died for all, and his death effectively paid for the sins of everyone, then all eventually will be saved.

The Saving Promise of God. The third group of biblical texts used by universalists are those that deal with the consummation of God's plan of redemption in history. Among those frequently cited are Acts 3:21 ("restoration of all things"), 1 Corinthians 15:26-28 ("all things [even death] are subjected to Him"), Ephesians 1:10 ("the summing up of all things in Christ"), and Philippians 2:9-11 ("that at the name of Jesus every knee should bow . . . that every tongue should confess that Jesus Christ is Lord").

I will offer a summary critique of these arguments in the next section, but first I will explain additional arguments that universalists propose for their position.

Philosophical/Theological Arguments

The first of these arguments is what could be called the argument from "Divine Love." N. T. Wright explains the basic logic of this view, admittedly in abbreviated form: "There are two Biblical ways of looking at salvation. One says that only Christian believers will be saved; the other says that all men will be saved. Since the latter is more loving, it must be true, because God is love."[45]

Nels Ferré advocates universalism in this manner by emphasizing *agape*. Ferré believes there are three possible teachings from the Bible concerning the eternal destiny of the "lost": eternal damnation, annihilation, and universalism. He claims that only universalism is "finally consistent with God as *agape*."[46] According to Ferré, God cannot condemn a human being to hell because that would violate his *agape*, which never fails.[47] Since God is sovereign, his *agape* will insure that all will be saved. Ferré writes:

> The logic of the situation is simple. Either God could not or would not save all. If He could not He is not sovereign; then not all things are possible with God. If He would not, again the New Testament is wrong, for it openly claims that He would have all to be saved. Nor would He be totally good. . . . The total logic of the deepest message of the New Testament, namely that God both can and wants to save all, is unanswerable.[48]

Why then does Scripture say that some will be lost? Why does it refer to a literal hell?

Ferré says that the teaching about eternal damnation is in Scripture because "preaching is existential. To preach to sinners that all will be saved will not reach them on their level of fear and hate of God. It will only secure them in their sin and self-sufficiency. Therefore, headed as they are away from God, they must be told: Repent or perish!"[49]

John A. T. Robinson claims that the New Testament teaches two eschatological "myths": universal restoration (universalism) and a final division into saved and lost. He asserts that they represent the two sides of the truth that is in Jesus: "Though both are the truth, one [universal restoration] is the truth as it is for God and as it is for faith the further side of decision; the other [heaven and hell] is the truth as it must be to the subject facing decision."[50]

Robinson argues that hell is a reality in the existential situation of the person facing the challenge of the Gospel; therefore the seriousness of his or her decision must not be watered down by any discussion of universalism. But since universal salvation is the reality that God wills, it will therefore come to pass. Universalism will have the last word. Only universal restoration is consistent with God's nature as omnipotent love. Robinson concludes, "Christ, in Origen's old words, remains on the cross as long as one sinner remains in hell. This is not speculation; it is a statement grounded in the very necessity of God's nature."[51]

Universalists use strong language in their condemnation of the traditional doctrine of hell. Ferré asserts that to "attribute eternal hell to God is literally blasphemy, the attributing of the worst to the best."[52] David Edwards says bluntly, "I would rather be an atheist than believe in a God who accepts it as inevitable that hell (however conceived) is the inescapable destiny of many, or of any of his children, even when they are prepared to accept 'all the blame.'"[53] Charles Duthie argues that the conclusion of universalism is "inescapable [for] any serious grappling with the issue of man's final destiny in the light of the revealed character of God."[54]

A second philosophical/theological argument for universalism relates to God's sovereignty. As I mentioned, proponents of universalism argue that if God is sovereign, he can and will bring universal salvation to pass. God will use his sovereign power and love to ensure that all persons eventually will be saved.

In addition to the arguments from "love" and "sovereignty," Duthie argues for universalism from what he terms "the witness of the Christian heart." By that he refers to the aversion that sensitive Christians share concerning the thought of human beings suffering eternally in hell. Duthie argues, "Although the last word cannot be with the Christian heart, what the Christian heart feels in this and in other matters must have *some* importance, since it is itself in some measure shaped by the Spirit of God."[55] To emphasize this "witness of the human heart," Duthie cites Paul's statement in Romans 9:3, "I could wish that myself were accursed from Christ for my brethren" (KJV).[56] This "witness," Duthie argues, adds powerful weight to the universalistic position.

An Evangelical Critique of Universalism

Biblical Critique. Space constraints prohibit a careful exegetical examination of each passage cited by proponents of universalism, and that task has been accomplished quite competently elsewhere.[57] But in general one can safely say there are not sufficient grounds for asserting that these verses teach universalism as explained by its adherents. Why? Several arguments can be set forth.

First, these verses all can be interpreted legitimately in a non-universalistic manner.[58] Second, and more important, the authors of each of the above statements clearly indicate that some persons will be lost.[59] Therefore, whatever these verses do mean, they cannot mean that ultimately *all* will be saved, for their contexts demand another interpretation. As Wright notes:

> Frequent appeal is made [by universalists] to Paul's use of the word "all" (e.g. in Rom. 5 and 11, and in 2 Cor. 5) with no apparent realization of the different shades of meaning that must be understood in the particular contexts. . . . The word "all" has several clearly distinct biblical uses (e.g. "all of some

sorts," "some of all sorts," etc.), and to ignore this frequently-noted fact is no aid to clear thinking.[60]

The basic problem with the universalists' use of these texts is that they separate them from their *immediate* context. For example, Paul's assertion that "God was in Christ reconciling the world to Himself" (2 Cor. 5:19) is separated from that which immediately follows: "be reconciled to God" (v. 20). The exhortation is not for the Corinthians merely to *recognize* that they have been reconciled, but for them to *become* reconciled to God.

Finally, there is no biblical warrant to legitimize the notion of any subsequent pleading of God with persons after death. However one interprets 1 Peter 3:19, this verse does not provide a basis for "asserting that there will be a preaching of our Lord after death to every soul in hell, nor does it provide a basis for saying that such preaching will be successful."[61] Harold Lindsell notes the tremendous alterations universalists must make to the biblical text:

> The universalist must change the Apocalypse of John into a love feast, the threats of the lake of fire into the sea of glass, and the fire of judgment into the waters of the river of life. Brimstone must become attar of roses, and blessing must be held out to those who are said to have no part in the final resurrection. The judgment of the great white throne, which witnesses to the opening of the book of life in which are to be found the names of men and "whosoever was not found written in the book of life was cast into the lake of fire," becomes poetic imagery designed to frighten men into coming into the kingdom of God earlier, although their failure to come now will not keep them out later. And heaven, despite John's contrary testimony, will be populated by liars, murderers, sorcerers, idolaters, the unbelieving and the abominable. The lake of fire is imaginary for it will be emptied of its occupants who will flood the corridors of heaven and mingle with the holy, the true, the righteous and the sanctified.[62]

Scripture clearly does not teach the doctrine of universalism.[63]
Theological Critique. How are we to evaluate the theological/philo-

sophical arguments set forth by adherents of universalism? Perhaps the most common error made by universalists is their practice of judging God and his actions by their standards instead of by how God has chosen to reveal himself in Scripture. Arthur Climenhaga says bluntly, "The issue of the new universalism is no longer 'God hath spoken' but 'Man hath reasoned.'"[64] Glasson illustrates this tendency quite well when he argues, "To affirm that any [persons] are kept alive for ever in a state of misery, without hope of any kind, is indefensible and is an affront to the *human* conscience."[65] Harold O. J. Brown summarizes this problem in universalism when he comments:

> This view contains the arrogant hidden assumption that God, if he is really to be God, must conform to our expectations. This is one feature that universalism has in common with feminist theology: it redefines God in terms of its own ideas of what is acceptable in deity, regardless of what God has revealed about himself in Scripture.[66]

Universalists claim that love is God's essential attribute. This position has several problems. First, is it legitimate to take one single attribute and subsume all of God's other attributes beneath it? Is any one single attribute superior in the divine essence? Second, even if it is acknowledged to be legitimate to focus on one attribute as superior, is love the best choice for the overarching attribute of God? Surely it would be just as possible, and in fact biblically preferable, to argue that holiness would be that attribute. When confronted by the living God (see Isa. 6 and Rev. 4), worshipers do not cry out, "Loving, loving, loving!" but "Holy, holy, holy!" Third, even assuming love to be the controlling characteristic, do the universalists really do justice to God's love as it is revealed in Scripture? Wright notes that

> . . . the great majority of the "hard sayings," the passages which warn most clearly and unmistakably of eternal punishment, are found on the lips of Jesus Himself. This is the point at which the usual argument comes dangerously close to cutting off the branch it sits on. It says "God is love": but we know that principally (since it is not self-evidently true) through the life and

death of Jesus Christ. We cannot use that life and death as an appeal against itself—which is precisely what happens if we say that, because God is love, the nature of salvation is *not* as it is revealed in the teaching of Jesus and in the cross itself, the place where God has provided the one way of salvation.[67]

The practice of judging God by human standards returns at this point. Harold Kuhn perceptively notes:

The supposed unthinkability of eternal punishment rests, in general, upon what we believe to be a faulty human analogy. Universalists tend to feel that the love of God must be like human love, raised to the *nth* power.[68]

Walter Martin adds that universalists "have set up their own standard of how God *must* act based upon what *they* believe is justice."[69] Joseph Bettis summarizes this tendency by stating, "The real question must be raised not about the universalist's premise that God's love is good and sovereign, but about his conclusion that the best way to describe the sovereignty and goodness of God's love is universalism."[70]

Another problem with the doctrine of universalism is that it ignores the Bible's emphasis on the decisive nature of this life's decision (e.g., Gal. 6:7; 2 Cor. 5:10; Matt. 25:46; Luke 16:26). The author of Hebrews warns, "It is appointed for men to die once, and after this comes judgment" (Heb. 9:27). There is no suggestion of a "second chance," much less of a successful one, in these verses. Eternal destinies are decided in this life.

The doctrine also undercuts the significance of real moral choices in this life. Indeed, Herbert Jones argues that the spread of universalism has precipitated a corresponding breakdown of morals.[71] He asks:

And—if we want to—why not? If Dr. [John A. T.] Robinson is right, if in some future state "the sinner must yield," if individual souls "must all of them ultimately reach heaven," if freedom is a delusion, if the law of consequence is nugatory, Why not? If it is all the same in the end, why not enjoy the pleasures of sin for a season? Why not fling to the winds all restraint? Why not, as so many are doing, go atheist all the way?[72]

Universalism also has difficulty explaining major parts of the preaching of Christ and the apostles. They warned people to turn; and therefore their preaching must be seen as either inept or immoral. Either they were wrong or they knew better but "did evil that good might come."[73] Tokunboh Adeyemo notes, "Unlike the Universalists, Jesus and the New Testament writers take the issue of man's destiny seriously. They do not romanticise heaven and hell or exploit the doctrine merely to induce right action."[74]

Finally, if everyone will eventually attain salvation, then there is no motivation to preach the Gospel or to pray for the conversion of those who do not yet know Christ.[75] Therefore, "preaching" done by universalists often focuses on temporal issues. Note the following description of what is taking place in many churches:

> People come to church seeking answers to their deep wonderings about life and death. But they hear sermons about the need to boycott certain brands of chocolate bars or grapes. They hear about the injustice of America's economic system. Timely topics, to be sure. But what relevance have they to a man whose wife is dying of cancer, to a widow whose years are dwindling and is terrified by thoughts of approaching death?[76]

T. F. Torrance bluntly writes, "No doctrine that cuts the nerve of that urgency in the Gospel can be a doctrine of love, but only an abiding menace to the Gospel and to mankind."[77] Well said.

The Primacy of Scripture

I have attempted to portray accurately and critique carefully the doctrine of universal salvation. Universalism is clearly unbiblical in its assertion that all will be saved. Yet, due to the pressures of pluralism, many people, even professed evangelicals, appear to be moving in the direction of belief in universal salvation. Hunter's conclusion from his massive research project deserves careful scrutiny:

> Overall, this cohort of Evangelicals has not, for all practical purposes, repudiated traditional Protestant theology on the matter of salvation. A dynamic is at work nonetheless. As with

their view of the Bible, it minimally represents a softening of
earlier doctrinal certainties. Of their own salvation, they are
confident. It is with regard to the salvation of others that there
is ambiguity and doubt. The certainties characteristic of previous generations appear to be giving way to a measure of hesi-
tancy and questioning.[78]

But as attractive as universalism and other theories that challenge
the traditional Christian teaching on heaven and hell might appear,
they fail to answer fundamental objections to changing our belief in
eternal punishment for those apart from Christ. Of these objections,
the most powerful are the sayings of our Lord, sayings that leave no
room whatever for the universalist's position.[79] J. I. Packer notes:

All the language that strikes terror into our hearts—weeping
and gnashing of teeth, outer darkness, the worm, the fire,
gehenna, the great gulf fixed—this is all directly taken from our
Lord's teaching. It is from Jesus Christ that we learn the doctrine of eternal punishment.[80]

Kenneth Kantzer echoes this sentiment when he writes:

So while I am deeply impressed by the arguments of brilliant
thinkers like Schleiermacher, Tillich, and others, I prefer our
Lord's words to theirs. Those who acknowledge Jesus Christ as
Lord cannot escape the clear, unambiguous language with
which he warns of the awful truth of eternal punishment. No
universalism, no annihilationism, no probation in the hereafter
satisfies his word.[81]

The simple fact remains that if we cannot trust Jesus Christ when
he speaks about hell and eternal punishment, then we cannot really
trust him when he speaks about heaven and eternal life.

How do we know that God is love? Through the person of Jesus
Christ. No one knows more about God's love than Jesus Christ. Do
universalists dare presume they can teach Jesus Christ something
about God's love? The One who embodied God's love spent more time

talking about the horrors of hell than the glories of heaven. Hell is real, and hell is eternal. We have Jesus Christ's word on that!

But what about the issue of justice? Is hell fair? Early in the biblical record Abraham asks, "Shall not the Judge of all the earth deal justly?" (Gen. 18:25). That question was answered affirmatively. Revelation 16:7 adds, "Yes, Lord God Almighty, true and just are your judgments" (NIV). No one will ever be able to say to God that he was unjust in his judgment. Every person receives one of two things from God: justice or mercy. No one receives injustice.[82]

We do not yet have the perspective of eternity to see life as God sees it. When we do, we will join with the chorus of those around the throne and exclaim, "Yes, Lord God Almighty, true and just are your judgments."

In the final analysis the issue comes back to the integrity of Scripture.[83] Kantzer notes:

> I wish I could say that God is too loving, too kind, and too generous to condemn any soul to eternal punishment. I would like to believe that hell can only be the anteroom to heaven, a temporary and frightful discipline to bring the unregenerate to final moral perfection. . . . On this all-important topic we have only two alternatives—dismal, helpless ignorance, or divine revelation.[84]

Can Scripture be trusted to give us the truth about God, man, and salvation? Is it not significant that a denial of eternal punishment has arisen during the same time as questions are being raised about the trustworthiness of the Bible? As history demonstrates, doubting God's Word is the starting point for universalism. In Eden the serpent told the woman, "You surely shall not die!"

The deceiver of mankind is still at work. His approach has not changed. Apparently, however, he is getting a greater audience today. "You surely shall not die" is a message being propagated by many voices.

Yet against these many voices the voice of Scripture states that persons who have not trusted Christ are lost. John 3:18 says, "He who does not believe has been judged already, because he has not believed in the name of the only begotten Son of God." Likewise, Peter declared, "There is no other name under heaven that has been given among men, by which we must be saved" (Acts 4:12).

CONCLUSION:
WHERE DO WE GO FROM HERE?

In closing, let me suggest three responses evangelicals should make to the doctrine of universalism. First, *we must rediscover and preach "the exceeding sinfulness of sin."* G. K. Chesterton once said it is surprising that people have rejected the doctrine of original sin because it is the only doctrine that can be empirically verified. We live in a culture that tries to sidestep the issue of sin. In *Whatever Became of Sin?* Karl Menninger states, "It [sin] was once a strong word, an ominous and serious word. . . . But the word went away. It has almost disappeared— the word along with the notion."[85] If Menninger could write that in 1973, what would he say today?

I believe this is the crux of the problem of universalism and other challenges to the orthodox view of judgment. Have some persons actually accepted the idea that people's sinfulness is not serious enough to merit as severe a punishment as an eternal hell? John Stott apparently has, for he has recently argued for a brand of annihilationism that allows sinners to cease to exist after having suffered "appropriately" for their sins. In his response to David Edwards concerning the issue of eternal, conscious torment, Stott asks, "Would there not, then, be a serious disproportion between sins consciously committed in time and torment consciously experienced throughout eternity?"[86]

Jonathan Edwards answered this objection forcefully in his powerful sermon "The Justice of God in the Damnation of Sinners":

> So that sin against God, being a violation of infinite obligations, must be a crime infinitely heinous, and so deserving infinite punishment. . . . The *eternity* of the punishment of ungodly men renders it infinite . . . and therefore renders [it] no more than proportionable to the heinousness of what they are guilty of.[87]

The lyricist Augustus M. Toplady summarizes well the biblical viewpoint with these lines from the hymn "Rock of Ages":

> *Could my tears forever flow,*
> *Could my zeal no respite know.*
> *All for sin could not atone;*
> *Thou must save and Thou alone.*
> *Nothing in my hand I bring.*
> *Simply to Thy cross I cling.*
> *Naked, come to Thee for dress;*
> *Helpless, look to Thee for grace.*
> *Foul, I to the fountain fly;*
> *Wash me, Savior, or I die!*

Second, *we must teach and preach on hell and judgment.* Our commitment must be to tell the truth, however unpopular it may seem to some. Telling the truth is indeed the most "loving" thing one can do.[88] Public opinion must not be allowed to change truth. Phillips Brooks challenges preachers with these words:

> Courage . . . is the indispensable requisite of any true ministry. . . . Courage is good everywhere, but it is necessary here. If you are afraid of men and a slave to their opinion, go and do something else. Go and make shoes to fit them. . . . But do not keep on all your life preaching sermons which shall say not what God sent you to declare, but what they hire you to say.[89]

Our culture disdains what is termed "fire and brimstone preaching." But as the great Puritan pastor Richard Baxter emphasized in his ministry, "fear must drive, as love must draw."[90] Both emphases are found in Scripture, and both must be preached. We must challenge people not only to flee *from* the wrath to come, but to flee *to* the One who bore that wrath for lost and guilty sinners. If in the past there was too much fire and brimstone preaching, today there is too little. The pendulum has swung too far in the direction of "love drawing," and many people do not understand the perils of being in a lost state.

Some Christian leaders today are telling us that people already know they are sinners—all they need to know is how to be saved. That statement is simply not true. A lot of people understand something is wrong, but they do not see themselves as guilty sinners under condemnation from a holy God. Most people think they are basically good. They throw out platitudes such as "If God grades on the curve, I'll make it" or "I'm as good as the next person—I'll take my chances."

Baxter asks a question that we need to ask today: How will they call on a Savior until they know they need one? Baxter maintains, "We persuade men to believe that they are sick, that they may go to the Physician."[91] Baxter shares the following powerful illustration about the importance of people understanding sin and condemnation before they can understand grace and the Gospel: "A man on the gallows will be glad of a pardon; but a stander-by, that thinks he is innocent, would not regard it, but take it for an accusation."[92]

Imagine a man on the gallows, with a rope around his neck, moments from being hanged to death. A messenger from the king rushes forward and hands the man a paper, declaring, "The king has pardoned you! The king has pardoned you!" Would not that man receive that news gladly and with rejoicing?

But consider if that messenger were to give that same message to a man in the crowd, an innocent bystander. How would that man receive the news of a pardon? That man most assuredly would revile the messenger. "What are you doing giving this message to me?" he might angrily ask. "Up there—on the gallows—he's the guilty party. He's the one who needs a pardon, not me." A pardon offered to an "innocent" bystander in the crowd would be considered an insult.

This illustration points out the wisdom in the oft-quoted statement, "We must get people lost before we can get them saved." If any preacher needs more motivation to do this, he need only study the preaching of Jesus. Jesus talked more about hell than he did about heaven. For example, in Matthew 10:28 he warned, "Do not fear those who kill the body . . . rather fear Him who is able to destroy both soul and body in Hell." Jesus Christ was what some might call today a "fire and brimstone preacher." He was not afraid of making people afraid.

C. H. Spurgeon recognized the importance of preaching on hell. He said:

We rob the gospel of its power if we leave out its threatenings of punishment. It is to be feared that the novel opinions upon annihilation and restoration which have afflicted the Church in these last days have caused many ministers to be slow to speak concerning the last judgment and its issues, and consequently the terrors of the Lord have had small influence upon either preachers or hearers. If this be so it cannot be too much regretted, for one great means of conversion is thus left unused.[93]

Because eternal judgment is part of the truth of God, we must proclaim it![94]

Third, *we must display a passion for lost souls.* How will lost people hear the unique message of hope in Christ? Human agents must be raised up by the Lord to share the message. And God has so willed it. As J. Herbert Kane points out, "There is not a single line in the book of Acts to suggest that God can save a human being without employing a human agent. On the contrary there are several examples of God's going to great lengths to secure the active cooperation of one or another of His servants."[95] If we truly believe in the reality of heaven and hell, we cannot say we love people if we refuse to share the Gospel with them. This point is emphasized in a booklet titled *Tract Written by an Atheist*:

> Did I firmly believe, as millions say they do, that the knowledge and practice of religion in this life influences destiny in another, religion would mean to me everything. I would cast away earthly enjoyments as dross, earthly cares as follies, and earthly thoughts and feelings as vanity. Religion would be my first waking thought, and my last image before sleep sank me into unconsciousness. I should labour in its cause alone. I would take thought for the morrow of Eternity alone. I would esteem one soul gained for heaven worth a life of suffering. Earthly consequences should never stay my hand, nor seal my lips. Earth, its joys and its griefs, would occupy no moment of my thoughts. I would strive to look upon Eternity alone, and on the Immortal Souls around me, soon to be everlastingly happy or everlasting miserable. I would go forth to

the world and preach to it in season and out of season, and my text would be, "WHAT SHALL IT PROFIT A MAN IF HE GAIN THE WHOLE WORLD AND LOSE HIS OWN SOUL?"[96]

Our Lord's commission constrains us to be faithful to take the Gospel to the ends of the earth, beginning in our own neighborhoods.

As John Stott himself has written:

Universalism, fashionable as it is today, is incompatible with the teaching of Christ and His apostles, and is a deadly enemy of evangelism. *The true universalism of the Bible is the call to universal evangelism in obedience to Christ's universal commission.* It is the conviction not that all men will be saved in the end, but that all men must hear the gospel of salvation before the end, as Jesus said (Matt. 24:14), in order that they may have a chance to believe and be saved (Romans 10:13-15).[97]

May we all prove to be thoroughgoing universalists in this sense.

CHAPTER 4

1. "We Face a Task Unfinished," lyrics by George J. Webb.
2. E.g., D. A. Carson, "The Challenges of Contemporary Pluralism," *Southern Baptist Journal of Theology (SBJT)* 1/2 (Summer 1997), 4-37; A. B. Caneday, "'Evangelical Inclusivism' and the Exclusivity of the Gospel: A Review of John Sanders's *No Other Name,*" *SBJT* 1/4 (Winter 1997), 24-39; and Thomas R. Schreiner, "Perseverance and Assurance: A Survey and a Proposal," *SBJT* 2/1 (Spring 1998), 32-62.
3. N. T. Wright, "Universalism and the World-Wide Community," *Churchman* 89 (July-September 1975), 200. J. I. Packer laments, "I am afraid that many of us have slipped into the practice of living and behaving as if universalism were true, even though we would never subscribe to it in writing." See Packer, "All Men Won't Be Saved," *Eternity* 16 (November 1965), 16.
4. In addition to eschatology, Blue lists theology proper, Christology, soteriology, biblical anthropology, hamartiology, and ecclesiology. See Ronald J. Blue, "Untold Billions: Are They Really Lost?" *Bibliotheca Sacra* 138 (October-December 1981), 341.
5. Fred Carl Kuehner summarizes the view as "all men are doomed to be saved." See Kuehner, "Heaven or Hell?" in *Fundamentals of the Faith,* ed. Carl F. H. Henry (Grand Rapids, Mich.: Zondervan, 1969), 242.
6. Someone has aptly summarized the shift in viewpoints as follows:
    Older forms of universalism: Man is too good for God to damn.
    Newer forms of universalism: God is too good to damn man.
7. Richard J. Bauckham, "Universalism: A Historical Survey," *Themelios* 4 (1979), 49.
8. James Davison Hunter, *Evangelicalism: The Coming Generation* (Chicago: University of Chicago Press, 1987), 34.

9. George Barna, *Absolute Confusion* (Ventura, Calif.: Regal, 1993), 15.

10. Hunter, *Evangelicalism: The Coming Generation*, 35. The Evangelical Academy project was a 1982-1985 attitudinal survey of students and faculty at nine liberal arts colleges and seven evangelical seminaries.

11. Ibid., 35. It must be noted, as Hunter does, that "it is important to recall that the majority still hold the traditional approach to the problem of salvation. Yet as the interviews suggest, even among these there is a pervasive uneasiness about the nature of hell and about who is relegated to it. It is an uneasiness which may portend a greater cultural accommodation." See Hunter, *Evangelicalism*, 47-48.

12. Ibid., 38. A survey taken at the 1967 Urbana Missions Conference bears this out. Out of 5,000 replies to over 8,000 questionnaires distributed, only 37 percent believed that "a person who doesn't hear the gospel is eternally lost." Only 42 percent believed that "unbelievers will be punished in a literal hell of fire," and 25 percent believed that "man will be saved or lost on the basis of how well he followed what he *did* know." See Arthur P. Johnston, "Focus Comment," *Trinity World Forum* 1 (Fall 1975), 3.

13. Jimmy Carter, quoted in "Power and Higher Power: Carter's Journey," *The New York Times* (December 15, 1996), 16. Note Carter's use of the term "innocent" in his quotation, implying a denial of the universality of sin and depravity.

14. Leighton Ford, *Worldwide Challenge* (September/October 1983), 20. David Wells notes that the doctrine of hell is being abandoned "not because of new light from the Bible but because of new darkness from the culture." See David F. Wells, "Foreword," in Robert A. Peterson, *Hell on Trial: The Case for Eternal Punishment* (Phillipsburg, N.J.: Presbyterian & Reformed, 1995), x.

15. See Bernard Ramm, "Will All Men Be Finally Saved?" *Eternity* (August 1964), 22. Harold O. J. Brown makes this same point in "Will Everyone Be Saved?" *Pastoral Renewal* 11 (June 1987), 13.

16. This is by no means a comprehensive history of universalism. For a more detailed presentation, see Richard J. Bauckham, "Universalism: A Historical Survey," *Themelios* 4 (1979), 47-54; Henri Blocher, "The Scope of Redemption in Modern Theology," *Scottish Bulletin of Evangelical Theology* 9 (Autumn 1991), 80-103; and Alan M. Fairhurst, "Death and Destiny," *Churchman* 95 (1981), 313-325.

17. For a differing perspective on Origen that defends his orthodoxy on the doctrine of universal salvation, see Frederick W. Norris, "Universal Salvation in Origen and Maximus," in *Universalism and the Doctrine of Hell*, ed. Nigel M. de S. Cameron (Grand Rapids, Mich.: Baker, 1992), 35-72.

18. Bauckham, "Universalism: A Historical Survey," 50.

19. Note the description of Erigena's teaching in *Christianity Today* 31 (March 20, 1987), 39.

20. Bauckham, "Universalism: A Historical Survey," 50.

21. Ibid.

22. Ibid., 51.

23. Ibid. Bauckham notes that the judgment was subsequently reversed on appeal by the Lord Chancellor.

24. Ibid. Bauckham notes that Farrar remained "agnostic as to the alternatives."

25. Ibid. Pusey's work was entitled *What Is of Faith as to Everlasting Punishment* (London: James Parker and Co., 1880).

26. Ibid.

27. Ibid.

28. James I. Packer, "The Way of Salvation. Part III: The Problems of Universalism," *Bibliotheca Sacra* (January-March 1973), 4.

29. Herbert G. Jones, "Universalism and Morals," *Scottish Journal of Theology* 3 (1950), 27.

30. Bauckham, "Universalism: A Historical Survey," 48. Those who argue in favor of universalism acknowledge that their position is not the historic one of the Church. But T.

F. Glasson dislikes the term *modification*, preferring instead to say that "elements which have all along been present in the N.T. and in some parts of our Christian heritage have now come into their rightful place." See Glasson, "Human Destiny: Has Christian Teaching Changed?" *Modern Churchman* 12 (July 1969), 291. When he wrote this article, Glasson was Lecturer in New Testament Studies, New College, London.

31. Note the article by Joseph D. Bettis, "Is Karl Barth a Universalist?" *Scottish Journal of Theology* 20 (December 1967), 423-436. Bettis argues that it is illegitimate to label Barth a universalist because Barth himself "consistently rejects universalism as a doctrine." Bettis also notes, however, that Barth leaves open the possibility that within God's freedom all men may indeed be saved. See p. 427.

32. Barth, *Church Dogmatics*, IV, Pt. I, trans. G. W. Bromiley (Edinburgh: T. & T. Clark, 1956), 295.

33. G. W. Bromiley, "Karl Barth," in *Creative Minds in Contemporary Theology*, ed. Philip Hughes (Grand Rapids, Mich.: Eerdmans, 1966), 54.

34. Barth, *Church Dogmatics*, 164ff. See also G. C. Berkouwer, *The Triumph of Grace in the Theology of Karl Barth* (Grand Rapids, Mich.: Eerdmans, 1956), 292-296. Emilio Antonio Núñez says, "The least that can be said of Karl Barth is that in his teaching about election and reconciliation he opens himself dangerously to universalism." See Núñez, "Universalism," in *Walvoord: A Tribute*, ed. Donald K. Campbell (Chicago: Moody Press, 1982), 173.

35. See Donald Bloesch, "The Legacy of Karl Barth," *TSF Bulletin* 9 (1986), 7. Note that Barth's view does not stem from man's participation in "religion" but from God's overwhelming grace. Bauckham notes that this "hopeful" universalism has had more appeal to conservative Christians than dogmatic universalism because it allows them to "hope for the salvation of all men without presuming to know something which God has not revealed." Bauckham, "Universalism: A Historical Survey," 52.

36. Barth, *Church Dogmatics*, IV, Pt. III, 478. Thus my labeling of Barth as a "hope-so universalist."

37. Barth, *The Humanity of God* (Richmond, Va.: John Knox Press, 1960), 62.

38. Carl E. Braaten, "The Meaning of Evangelism in the Context of God's Universal Grace," *Journal of the Academy for Evangelism in Theological Education* 3 (1987-1988), 16.

39. Ibid., 17.

40. Ajith Fernando utilizes the term "wishful universalists." See his *Crucial Questions About Hell* (Wheaton, Ill.: Crossway Books, 1991), 22.

41. I am indebted to Emilio Núñez for this helpful grouping. See Núñez, "Universalism," 173.

42. For an in-depth exegetical treatment of these texts from an evangelical perspective, see Ajith Fernando, *A Universal Homecoming?* (Madras, India: Evangelical Literature Service, 1982) and also his more recent work, *Crucial Questions About Hell*. N. T. Wright makes an interesting observation concerning the universalists' use of Scripture, usually from the Pauline corpus. Wright says: "An odd inversion, this, of the old liberal position where Jesus was the teacher of heavenly truths and Paul the cross-grained dogmatic bigot." See Wright, "Towards a Biblical View of Universalism," *Themelios* 4 (1979), 55.

43. Unless otherwise noted, all Scripture quotations are from the NASB.

44. Glasson, "Human Destiny: Has Christian Teaching Changed?" 296.

45. Wright, "Towards a Biblical View of Universalism," 54. Wright is not espousing this view, but is merely presenting it. Wright's article argues against universalism.

46. Nels F. S. Ferré, "Universalism: Pro and Con," *Christianity Today* 7 (March 1, 1963), 24. Ferré criticizes P. T. Forsyth for making holiness God's dominant attribute; yet, as Kenneth Hamilton points out, Ferré's criticism can apply equally to his own view that love is God's dominant attribute. See Kenneth Hamilton, "Love or Holy Love? Nels Ferré versus P. T. Forsyth," *Canadian Journal of Theology* 8 (October 1962), 229.

47. Ferré claims, "That such a doctrine [hell] could be conceived, not to mention believed, shows how far from any understanding of the love of God many people once were and, alas, still are!" See Ferré, *The Christian Understanding of God* (New York: Harper & Brothers, 1951), 228.

48. Ferré, *Evil and the Christian Faith* (New York: Harper & Brothers, 1947), 118. Lindsell answers this "unanswerable logic" by saying, "When Ferré says that if God could not save all He is not sovereign, his own logic can be turned against him by saying that if God cannot send anyone to eternal perdition then He is also not sovereign! In either statement (Ferré's or its opposite), one is left with a finite God. Therefore there is a standoff. Assuming either argument, God is finite." See Harold Lindsell, "Universalism Today: Part Two," *Bibliotheca Sacra* 122 (January-March 1965), 32.

49. Ferré, "Universalism: Pro and Con," 24. Apparently the logic of what this does to Ferré's concept of a loving God escapes him. Is it loving to deceive people deliberately to get them to act in a certain way? Blum notes, "The idea of scaring people with notions that God knows to be untrue even if it results in a good end is unworthy of God." See Edwin A. Blum, "Shall You Not Surely Die?" *Themelios* 4 (1979), 59.

50. John A. T. Robinson, *In the End God* (New York: Harper & Row, 1968), 130.

51. John A. T. Robinson, "Universalism: Is It Heretical?" *Scottish Journal of Theology* 2 (1949), 155. Packer correctly notes, "But it is a speculation, of course; all statements about 'the necessity of God's nature' which go beyond Scripture are speculative." See J. I. Packer, "Universalism and Evangelism," in *One Race, One Gospel, One Task*, Vol. 2, eds. Carl F. H. Henry and W. Stanley Mooneyham (Minneapolis: World Wide Publications, 1967), 183.

52. Ferré, "Universalism: Pro and Con," 24.

53. David L. Edwards, *Evangelical Essentials: A Liberal/Evangelical Dialogue. With a Response by John Stott* (Downers Grove, Ill.: InterVarsity Press, 1988), 295.

54. Charles S. Duthie, "Ultimate Triumph," *Scottish Journal of Theology* 14 (1961), 168.

55. Ibid., 157.

56. Ibid., 169. Duthie has overlooked, however, the fact that Paul definitely believed people would be cursed if they rejected Christ! To use Paul as an example of a "universalist's heart" certainly gives back more than it takes.

57. See Ajith Fernando, "A Critique of Exegetical Arguments for Universalism," unpublished Th.M. Thesis, Fuller Theological Seminary, 1976.

58. Packer argues that the non-universalistic interpretation of these texts is "more germane to their context than the universalist one." See Packer, "All Men Won't Be Saved," 17.

59. E.g., John 5:28-29; John 10; Rom. 2:9, 12; 2 Cor. 13:5; 1 Cor. 15:1; Eph. 5:5; 1 John 5:14-15; 2 Pet. 2. Note that some of these assertions are found within the same passage as that which supposedly teaches universalism! Harold Lindsell notes that an objective observer will be "struck by the amount of data against universalism when contrasted with the few references which seem to favor it." See Lindsell, "Universalism Today: Part Two," 36.

60. Wright, "Universalism and the World-Wide Community," 200.

61. Packer, "All Men Won't Be Saved," 17.

62. Lindsell, "Universalism Today: Part Two," 39.

63. Packer claims that many universalists have seen the futility of the above exegetical arguments and that therefore they have moved from exegetical to philosophical/theological arguments. See Packer, "All Men Won't Be Saved," 17. Bauckham concurs, saying that in the twentieth century, "exegesis has turned decisively against the universalist case." See Bauckham, "Universalism: A Historical Survey," 52.

64. Arthur M. Climenhaga, "The New Universalism," *United Evangelical Action* 23 (December 1964), 18.

65. Glasson, "Human Destiny: Has Christian Teaching Changed?" 294 [emphasis mine].

66. Harold O. J. Brown, "Will Everyone Be Saved?" 13.

67. Wright, "Towards a Biblical View of Universalism," 55.

68. Harold B. Kuhn, "Universalism in Today's Theology," *Christianity Today* (September 16, 1957), 10-11.

69. Walter R. Martin, "Universal Salvation: Does the Bible Teach It?" *Eternity* 7 (September 1956), 39.

70. Bettis, "Critique of the Doctrine of Universal Salvation," *Religious Studies* 6 (December 1970), 336. Ajith Fernando critiques Barth's use of God's sovereignty as an argument for universalism: "Barth's point is that God will do as he chooses, and we have no right to make pronouncements as to whether all will be saved or not. Barth must be lauded for his emphasis on the sovereignty of God. But if the sovereign God has disclosed to humanity what he will do, then the appropriate response to his sovereignty is to believe what he has revealed. God has revealed unmistakably in the Scriptures that there will be some who will be lost eternally. Therefore, it is Barth who has been disrespectful of God's sovereignty by denying that we cannot know the answer to a question which God has answered for us." See Fernando, *Crucial Questions About Hell*, 121-122.

71. Jones, "Universalism and Morals," 27.

72. Ibid., 29.

73. Paul Helm argues that if "it is immoral to punish the impenitent in hell then it is immoral genuinely to threaten such punishment." See Paul Helm, "Universalism and the Threat of Hell," *Trinity Journal* 4 (Spring 1983), 43.

74. Tokunboh Adeyemo, "The Salvation Debate and Evangelical Response: Part Two," *East Africa Journal of Evangelical Theology* 2 (1983), 11. Packer notes that according to the gospel of universalism, Paul would have added to his assertion to the Philippian jailer, "And if you don't believe you will be saved anyway, but it will hurt badly, and I would like to spare you that." See Packer, "The Way of Salvation, Part III: The Problems of Universalism," 3.

75. Harold Lindsell argues that statistics bear this out quite well: "Perhaps the best way to show how dramatic the missionary retreat has been is to look at the percentage decline in the number of overseas missionaries among some of the major denominations between 1962 and 1979: Episcopal Church, 79 percent decline; Lutheran Church of America, 70 percent; United Presbyterian Church in the U.S.A., 72 percent; United Church of Christ, 68 percent; Christian Church Disciples, 66 percent; United Methodist Church, 46 percent; American Lutheran Church, 44 percent." See Lindsell, "The Major Denominations Are Jumping Ship," *Christianity Today* 25 (September 18, 1981), 16. The article concludes, "Though many factors contributed to this decline, it is legitimate to reckon that these figures are a rough index of the depth of conviction about basic Christian doctrine—the nature of the gospel, the lostness of mankind apart from Christ, and the necessity of obeying biblical mandates calling for sacrifice and discipline for the sake of advancing the kingdom of Christ." T. F. Glasson tries to counter such charges: "It used to be said that the very lever of missionary endeavour would be broken if there were any deviation from the old eschatology. But this has proved to be untrue. Our grandfathers were impressed with the horror that men should die without Christ. We are more concerned with the tragedy that they should live without Him." See Glasson, "Human Destiny: Has Christian Teaching Changed?" 292. Glasson's argument is theologically and historically flawed.

76. Charles W. Keysor, "What Has Become of Eternity?" *Pastoral Renewal* (April 1985), 132.

77. T. F. Torrance, "Universalism or Election?" *Scottish Journal of Theology* 2 (1949), 318.

78. Hunter, *Evangelicalism: The Coming Generation*, 40.

79. N. T. Wright notes that universalists approach these texts in one of three ways: (1) Ignore them and base their theology on a supposed overview of the Gospels or on philosophical ideas instead; (2) claim they were not the actual words of Jesus; (3) claim Jesus was mistaken in what he said about hell. Obviously, when someone adopts any of these three approaches, they have already departed from historic orthodoxy in their

methodology, even before getting to their conclusion. See Wright, "Universalism and the World-Wide Community," 202.

80. Packer, "All Men Won't Be Saved," 156. William G. T. Shedd agrees: "Jesus Christ is the Person who is responsible for the doctrine of Eternal Perdition. He is the Being with whom all opponents of this theological tenet are in conflict. . . . The Christian ministry never would have invented it in all the Christian centuries." See Shedd, *Dogmatic Theology*, Vol. 2, 2nd ed. (Grand Rapids, Mich.: Zondervan, 1953), 680.

81. Kenneth S. Kantzer, "Troublesome Questions," *Christianity Today* 31 (March 20, 1987), 45. See also Kantzer, "The Claims of Christ and Religious Pluralism," in *Evangelism on the Cutting Edge*, ed. Robert E. Coleman (Old Tappan, N.J.: Fleming H. Revell, 1986), 15-29.

82. For an excellent discussion of this issue see R. C. Sproul, *Chosen by God* (Wheaton, Ill.: Tyndale House, 1986), 38ff.

83. William Hendriksen says, "The passages in which this doctrine of everlasting punishment . . . is taught are so numerous that one actually stands aghast that in spite of all this there are people today who affirm that they accept Scripture and who, nevertheless, reject the idea of never-ending torment." See Hendriksen, *The Bible on the Life Hereafter* (1959; rpt. Grand Rapids, Mich.: Baker, 1975), 197-198. Fernando argues that evangelicals do not generally *reject* the doctrine of eternal punishment; they simply *neglect* to mention it in their preaching and teaching. Fernando fears that if "one generation of evangelicals neglects these doctrines, it is quite likely that the next generation will reject it. People will grow up without the serious side of the gospel as part of their worldview." See Fernando, "Rediscovering the Doctrine of Lostness—Part 1," *World Evangelization* 13 (November/December 1987), 21-22.

84. Kantzer, "Troublesome Questions," 45.

85. Karl Menninger, *Whatever Became of Sin?* (New York: Hawthorn Books, 1973), 14.

86. Stott, *Evangelical Essentials*, 318.

87. Jonathan Edwards, "The Justice of God in the Damnation of Sinners," in *The Works of Jonathan Edwards*, Vol. 1 (Edinburgh: Banner of Truth Trust, 1974), 669. This sermon was first published in 1738. See also Edwards's sermon, "The Eternity of Hell Torments," *Works*, Vol. 2, 83-89. This sermon was preached in 1739.

88. Roger Nicole observes, "If a person is struck with a deadly disease for which there is a known cure, it is neither wise nor loving to try and convince him that nothing is wrong." See Nicole, "Universalism: Will Everyone Be Saved?" *Christianity Today* 31 (March 20, 1987), 38.

89. Phillips Brooks, *Lectures on Preaching* (New York: E. P. Dutton and Co., 1877), 59.

90. Richard Baxter, "The Life of Faith" (1669), in *The Practical Works of Richard Baxter*, Vol. 3 (London: George Virtue, 1838), 665.

91. Baxter, *Catholick Theologie: II* (1675), 221.

92. Baxter, "Directions and Persuasions to a Sound Conversion" (1658), in *The Practical Works of Richard Baxter*, Vol. 2, 603.

93. C. H. Spurgeon, *Lectures to My Students* (1875; rpt. Grand Rapids, Mich.: Baker, 1977), 339.

94. Fernando wisely cautions, "Because many have preached about hell in the wrong way, we must not avoid preaching about it. Misuse does not warrant disuse." See Fernando, "Rediscovering the Doctrine of Lostness—Part 2," *World Evangelization* 14 (January/February 1988), 14. For additional material in preaching on hell and judgment see John Blanchard, *Whatever Happened to Hell?* (Durham, England: Evangelical Press, 1993; also Wheaton, Ill.: Crossway Books, 1995); Tim Keller, "Preaching Hell in a Tolerant Age," *Leadership* (Fall 1997), 42-48; and Kenneth S. Kantzer, "Do You Believe in Hell?" *Christianity Today* 30 (February 21, 1986), 12.

95. J. Herbert Kane, *Understanding Christian Missions* (Grand Rapids, Mich.: Baker, 1974),

102. As G. C. Berkouwer asserts, "The Church is not to speculate but to preach." See Berkouwer, "Universalism," *Christianity Today* 1 (May 13, 1957), 6.

96. Norman P. Grubb, *C. T. Studd* (Fort Washington, Penn.: Christian Literature Crusade, 1982), 35-36.

97. Stott, "Response to Bishop Mortimer Arias," *International Review of Missions* 65 (1976), 33 (emphasis mine). J. I. Packer similarly describes "biblical" universalism in terms of its universal claim (Rom. 1:16), its universal summons (Acts 17:30), and its universal mission (Matt. 28:19). See Packer, "All Men Won't Be Saved," 15.

FIVE

"MISGIVINGS" AND "OPENNESS"

A Dialogue on Inclusivism Between R. Douglas Geivett and Clark Pinnock

SOME MISGIVINGS ABOUT EVANGELICAL INCLUSIVISM
R. DOUGLAS GEIVETT

Max Warren has observed that "the impact of agnostic science will turn out to be child's play compared to the challenge to Christian theology of the faiths of other men."[1] One sort of response to this challenge is what I will call "evangelical inclusivism." Whether evangelical inclusivism is growing in popularity or not, I cannot say;[2] it certainly attracts a great deal of attention these days. At any rate I find the recent recrudescence of inclusivism among evangelicals somewhat unsettling—and I sense that I am not alone.

As it happens, it is difficult to conduct a fully general assessment of inclusivism. This is partly because the label *inclusivism* means different things to different people. It even means different things to different self-described inclusivists. Whereas inclusivists seem to agree that there are varieties of inclusivism, self-described inclusivists do not agree about what counts as a variety of inclusivism. Thus, from the point of view of one self-described inclusivist, another self-described inclusivist may not be an inclusivist at all. (From now on I will dispense with the term *self-described inclusivist* and let the unqualified term *inclusivist* do the same semantic work.)

Clark Pinnock and I will be exploring the strengths and weaknesses of his own inclusivist proposal, familiar to many through his various publications. The topic and format of this exchange was proposed by the president of the Evangelical Philosophical Society and agreed to by the two of us. It should not be inferred from this arrangement, however, that I assume Pinnock owns a special burden of proof in all exchanges between himself and his detractors. Inclusivists have sometimes complained that exclusivists have generally neglected to state and defend their own positions clearly.[3] Anyone interested in my positive account of the uniqueness of Christianity in a religiously pluralistic world is encouraged to consult the essays I have contributed to the books *Jesus Under Fire* and *Four Views on Salvation in a Pluralistic World*.[4]

The focus of the present discussion is a series of misgivings I have about Pinnock's "wider hope" proposal. I characterize my objections to Pinnock's inclusivism as "misgivings" for reasons I will explain later. To begin, however, let me identify the most salient feature of Pinnock's inclusivism as I understand it.

It may seem obvious that Clark Pinnock is an inclusivist. He certainly uses the term as a label for his position. But what is perhaps not so well understood is how he *defines* inclusivism.[5] Part of what it means to be a Christian inclusivist is to insist "that Jesus is the only mediator and that all must come to him and through him."[6] But inclusivists also embrace what Pinnock calls "a wider hope." They affirm the possibility of salvation for non-Christians—in particular, the unevangelized.[7] Even this, however, is not enough to make one an inclusivist. One must also hold that non-Christian religions have some sort of saving value.[8] Though inclusivists differ with respect to the role they assign to religions in salvation, they do not differ in assigning some role or other.

Let us call this claim about the soteriological significance of non-Christian religions the Strong Inclusivist Condition. Rather than take a firm stand on how best to define Christian inclusivism, let us distinguish between an inclusivism that embraces the Strong Inclusivist Condition (Strong Inclusivism) and an inclusivism that either repudiates the Strong Inclusivist Condition or is neutral with respect to it (Weak Inclusivism). Pinnock is a Strong Inclusivist. I turn now to some misgivings about Pinnock's acceptance of the Strong Inclusivist Condition.

First, a minor misgiving. Notice that it becomes impossible, due to his acceptance of the Strong Inclusivist Condition, for Pinnock to allow the designation *inclusivist* for others who call themselves inclusivists. John Sanders, for example, is an evangelical inclusivist who appears unwilling to accept the Strong Inclusivist Condition. The irony here is that Pinnock and Sanders have, through their collaborative efforts, created an impression that they represent a more or less united front, that they stand shoulder to shoulder in the vanguard of Christian inclusivism. Despite the fact that from Pinnock's vantage point Sanders must be represented as an exclusivist rather than an inclusivist, Pinnock had this to say in the foreword to Sanders's 1992 book: "Sanders provides an exposition of the wider hope that is superior to anything we presently possess."[9] (During the same year, Pinnock's own book *A Wideness in God's Mercy* was published.) How are we to escape the impression that there is mischief in this commendation?

Second, turning to a more serious misgiving, Strong Inclusivism is severely undersupported by the evidence of Scripture. Any biblical argument for Strong Inclusivism must make the case for the Strong Inclusivist Condition from the Bible. But what is the biblical evidence that non-Christian religions have saving value? Even if there is room for a wider hope within the framework of biblical teaching, Pinnock has not made the case that such a hope is secured in some way by elements within non-Christian religions. If the appeal to Scripture on behalf of this wider hope is dubious without the Strong Inclusivist Condition Pinnock endorses, it is doubly so when the Strong Inclusivist Condition is included.

Pinnock says he finds Luke saying things in the book of Acts "that bear lightly on this matter."[10] He has in mind the example of Cornelius in Acts 10, the sympathetic allusions to pagan religion in Paul's preaching at Lystra in Acts 14, and Paul's conciliatory reference to the Athenian worship of "an unknown God" in Acts 17. In support of the Strong Inclusivist Condition, Pinnock also references the assimilation of non-Jewish elements in Israelite religion, Abraham's identification of Melchizedek's God with Yahweh (Gen. 14:17-24), Abimelech's fear of God (Gen. 20:1-18), Jethro's sacrifice for Israel (Exod. 18:1-12), Balaam's prophetic success concerning God's will for Israel (Num. 23—24), and the worship of Christ by the Magi (Matt. 2:1-12).[11] Note that the whole of Pinnock's exposition of "the holy pagan tradition" of the Bible takes less than six pages.[12]

These passages can hardly bear the weight of the Strong Inclusivist Condition essential to Pinnock's version of inclusivism. They surely do not warrant the degree of confidence Pinnock exudes in his writings about the soteriological value of non-Christian religions.

Third, Pinnock clearly desires to be understood as endorsing some role for non-Christian religions in salvation. But what precisely is that role? He says he "agrees about the uniqueness of the Christian message but does not refuse to see prevenient grace operating in the sphere of human religion."[13] What does he mean by "prevenient grace"? While his concept of prevenient grace is never fully explicated, he does speak of various non-Christian religions as more-or-less suitable "vehicles of salvation." Using some complex criteria, Pinnock concludes that the religions of Melchizedek and Jethro "seem to have been vehicles of salvation for them," but that Islam "is not a reliable vehicle of salvation."[14]

So how does a religion function as a vehicle of salvation? Things come into somewhat sharper focus with the idea of religion as "preparation for the gospel." When something called "the faith principle" is operative in the life of a non-Christian and in the context of his non-Christian religion, the non-Christian is converted into a "premessianic believer."[15] As near as I can tell, a pre-messianic believer is someone who has or would have a disposition to believe in Jesus Christ upon being adequately presented with the Good News. Pre-messianic does not have a temporal reference but an informational reference. Some pre-messianic believers become Christians during this life, whereas others do not because they never actually hear. But the pre-messianic believer, who is as such a non-Christian, does receive the gift of "eschatological salvation."[16]

So the promise of eschatological salvation is grounded in the pre-messianic believer's faith, if the pre-messianic believer would believe upon hearing the Gospel, whether or not the pre-messianic believer ever hears the Gospel. If I have this right, the question is whether the elements of non-Christian religions can be responsible for inculcating in one the requisite disposition to believe upon hearing the Gospel. Since it is likely that most non-Christian religions harbor tenets that are antithetical to this sort of disposition, it seems highly unlikely that this disposition could find fertile ground or a natural home within the non-Christian religions.[17]

Fourth, how is the operation of the faith principle within the life of a non-Christian related to the doctrinal content of that non-Christian person's religious orientation? Pinnock "stops short of saying that the religions themselves as such are vehicles of salvation."[18] "What God really cares about," he stresses, "is faith and not theology, trust and not orthodoxy."[19] "[P]eople are saved by faith and not the content of their theology."[20] But if it is the exercise of faith itself that is soteriologically effectual, in total abstraction from the specific content of the non-Christian's religious faith, then what is the salvific role of the non-Christian religion exactly? Alternatively, if the very elements of non-Christian religion function as "means of grace,"[21] how do they function that way without procuring salvation for the non-Christian?

Fifth, is the faith that is exercised within the framework of a non-Christian religion of the right specific quality to have the salvific effect Pinnock envisages? It could be argued that faith requires an object and that the *quality* of faith (and therefore its effect) is conditioned by its *object*. Another way to put this is to say that the specific quality of a religious believer's faith is "in-formed" and made to be the sort of faith it is by the object to which it is directed. The object of faith, then, is at least partly constitutive of the character of faith. This may be true even if faith is a completely free response to the object.

The problem may be described two ways, with each description focusing on either faith or object. On the object side, the question is whether anything within the non-Christian religions has the properties that give form to the response of faith such that the faith that responds is of the right quality. The answer to this question would require a detailed consideration of the various non-Christian religions.[22]

On the faith side, the question is whether pre-messianic faith, which is characterized by the disposition to believe the Gospel upon hearing it, is a response to anything identifiable within the non-Christian religions that, as Pinnock says, form the context of that act of faith. Again, answering this question calls for a detailed acquaintance with non-Christian religions. But a carefully developed phenomenology of religious faith is also needed. Unfortunately, it is probably rare that the sort of faith required for eschatological salvation is tied to features of non-Christian religions in the way implied by the Strong Inclusivist Condition.

In short, does the actual faith of non-Christians, under the realistic phenomenological description, conform to the special contours of faith required for salvation, and is that faith rooted in a suitable way to features of non-Christian religions as envisaged by Pinnock?

Sixth, Pinnock's language is uniformly ambiguous when he speaks about the "possibility" that (some) unevangelized persons are helped along by their pre-messianic faith operating within some non-Christian religious framework. For example, he says that "we must be alert to the possibility that God is effectively at work in the religious dimension in a given instance, but there are no guarantees of it";[23] and inclusivism "entails the possibility that religion may play a role in the salvation of the human race."[24] Does he mean (1) that it is possible though not certain that God sometimes works through non-Christian religions to bring people to saving faith, or (2) that working through non-Christian religions is but one of several modalities that God uses to bring people to saving faith, and that for any given non-Christian it is always a possibility that this is the modality God chooses to use?

My remarks so far have focused on the Strong Inclusivist Condition that plays such an important role in Pinnock's inclusivism. I now want to shift the focus slightly to examine what I will call the Universal Access Requirement, which is also a feature of his position. In particular, I am interested in the relationship between this requirement and another component of his system. But even here Pinnock's commitment to the Strong Inclusivist Condition contributes to the generation of misgivings about his version of evangelical inclusivism.

Pinnock is committed to the view that "everyone must have

access to salvation," that everyone must have the opportunity to "participate in the salvation of God."[25] This is the Universal Access Requirement. As Pinnock says, it "raises a difficult question. How is salvation within the reach of the unevangelized? How can anyone be saved without knowing Christ?"[26] He answers that "the faith principle is the basis of universal access."[27] By distinguishing between the act of faith and the specific object of faith, Pinnock attempts "to explain how the unevangelized gain access to God and are finally saved."[28] He asserts that "we cannot reasonably suppose that a failure of evangelization that affects many millions would leave them completely bereft of any access to God." He then presents the biblical evidence for the faith principle.[29]

Other statements suggest that Pinnock confidently believes many unevangelized persons will be saved because of the faith they exercise in this life. (Because he accepts the Strong Inclusivist Condition, this probably means that non-Christian religions will be a vehicle through which some of the unevangelized will exercise the faith that saves.) Consider these remarks:

The Bible does not teach that one must confess the name of Jesus to be saved.[30]

This [appeal to the faith principle] is the path I will take to explain how the unevangelized gain access to God and are finally saved.[31]

Obviously the unevangelized can be saved by faith just like anyone else.[32]

[T]he Bible teaches that many varieties of unevangelized persons will attain salvation. This will happen according to the faith principle.[33]

These statements, and the contexts in which they are embedded, all indicate that acting according to the faith principle, without the benefit of hearing the Good News, is sufficient for salvation. Hence it would appear that the Universal Access Requirement is fully satisfied by this proposal.

Immediately following his discussion of the faith principle,[34] Pinnock considers "another way of conceiving universal access to salvation." This is "the idea that people would have an opportunity to respond to Christ after death, if they had not had the opportunity to respond before." The goal of this section of Pinnock's material is "to weigh this possibility alongside the faith principle and see if they can be combined."[35]

Here we come to a seventh misgiving. If Pinnock sanctions postmortem opportunities for the unevangelized to believe in Jesus Christ, can he insist on the Strong Inclusivist Condition? His transition from a consideration of the faith principle to a discussion of the possibility of postmortem opportunities to believe initially suggests that there are two different ways to meet the Universal Access Requirement. Each way appears to be sufficient for the satisfaction of this requirement, and, since there is more than one way to satisfy the requirement, neither way is necessary. If Pinnock allows that the Universal Access Requirement may be satisfied during a postmortem encounter, then how is the faith principle necessary to his system? But if the faith principle is not necessary, then neither is the Strong Inclusivist Condition.

But can Pinnock, given his commitment to the Strong Inclusivist Condition, really allow that acting on the faith principle within the context of non-Christian religions is not necessary to secure the salvation of certain unevangelized persons?

But now we must ask: Is the exercise of faith on the part of the pre-messianic believer even sufficient for salvation? There are at least two reasons for thinking that pre-messianic faith may not be sufficient for salvation. First, Pinnock himself says:

> If pre-Christian faith is inherently prospective, how does it experience fulfillment if the gospel does not arrive in time? . . . If God desires to save sinners, and if sinners have responded positively to the light they have, then it follows that at some point in the future the opportunity to encounter Christ will present itself.[36]

Perhaps Pinnock agrees with the exclusivist that explicit faith in Jesus Christ is ultimately required for salvation.

Further, earlier in this chapter I interpreted Pinnock's concept of a "premessianic believer" as the concept of a person whose faith is a sign that if he heard the Good News under satisfactory conditions he would be disposed to believe in Jesus Christ. But given Pinnock's views about God's foreknowledge of future free acts,[37] he can hardly countenance the claim that God knows what every person would do if given the opportunity to believe in Jesus Christ. Presumably, signs that one has a disposition to believe given the opportunity is no guarantee that one would believe. So the postmortem encounter represents the crucial test of every pre-messianic believer's faith. How would God know that one really was a pre-messianic believer in Pinnock's sense without performing the crucial experiment in which the hitherto unevangelized person finally hears the Good News and is given the opportunity to believe in Jesus Christ?

These are just a few of the misgivings I have about Clark Pinnock's inclusivism. I have not pursued the details of his use of Scripture to support his position, nor have I raised any of the missiological problems I associate with his position. Instead, I have concentrated on the logic of certain major components in his system. It is quite possible that I have misunderstood him and that this will be cleared up in the ensuing discussion. For that reason I settle for representing the objections raised here as "misgivings." I have cast these misgivings in the form of questions, and I look forward to hearing Pinnock's replies.

OVERCOMING MISGIVINGS
ABOUT EVANGELICAL INCLUSIVISM
CLARK H. PINNOCK

Introduction

Inclusivism is a term I use for a theology that observes two axioms: (1) that Jesus Christ is humanity's exclusive savior and only mediator; and (2) that divine grace and truth are found outside the Church and Christian revelation. Inclusivism seeks a middle path between two extremes—restrictivism and pluralism.

Doug notices varieties of inclusivism and asks for an explanation. This definition is a broad one and includes all who hold the two axioms, whatever their differences. Some inclusivists believe other religions play a role in God's grace, while others do not. I take this difference to be a variation within inclusivism as to how things work out. I would not make it the distinction between weak and strong versions, as Doug does. It seems to me to be a detail in how they think the grace of God works in people who have not heard the Gospel. I suppose it could be the basis for a weak/strong distinction. My view is that if God works through other channels than religion, all well and good. In either case, grace is at work. In note 8, Doug picked up an inconsistency in my remarks about McGrath. Given his wider hope, I should really have claimed him as an inclusivist. It is a small slip but important for the typology.

Most terms have limitations. The term *exclusivism* is often used in opposition to *inclusivism*, even though it is not really its opposite, since the latter also holds to the exclusiveness of God's saving work in Christ as an objective fact. One might call inclusivism an exclusivist position with a wider hope for the unevangelized. In regard to definitions, fuzziness seems to be part of the territory.

Doug and I both think that inclusivism is worth examination. I think so because it is influential almost everywhere in the churches—in the Catholic Church after Vatican II, in the Orthodox churches unburdened by *filioque*, and in the Protestant mainline denominations. Recently the Doctrine Commission of the Church of England issued a study entitled *The Mystery of Salvation* (1995) that endorses inclusivism and cites my book *A Wideness in God's Mercy*, page 176ff. This may be becoming the standard view. I think of it positively as a development of doctrine in the Church's thinking. Recently I came across a study that finds inclusivism in Edwards's thinking.[1] Perhaps this will spur evangelicals to give it a more sympathetic look.

Doug's interest in inclusivism is rather different. He speaks of a "recrudescence" of it among evangelicals, something that he finds unsettling. This is understandable because the evangelicals are the largest group in the Church not to go along with inclusivism. His language is revealing of how he feels about that, since "recrudescence" is

used for the outbreak of a disease that has been quiescent. Evidently
he does not see it as a valid development of doctrine.

I am not comfortable with his reference to inclusivism as a disease. I think it deserves more respect than that since it seems to be the
view now held by large numbers of Christians. I would prefer to speak
of it as a "disputed question" on which people differ. The term puts
me in a bad light, as if I were the carrier of a virus. Do we want to use
such language with each other? Do we want to put each other down
rhetorically? The word "quiescent" crops up in the definition and
pleases me more because it recognizes that the "virus" has been
around evangelical traditions (in Wesley, Strong, Kraft, C. S. Lewis,
Hackett, etc.) and is not a foreign disease. Maybe it is a good infection,
as Lewis might say.

Obviously there is strength of feeling here. Such is always the
case with disputed questions of significance. Here is the framework
I suggest we use. In the history of doctrine, wheat and tares grow up
together. Normally, rather than rooting up the tares, it is best to let
the plants grow, because we do not know which plant is which as of
yet. It is best to give the discussion time to sink in and watch for the
fruit—fruit in terms of positive or negative impact on Christian character and mission. In the spirit of Acts 15, let us ask what the Spirit
is leading us to think about this matter and what the directions are
in which the Spirit is leading as we move in mission toward the
Kingdom of God.

Section One

I want to start, not with Doug's order of questioning, which places
me on the defensive, but with what I consider the most weighty issue
for us and one that may relativize the importance of the specific
objections. This will give me a chance to say what moves me most,
after which I can return to specific queries. I am speaking of axiom
two—God's universal salvific will. It is the nature of God as *abba* that
funds wider-hope theories in general. Inclusivism is one possible
implementation of that axiom and is of less significance than the
axiom itself.

Support for it arises from the growing recognition among

Christians of the priority of God's love relative to other issues. It has
developed from the vision of *abba* who seeks every lost coin and every
lost sheep and who longs for the return of each of his lost sons. This
(I think) is the factor that accounts for the more positive attitude
toward those outside the Church among Christians today—not liberalism, not sentimentality, but the Gospel. Large numbers are coming
to accept that at the top of the hierarchy of Christian truths, and of
primary importance, is the will of God for the salvation of the race.
Issues such as baptism and church membership have become subordinate to it and are being reformulated in order to confirm rather than
conflict with it. This shift is helping us move from a ghetto mentality
typical of many traditions in the past that saw little grace outside the
Church toward a spirit of greater openness to people outside the
Church and those who have not yet heard the Gospel. This shift fos-
ters the quest for some sort of wider hope, of which inclusivism is a
variety. It explains the reduced inclination to dogmatize about who is
in and who is out of God's Kingdom. It leads one to hope for the other
person however dismal the situation.

The conviction is growing in evangelical circles that God is not
planning to cast into hell the majority of the race who, through no
fault of their own, have had no opportunity to become Christians.
There are others, of course, who still wish to assert that is what will
happen. For them, the love of God is not higher than, but on a level
with, God's freedom and wrath. The view is coherent but seems to be
getting harder to maintain. Many are thinking there is more hope than
that in the Christian message. They are loath to say God created
human beings only to damn most of them and save but a few of them.
I think it is God's universal salvific will that gives inclusivism basic
plausibility and makes restrictivism seem unlikely. I begin my
response with this statement because it is the presupposition that gives
rise to wider hope and inclusivist theory and should be acknowledged.

In making this point, I am admitting that presuppositions are at
work in the discussion of inclusivism. The proposition that God wills
the salvation of every human being is itself contested. More and more
may believe it, but not everyone agrees. Reformed traditions in particular maintain double predestination, which leads some to say that

God does not care for every human but has from the beginning decided whom to save and whom not to save. They believe that God is within his rights to refuse grace to anyone he has decided to deprive of it. His freedom is complete, and his love may discriminate. Although I find this way of thinking difficult, some evangelicals look at things this way and will have little sympathy for my thinking. Yet in their own way they could bridge the gap—if, for example, they were to think of the elect as numerous and not sparse, or of them sprinkled among non-Christian peoples and loved by God, or of every child of Adam as presumptively elect, as Hodge does. Even from this theological model, one could regard people optimistically, based not upon their worthiness, but upon the breadth of sovereign divine grace. Conflicting theological paradigms are not likely to disappear, but it is possible to build bridges to one another on matters of consequence.

Section Two

I turn now to Doug's specific concerns concerning the wider hope of inclusivism itself and its workings. The fact that God loves the world moves one in the direction of wider hope but does not establish a theory of it. Recall that John Stott, who hopes for the salvation of most people, refuses to say how he thinks this will be accomplished. Although we would like him to offer reasons for his hope, he leaves us without an explanation. Most of us would prefer a reason to be offered, which is what I have attempted to do in my theory, though (I would admit) it is not the only way to think about these things and may be flawed, as Doug believes it is.

It is my opinion that, whereas objective salvation is clear (i.e., through Christ alone—John 14:6), subjective salvation is not so straightforward (i.e., *how* one is saved by Christ). Scripture speaks in different ways about how people are saved subjectively. For example, it says that God loves seekers and rewards them, even if they are not Jews or Christians (Heb. 11:6). It says that Christ will save some people who have no idea who Jesus is but who showed by their deeds that they love God's Kingdom (Matt. 25:37). A response is required in each case, but there can be more than one kind of response. I presume that faith may be based on the true light that enlightens everyone (John

1:9). I find support in Paul's statement that people may search for God and find him from anywhere in the world (Acts 17:27). I appreciate his saying that the Gentiles have God's Law written on their hearts (Rom. 2:15) and may be given eternal life when, by patiently doing good, they seek for glory and honor and immortality (Rom. 2:7). As a Catholic might put it, there are people with a desire for baptism who have not been able to be baptized. Inclusivism responds to such generous sentiments.

It would be nice to be able to be more precise in explaining how a saving yet non-Christian faith works. Some of Doug's questions ask for that, and I wish I/we knew more about it than we do. Nevertheless, the fact remains that Scripture supports the position that it is possible (however it may be possible) to have faith on the basis of an uncertain amount of revelational information. I adduce the slogan in this connection: If something is actual, it must be possible. We do not have to know how it works in order to acknowledge it.

The Old Testament is clear that one can be saved without knowing about the incarnate Christ. What was required of people during that time (as far as I can tell) was that they seek, repent, and believe. God rewards those who seek him; the wicked must forsake their ways; faith itself is based on what they already know about God. We cannot quantify how much knowledge they must have in order to be saved. Knowing facts can be quantified, but not knowing a Person. God sees the heart and knows who loves him. We agree that people know enough to make them responsible before God; by the same token grace can reach the heart of people even when the propositional content is minimal. I like what Peter Kreeft and Ronald Tacelli say: "Socrates (or any other pagan) could seek God, could repent of his sins, and could obscurely believe in and accept the God he knew partially and be saved."[2]

We do not know how common these responses are—only that they are possible. Because of biblical promises for a large salvation outcome, I myself hope that it is very common. This optimism is a feature of my version of inclusivism that differs from others. Sanders makes no such claim. My view agrees with John Stott but goes further than he does in trying to explain it.

Control beliefs are at work. The presupposition about God's universal salvific will biases me toward favoring inclusivist arguments. Maybe it makes me think better of them than I should, because I want them or something like them to be true. I know that necessity can be the mother of invention. At the same time, accepting the doctrine of restrictivism, that God is free to damn people in large numbers, seemingly arbitrarily disposes a person against seeing the biblical evidence for inclusivism or makes them feel it is unacceptably slight. I agree that inclusivism is not a central topic of discussion in the Bible and that the evidence for it is less than one would like. But the vision of God's love there is so strong that the existing evidence seems sufficient to me. I understand, however, why someone might not find it sufficient.

Another feature of my version of inclusivism is an openness not only to grace outside the Church like all inclusivists have, but to the possibility that other religions might play a role in making faith possible. In my book I appeal to Scriptures addressing the accounts of Melchizedek, Abimelech, Jethro, the Magi, Cornelius, etc. that seem to suggest this. I agree with Doug about the evidence being slim. In their contexts, biblical authors usually denounce and rarely credit the truth of other religions (for good reasons, I presume). I acknowledge that religions can be very bad; but the possibility of a religion being helpful in some way cannot be ruled out. Religions are not salvific as systems. Still, they are partly true. God has not left himself without witness, and this witness has (presumably) registered in the religious realm. There may be aspects of religions that the Spirit can use in someone's life. Don Richardson, for example, speaks of redemptive bridges, and C. S. Lewis speaks of God using parts of a religion in agreement with Christianity. Lewis also wrote in the Chronicles of Narnia series of Tash being saved even though he was ignorant of Aslan's claim on him, because Aslan was the one he really sought. It seems plausible to think after this manner and to be watchful for such possibilities in those we meet. We must not suspend critical judgment, but it does allow us to hope that among non-Christians there are seekers who have found something, if not yet Christ.

I appreciate what Vatican II said: "The Catholic Church rejects nothing which is true and holy in these religions. She looks with sincere respect upon those ways of conduct and of life, those rules and teachings which, though differing in many particulars from what she holds and sets forth, nevertheless reflect a ray of that truth which enlightens all men."[3] I think we should be open to the possibility of God's gracious presence there. I cannot understand why Doug is not open in principle to that possibility. The Spirit of God is present throughout creation, ministering the presence of the divine Suitor. It seems that Doug doubts that it is within the Spirit's power to make positive use of truth components in another religion. Why is he so pessimistic? Why can it not be one of the modalities that God uses? How is it that the darkness always overcomes the light in his view (John 1:5)? I cannot grasp why God would bypass the realm of human religion in his seeking of sinners when that realm is the place where so many seek ultimate truth and meaning.

Doug asked about the role which postmortem experience plays in my inclusivist theory. Here is what I think. After death we meet God face to face. At that point the faith in all of us is completed in this encounter. For everyone it will be a great leap forward, both in understanding and love. For an unevangelized person like Job, who was on earth before Christ, this would be a time when his desire for God opens up to a secure and complete picture of the triune God. I assume that persons who had not responded to God in this life would not change their minds and do so then. As for God knowing whether a Job who loved God in life would love him in death, I think he would know what his friend would do in the presence of even more truth and love. Or more adequately, he would know what the beloved would do at the wedding.

R. DOUGLAS GEIVETT'S NOTES

1. As quoted in Daniel B. Clendenin, *Many Gods, Many Lords: Christianity Encounters World Religions* (Grand Rapids, Mich.: Baker, 1995), 11.

2. Clark H. Pinnock, "An Inclusivist View," in *Four Views on Salvation in a Pluralistic World,* eds. Dennis L. Okholm and Timothy R. Phillips (Grand Rapids, Mich.: Zondervan, 1995), 251, 253-254; John Sanders, *No Other Name: An Investigation into the Destiny of the Unevangelized* (Grand Rapids, Mich.: Eerdmans, 1992), 216, n. 1; Ronald Nash, *Is Jesus the Only Savior?* (Grand Rapids, Mich.: Zondervan, 1994), 108-109.

3. Sanders, "Inclusivism," in *What About Those Who Have Never Heard? Three Views on the Destiny of the Unevangelized* (Downers Grove, Ill.: InterVarsity Press, 1995), 140.

4. R. Douglas Geivett, "Is Jesus the Only Way?" in *Jesus Under Fire: Modern Scholarship Reinvents the Historical Jesus*, eds. Michael J. Wilkins and J. P. Moreland (Grand Rapids, Mich.: Zondervan, 1995); and Geivett and W. Gary Phillips, "A Particularist View: An Evidentialist Approach," in *Four Views on Salvation in a Pluralistic World*.

5. Pinnock, *A Wideness in God's Mercy: The Finality of Jesus Christ in a World of Religions* (Grand Rapids, Mich.: Zondervan, 1992), 15; Pinnock, "An Inclusivist View," 98.

6. Pinnock, "The Finality of Jesus Christ in a World of Religions," in *Christian Faith and Practice in the Modern World: Theology from an Evangelical Perspective*, eds. Dennis L. Ockholm and Timothy R. Phillips (Grand Rapids, Mich.: Zondervan, 1988), 162.

7. Pinnock, *Wideness*, 157.

8. Ibid., 15. This conviction comes out most clearly in a passage where Pinnock contrasts his position with Alister McGrath's. He acknowledges that McGrath's position is soteriologically inclusive in the sense that "salvation is possible for non-Christians. . . . God can bring the unevangelized to faith in this life." But McGrath's position is "exclusive when it comes to other faiths. That is, it differs from inclusivism in its assessment of the role of religion in salvation. . . . McGrath does not look to religion as a locale of prevenient grace." This is why Pinnock calls McGrath's position "nonrestrictive exclusivism": it is "'nonrestrictive' because of [McGrath's] wider hope and 'exclusivist' because he sees no saving value in other religions." McGrath's position, though it allows "that salvation is possible for non-Christians, that God can bring the unevangelized to faith in this life," is quite clearly considered by Pinnock to be a variety of exclusivism—and this is because the position "sees no saving value in other religions" (Pinnock, "An Inclusivist View," 187-188).

9. Pinnock, Foreword to *No Other Name: An Investigation into the Destiny of the Unevangelized* by John Sanders, XV.

10. Pinnock, "Acts 4:12—No Other Name Under Heaven," in *Through No Fault of Their Own*, eds. William Crockett and James Sigountos (Grand Rapids, Mich.: Baker, 1991), 114.

11. Pinnock, *Wideness*, 93-95; "Finality," 153, 158; *Wideness*, 95-98.

12. Pinnock seems to regard the cases of Melchizedek and Cornelius as most promising. See Pinnock, "An Inclusivist View," 109.

13. Ibid., 188.

14. Pinnock, *Wideness*, 107, 110.

15. Ibid., 157-168.

16. See Pinnock, "Acts 4:12" for this use of the term "eschatological salvation."

17. Pinnock holds that the truth and goodness discoverable in other religions anticipates salvation through Jesus Christ (Pinnock, *Wideness*, 113). But about the only evidence for this assertion is that people from non-Christian traditions have been known to convert to Christianity. It is hard to see how the inclination to embrace Jesus Christ can be positively inspired by acceptable features of non-Christian religions, except in the case of Judaism.

18. Pinnock, "An Inclusivist View," 99. See also his comments on page 116 in the same article.

19. Pinnock, *Wideness*, 112.

20. Ibid., 157.

21. Pinnock, "An Inclusivist View," 116.

22. Cf. Winfried Corduan's article in this volume.

23. Pinnock, "An Inclusivist View," 116.

24. Ibid., 98.

25. Pinnock, *Wideness*, 157.

26. Ibid.

27. Ibid.

28. Ibid., 158.
29. Ibid., 159.
30. Ibid., 158.
31. Ibid.
32. Ibid., 161.
33. Ibid., 168.
34. Ibid., 157-168.
35. Ibid., 168; cf. 168-175. See also "Finality of Jesus," 165-167.
36. Pinnock, "Finality of Jesus Christ," 165. See *Wideness* for intimations of this same attitude.
37. Pinnock, *Wideness*, 160-161; "Systematic Theology," in *The Openness of God: A Biblical Challenge to the Traditional Understanding of God* (Downers Grove, Ill.: InterVarsity Press, 1994), 121-124; "An Inclusivist View," 144-145.

CLARK PINNOCK'S NOTES

1. Anri Morimoto, *Jonathan Edwards and the Catholic Vision of Salvation* (Pittsburgh: Pennsylvania State University Press, 1995), 62-67.
2. Peter Kreeft and Ronald Tacelli, *Handbook of Christian Apologetics* (Downers Grove, Ill.: InterVarsity Press, 1994), 328.
3. Vatican II statement, "Declaration on the Relationship of the Church to Non-Christian Religions," par. 2, in *The Documents of Vatican II*, ed. Walter M. Abbott, trans. ed. Joseph Gallagher (New York: Herder & Herder, 1966), 662.

SIX

BUDDHA, SHIVA, AND MUHAMMAD

Theistic Faith in Other Religions?

WINFRIED CORDUAN

What is the destiny of the unevangelized? Clark H. Pinnock has argued that a person who has not had the opportunity to hear the Gospel and so has not exercised explicit conscious faith in Christ may yet partake of the effect of Christ's atonement for salvation.[1] Pinnock supports his case with a number of arguments,[2] only a minor one of which is the presence of true and noble beliefs found in non-Christian religions.

In this paper I will respond to some of Pinnock's references to non-Christian religions. In these references Pinnock attempts to show that there are some aspects of some religions that offer a potential for fruitful faith in God. I will show that Pinnock distorts the content of these religions in order to provide more common ground than there really is. In the process, however, it becomes apparent that Pinnock does not really need these cases because his subjective understanding of salvific faith overrides the objective content anyway.

Pinnock appeals to four specific areas of non-Christian religions' rapprochement with biblical theism: the teachings of the Buddha, particularly with regard to *nirvana*; the Jodo Shin-Shu school of Buddhism and the free grace of Amida Buddha; the Shaivite school of Bhakti Hinduism with its emphasis on an all-pervasive divine love;

and the teachings of Muhammad in reaffirming monotheism.[3] None of these four cases is as helpful as Pinnock would like them to be.

I approach Pinnock's work, and my response to his views on salvation in other religions, with a few presuppositions. I believe that goodness can be found in other religions and that God has given witness to his existence outside of Scripture. However, neither of these have the weight with which Pinnock invests them. I present these presuppositions because I want the reader to understand these underlying basic beliefs through which I interact with Pinnock's work.

PRESUPPOSITION A:
GOODNESS IN OTHER RELIGIONS

We need not question whether there can be good and true beliefs in other religions. Of course there are. Many religions present helpful insights into some aspect of life or command important virtues. Even though it is false that all religions have the same essential moral teaching, it is true that many religions have moral teaching of high standards. To show that a specific religion is false, you do not have to show that every single proposition within it is false—only that its core beliefs are false, or that its set of beliefs as a whole is false.

PRESUPPOSITION B: NATURAL THEOLOGY

Romans 1 teaches that God has left himself a witness in creation so that there is enough evidence to recognize his existence, power, and deity. It is possible to know him and thereby to be responsible to him. In addition to the fact that this belief is taught in Scripture, it has also received support through anthropological studies, thereby making a clear case for an original theism.[4] The following points can be demonstrated:

1. Historically, the origin of religion lies with the self-revealing God.
2. A relatively pure theism has been perpetuated among some of the least developed peoples of the world—e.g., Asian

and African pygmoids, certain Native American tribes, and Australian aborigines.

3. A remnant of theism can be detected in the history of most of the complex religions of the world—e.g., Dyaus Pitar in the history of Indic religion, Allah in the Arabian peninsula, and Shangdi in China.

4. God, as evidenced in these contexts, has roughly the properties associated with biblical theism. Within the particular descriptive limitations of a culture, he is considered to be personal, omnipresent, omniscient, omnipotent, transcendent, immanent, Creator, and the supreme moral authority.

In the ensuing discussion I am going to address the crucial theological question of whether devotion to God on the basis of natural theology has the potential to save a person. I will limit myself to the more factual issue: To what extent is there a legitimate tie-in of Pinnock's four cases to this original theism and, by extension, to biblical theism?

SAKYAMUNI AND NIRVANA

Pinnock's interaction with Buddhism is highly subjectivized,[5] relying to a large extent on the positive feelings that we might get about the Buddha or Buddhism. "But how does one come away after encountering Buddhism," he asks, "and deny that it is in touch with God in its way?"[6] Surely, even though this question sounds rhetorical, it has a very clear answer: By listening to what Buddhism actually teaches. Pinnock rightly objects to John Hick's method of forcing Christian beliefs into a straitjacket of religious monism.[7] But it would be just as wrong for Pinnock to reinterpret Buddhism to fit a theistic pattern that the Buddhist himself would reject. Pinnock recognizes that "Buddhism is not Christianity"[8] but still attempts to make the Buddha's teachings more amenable to Christianity than is reasonable. Let me take several of Pinnock's statements summarizing Buddhism and show how a more accurate analysis of these concepts leads us in a different direction.

"[Buddha] taught people that a man's proper relationship to the created world is not to give it ultimate value or devotion, because much human suffering derives from that."9

Allow me to refer to the historical Buddha (Siddhartha Gautama) by the title that Buddhists themselves prefer in order to distinguish him in his earthly life from his spiritual existence or from the many other Buddhas—namely, Sakyamuni ("the sage of the Sakya tribe"). Sakyamuni's teaching was far more radical than Pinnock's summary indicates. He located the root of all human suffering (*dukha*) in the very fact of our existence and our attachment (*tanha*) to the phenomenal world per se. There is no "created world" in the sense in which a god created something to exist, but only the deception that is engendered by our considering our life-world to be real. True reality is emptiness (*sunyata*); we ourselves are non-self (*anatman*). The world, all beings within the world, even the very gods who assisted Sakyamuni toward enlightenment, are products of an illusionary causal nexus. Until a person internalizes this awareness, he or she will continue to be stuck in a cycle of reincarnations and will suffer. Thus what Sakyamuni taught was far more than wise counsel not to lay up our treasures on earth; it was the denial of a created order.

*He also spoke of a power he called the *dharma*, which seems to be a gracious and good power, and which promotes redemption and salvation."10

Dharma, literally "the way," is a concept that occurs in all Indic religions. It is primarily not a power, though it engenders power. Because it is not a power, it also does not promote redemption or salvation by itself. Rather, the *dharma* is a method of living according to correct spiritual insights. In early Buddhism, *dharma* specifically refers to the way of the monks and is embodied in the noble eightfold path: right view, right intention, right speech, right action, right livelihood, right effort, right meditation, and right concentration. The practical outworking of right actions is summarized in the ten precepts. A monk is forbidden to harm any living being, steal, have sex, lie, take intoxicating drinks, eat after noon, attend entertainment, decorate himself or herself, sleep in a comfortable bed, or touch gold or silver. Following this path will lead a person to release from the cycle of reincarnations and to find his or her place in the emptiness of *sunyata*. At this point the person has attained the state of *nirvana*.

"There is in *nirvana* a quasi-personal aspect, a sense of possible friendship and intimacy with the good and the lovely, and there is the blessing of spiritual insight suggestive of revelation."[11]

Sakyamuni consistently refused to describe the state of *nirvana*. Literally the word means "blowing out," as in extinguishing a candle. What has been blown out is usually the following: a person's mistaken sense of individual identity, the describable phenomenal world, the cycle of reincarnations, and the suffering that goes along with existence. Sakyamuni insisted, however, that *nirvana* is not purely negative; it is something to anticipate joyfully. In later developments after Sakyamuni, *nirvana* took on a greater meaning as the distillation of absolute compassion and thus began more closely to resemble a pantheistic monism. But it still did not turn into a personal deity. Furthermore, it was said from Sakyamuni's time on that the person who achieves *nirvana* has an immediate intuition of its nature, though it is an awareness beyond all words and concepts. This knowledge, however, can hardly be construed as self-revelation from a deity.[12]

"Granted, being anti-metaphysical in reaction to Hinduism, the Buddha did not teach personal theism with force or clarity."[13]

Assuming that the words "personal theism" have any meaning, this statement is true simply because Sakyamuni did not teach theism at all. *Nirvana* is not a personal deity. The Indian gods occupy a paradoxical place in the myth of Siddhartha Gautama, the Buddha. They assured his calling to a religious life by providing the four visions (old age, sickness, death, and religious devotion) that propelled Gautama to monkhood. The earth mother gave witness to his enlightenment, and Brahma encouraged the new Buddha to preach the *dharma*. However, in the core teaching of Sakyamuni's insights, the gods play no helpful role. In fact, as long as a person keeps looking to a deity for help, he or she is going to remain trapped in the vicious cycle of suffering. Traditional Buddhism is not theistic.

In sum, it would appear that Pinnock, motivated by a desire to find bridges to Buddhism, has reinterpreted Sakyamuni's teachings beyond what was intended.

JODO SHIN-SHU

Pinnock asks, "Why turn up our noses at . . . the insights into grace in the Japanese Shin-Shu Amida or other positive changes in Buddhism?"[14] Let us focus on Amida in Jodo Shin-Shu, the most popular Japanese school of Pure Land Buddhism. And let us agree that to reject something as false is not necessarily to turn up our noses; the latter would be disdainful, while the former could be prudent.

Pure Land Buddhism is one of the many branches of Buddhism that are usually classified together as *Mahayana*, the "greater raft." Mahayana Buddhism diverges from the older schools of Buddhism and the teachings of Sakyamuni himself in a number of respects.[15] One of the most important differences is the accretion of numerous Buddhas and Bodhisattvas—beings who are in a state immediately prior to becoming Buddhas. In most Pure Land schools, the central Buddha is not Sakyamuni, the historical founder of Buddhism, but Amitabha, known in Japan as Amida Buddha.

Amida has his own story. In remote history he was a king who heard the teaching of another Buddha while on earth. Under this influence he vowed that someday he would provide for the salvation of all humankind, and countless incarnations later he was able to achieve enlightenment. To this point the story is similar to that of Sakyamuni, but now an important difference emerges. Whereas Sakyamuni received enlightenment on earth and departed from the earthly sphere of influence upon death, Amida took the final step of enlightenment in heaven,[16] where he continues to dwell as a celestial being.

Amida is one of four such Buddhas (*Dhyani* Buddhas), each of whom has received one of the cardinal directions as his domain. Amida is associated with the West. Having attained Buddhahood, he was now able to complete his vow. He created a "paradise" or "pure land" into which anyone can be reincarnated as long as they have faith in him.

Jodo Shin-Shu distinguishes itself by its emphasis on the grace of Amida. Shinran, its founder, taught that all that was necessary for a person to attain the pure land after death was to call on Amida Buddha once. All pure land schools (as well as other schools of Buddhism) chant the phrase *Namu Amida Butsu* (or *Nembutsu*): "I bow down (to worship) the Buddha Amida." In this particular school the single utterance of the statement is enough to guarantee paradise.

Amida's western paradise is a place of beauty and serenity. Everyone is born into it as a male, and everyone who abides there can take the final step into *nirvana* without hindrance. Let me now respond to some questions concerning this teaching.

Does Jodo Shin-Shu teach salvation "by grace through faith"? Yes, of course it does. Amida's pure land is graciously bestowed on anyone who simply has faith in him. Christian apologists do not gain anything by needlessly parsing away those two concepts. One wishes that more Christian thinkers would have as straightforward an understanding of grace and faith as Shinran did! But difficulties arise from the meaning of salvation and of the being who grants it.

Is Amida a god? Here the answer is clearly no. Amida was a man named Dharmakara who was able to transform himself into a *Dhyani* Buddha by his own devotion and discipline. Although as a celestial Buddha he now receives devotion similar to the worship of a god, he is not a god; but he is superior to the gods in his knowledge and power. In fact, the gods can also be granted bliss in the pure land, thanks to Amida. More importantly, neither by historical origin nor by description can one say that Amida is the God of theism; he is a different sort of being who has merely taken the functionally equivalent place of God in this religion.

Is rebirth in the pure land the equivalent of salvation? The answer to this question is ambivalent. Within Jodo Shin-Shu it is precisely what salvation is all about; even though being in paradise is not yet the attainment of *nirvana*, for practical purposes the two are equated. However, it should hardly need to be pointed out that escaping the cycle of reincarnation and its attending suffering is distinct in all respects from the Christian understanding of salvation as reconciliation with God based on the propitiation of Christ. One can classify the two together under some large umbrella—both provide a way of release from the human predicament; but fill out the meaning and all similarity vanishes.

Obviously, what attracts Pinnock is the subjective side of the Pure

Land School. I certainly would not wish to dismiss the potential for finding a bridge to communicate the Gospel in these ideas, but the content of the Christian Gospel is the Redeemer who has made atonement, not the subjective faith of the Christian.

Having made reference to Jodo Shin-Shu and some other religions, Pinnock contends that "religions do not present only the way of human self-justification. At times they also announce the grace and love of God."[17] Jodo Shin-Shu may present the love and compassion of Amida, but not of God—as long as the word *God* refers to the infinite personal Creator described in theism.

SHIVA AND BHAKTI HINDUISM

The aforementioned quotation from Pinnock actually begins with, "Why turn up our noses at the bhakti tradition in Hinduism . . . ?"[18] In another place he writes:

> The theistic Saiva Siddhanta literature of Hinduism, to take another example, celebrates a personal God of love. It expresses the belief that all God's actions in the world are intended to express love for his creatures and to lead them into loving union with himself.[19]

Saiva Sidhanta is a school of devotion to Shiva; its adherents consider Shiva to be the highest form of God.

Pinnock is to be commended here for recognizing the theistic nature of much of Hinduism. Too many evangelicals today try to understand all of Hinduism as pantheistic, which many of its schools are not. Again though, similarities to original theism are more apparent than real and vanish entirely when the surrounding context is taken into account.

Historically Shiva's beginnings are not in the God of original theism. His first appearance in the Vedas, the first scriptures of Hinduism, is as the fierce mountain god Rudra. Under the praise name Shiva ("the auspicious one") he took on greater significance but maintained his capricious character long into the history of Hinduism. Then in the bhakti revolt toward the end of the first millennium A.D. in southern

India, he became the first bhakti deity to receive wide acclaim. Subsequent developments elevated Vishnu as well, but Shiva continues to be the most popular bhakti god today.

Bhakti Hinduism has roots going back to the much earlier *Bhagavad Gita*. In the *Gita*, Krishna, who is an incarnation (avatar) of the god Vishnu, instructs the archer Arjuna to trust in him alone, and he will then provide for Arjuna's salvation (*moksha*). Similarly, the various schools of bhakti Hinduism identify certain gods as supreme, and the adherents devote themselves primarily (though not necessarily exclusively) to their chosen deity. The most popular bhakti god is Shiva, followed by Vishnu and his avatars (such as Krishna and Rama), with a sizable following also going to the less clearly defined goddess.

We need to be aware of two important points concerning bhakti:

1. Although there is a certain notion of grace and faith within these schools, for the most part, in their original contexts, these words have a fairly weak meaning at best. Usually bhakti practices focus on acts of devotion that are necessary to partake of the deity's mercy; and so in most bhakti schools we are looking at synergism at best, salvation by works at worst. The Shaivite school (the school of Shiva bhakti) is particularly prone to emphasizing works of devotion as essential for a true relationship to Shiva.

2. Only in certain bhakti schools centered on Rama is there a genuine conception of grace. Here the god truly does not require any contributory works by the human being; all acts by the man or woman are simply deeds of gratitude. Nevertheless, as with Jodo Shin-Shu, the context of grace and faith certainly negates any resemblance to their biblical counterparts. As Rudolf Otto pointed out,[20] the deity's supposed work of releasing a person from the cycle of incarnations incurred by karma is pervasively different from the Christian notion of redemption from sin through Christ's atonement.

To return to Shiva, reference to him as a "god of love" is valid as far as it goes, but it misses some of the most salient aspects of Shiva's character, particularly the eroticism. Shiva's most common representation in temples is as a *lingam*, a phallus. Frequently he is shown together with the goddess in the *lingam-yoni* configuration. These depictions are not obscene by usual standards, but they do call attention to a side of the deity that is clearly incompatible with original theism, which centers around a self-revealing God. In fact, it appears to resemble more closely some of the concepts of Canaanite fertility religions (which Pinnock has no trouble dismissing),[21] though it only rarely produces sexual practices in Tamil India, its most important region.[22] But even aside from the erotic side of Shiva, his attributes are still largely removed from original theism. He is capricious, wantonly destructive, and demanding. Shaivite bhakti is known for its austere practices that sometimes verge on self-immolation. Yes, Shiva is referred to as a "god of love," but it is the love of passion only. Once again we are further removed from original theism than a superficial summary might lead us to suspect.

MUHAMMAD AND ALLAH

Pinnock asks, "Who can deny the striking similarities between the prophet Muhammad and the Old Testament prophets? Would not admitting this have momentous consequences for our witness to Islam?"[23]

Here we can make a greater number of positive comments than with regard to the previous three examples.

1. Allah, the God of ancient Arabia whose worship was revived by Muhammad, is historically the God of original theism.

2. Muhammad courageously led a profound movement to restore Arabian religion to these theistic foundations.

3. In the teachings of Muhammad, Allah shares most of the traits of not only original theism but biblical theism as well.

Still, despite the common origin, there are also some crucial differences between Muhammad's understanding of God and the biblical one, which we can point out without impugning the goodness and love of Allah, as evangelical apologists sometimes do. After all, five times a day Muslims begin their prayers with "In the name of Allah, the most gracious, the most merciful."

One important distinction lies in the obvious point that the Qur'an denies the deity of Christ. Since the outright contradiction of this doctrine is placed into the mouth of Allah himself in the Qur'an,[24] Islam cannot just be unfulfilled pre-Christian religion.

But one of the most fundamental incongruities between God as depicted in Islam and in biblical theism lies in Allah's capacity to overlook sin. In contrast to the biblical teaching, epitomized by 1 John 1:5 ("God is light, in him is no darkness at all"), Allah is free to pardon sin at his discretion without any provision such as an atonement. His holiness is not violated by human sin. Consequently there is no need for an atonement; in fact, the Qur'an censures the very notion of a substitutionary death.[25]

This is why even recognizing the theistic truth within Islam does not really constitute a boon for evangelism to Islamic countries. The statement of Pinnock's that I quoted at the beginning of this section commits two errors. First, he makes it appear as though evangelists to Islam have not appreciated the truths within this religion. At least since the time of Samuel Zwemer early in this century this is not the case. Second, he does not take cognizance of the fact that, nevertheless, Muslims have shown themselves exceptionally unreceptive to the Gospel. It would appear that the very similarity has made it more difficult for Muslims to understand the crucial need for faith in Christ.

ASSESSMENT

I have tried to show that Pinnock's short references to some non-Christian religions are far too positive. In three of the four cases the differences are much greater than Pinnock lets on, and even in the fourth case the relatively smaller differences are still momentous. In all cases, including the original theism that has been preserved in Islam, the actual content of the beliefs is not merely incomplete compared to biblical theism but is incompatible with it. Pinnock's rejoicing at these teachings is at least premature.

What makes this discussion so poignant is the fluid use that Pinnock attempts to make of his interpretations. He follows up the statements in question with a theology of general revelation and prevenient grace, according to which there may be a remnant of true self-revelation of God in these religions. Despite the factual concerns raised above, this inference could be acceptable if he were to find better examples than the first three or if he would not gloss over the differences to Allah in Islam. After all, there *is* general revelation, and we can demonstrate the reality of an original theism. But there is nothing in the objective beliefs of these religions to lead us to expect salvific efficacy within them.

Surprisingly, Pinnock agrees with this last statement. Having exaggerated the positive contributions of the religions in question, he is also able to see deficiencies in them. For example, "The dharma of Buddhism may be an effective way of overcoming egoism and attaining inner peace and compassion, but it does not intend to lead people into a personal relationship with God. . . . Salvation in this sense is something Jesus and not the Buddha opens for humanity. Jesus is the way to the Father."[26] Or, "[Islam] as a system is not a reliable vehicle of salvation. On the contrary, it enslaves millions by its emphasis on works righteousness."[27]

How can Pinnock be so positive on the one hand and turn right around and be so negative? The key to understanding him on this point is that the conceptual and objective hindrances to the Gospel in these religions are important to Pinnock, but not crucial. In between the two quotations excerpted above, he asserts:

> This does not mean Buddhism has nothing to offer, or that Buddhists cannot move in Christ's direction *from where they presently are*. The same can be said of Islam. There is truth aplenty in it on which the sincere soul can feed. God can call people to himself *from within Islam*.[28] (emphasis mine)

Thus Pinnock's position boils down to this: Despite objective hindrances to salvation within a religion, it is still possible to come to saving faith within that religion.

He is not just saying that a Buddhist could come across New Testament truth while living in a Buddhist context, renounce Buddhism, and obtain salvation outside of his former Buddhist allegiance. There would be nothing different from an exclusivist position in that interpretation. Pinnock's point can be stated in this way: Even though Buddhism as a whole is contrary to the truths of salvation, an individual Buddhist can continue to practice Buddhism and receive salvation from the God he never knew while remaining a Buddhist.

Here we see the real ambivalence in Pinnock's treatment of non-Christian religions. He recognizes some serious flaws in those religions that the Bible opposes—e.g., the Canaanite fertility cults. Still, while trying to be aware of the deficiencies in contemporary religions, he attempts to find positive contributions within them. And even recognizing the fundamental opposition to God's revelation in non-Christian religions does not prevent Pinnock from believing that a person can come to God without shedding the false concepts.

Pinnock's solution to this apparent paradox is to make a distinction between subjective and objective religion. In his approach, "objective" religion refers to what is actually true and real, while "subjective" religion denotes how the human being relates to his or her religious beliefs, specifically faith and devotion. He claims that "objective religion does matter, and it must be confronted on truth issues, even though subjective religion is more important to God."[29] And thus we come to the theological issue that goes beyond the intent of this paper. Pinnock wishes to defend the notion that the sincere seeker after God, no matter how entrapped in deficient beliefs, can still experience God's grace and mercy.[30] But if this is so, one wonders why Pinnock even attempts the forays into non-Christian belief systems since he had to distort them to serve his purposes anyway. Even though he counsels discernment on objective belief systems and even protests that they are important, they do not appear to hold any lasting importance since they can be overridden by subjective attitudes in many conspicuous cases.

Rather than following Pinnock's procrustean analysis, we can draw the following conclusions concerning other religions. First, the religions clearly derived from original theism contain elements that can be seen as preparatory for the Gospel. But they also contain beliefs inimical to the Gospel, and so the Gospel cannot merely be the fulfillment of such religions.

Second, despite the availability of general revelation, actual non-Christian religions include beliefs inconsistent with biblical and theistic truth. Romans 1 teaches a general awareness of God, but it teaches just as strongly the human denial of God and the substitution of idols for the true God. I cannot think of one teaching of a major non-Christian religion that, given its own formulation rather than one imposed on it, is actually competent to open a person to the grace of God within its own framework.

The stumbling block of the cross cannot be avoided with an objective examination of world religions; more likely it is exacerbated by it, for the cross does not find common ground with Sakyamuni, Amida, Shiva, or Muhammad.

CHAPTER 6

1. Clark H. Pinnock, "Toward an Evangelical Theology of Religions," *Journal of the Evangelical Theological Society (JETS)* 33/3 (June 1990), 359-368; *A Wideness in God's Mercy: The Finality of Jesus Christ in a World of Religions* (Grand Rapids, Mich.: Zondervan, 1992). Similar cases have been made by John Sanders, *No Other Name: An Investigation into the Destiny of the Unevangelized* (Grand Rapids, Mich.: Eerdmans, 1992) and J. N. D. Anderson, *Christianity and World Religions: The Challenge of Pluralism* (Downers Grove, Ill.: InterVarsity Press, 1984). A critique of this view has been issued by Ronald H. Nash, *Is Jesus the Only Savior?* (Grand Rapids, Mich.: Zondervan, 1994).

2. The heart of Pinnock's contention is that God rewards those who sincerely seek and serve him regardless of how much cognitive content they have of him. Pinnock, *Wideness*, 149-180.

3. Nash has already commented, "I believe that the parallels and analogies Pinnock offers do not really establish anything." Nash, *Is Jesus the Only Savior?*, 114.

4. Wilhelm Schmidt, *Der Ursprung der Gottesidee* (zwölf Bönde; Münster: Albrecht, 1926-1955). Also, the shorter one-volume work by Schmidt, *The Origin and Growth of Religion: Facts and Theories*, trans. H. J. Rose (London: Methuen, 1931) and Schmidt, *Primitive Revelation*, trans. Joseph J. Baierl (St. Louis: Herder, 1939). Further, Don Richardson, *Peace Child* (Glendale, Calif.: G/L Publications, 1974) and *Eternity in Their Hearts* (Glendale, Calif.: G/L Publications, 1981).

5. Pinnock, *Wideness*, 100.

6. Ibid.

7. Ibid., 69-74.

8. Ibid.

9. Ibid.

10. Ibid.

11. Ibid.

12. A twentieth-century Buddhist teacher writes (using the Pali words for *nirvana* and *dharma*), "*Nibbana* of the Buddhists is neither a mere nothingness nor a state of annihilation, but exactly what it is no words can adequately express. It is a *dhamma* which is uncreated and unformed, hence it is boundless, to be sought after, happy, because it is free from all suffering, free from birth, death and so on. *Nibbana* is not situated in any place, nor is it a sort of heaven where a transcendental ego resides, it is *a state which is dependent upon ourselves.*" Ashin Thittila, *Essential Themes of Buddhist Lectures*, 2nd ed. (Bangkok, Thailand: James Patrick Stewart Ross, 2532 Buddhist Calendar), 166 (emphasis mine). As a Burmese Therevada monk, Thittila represents the original teachings of Sakyamuni more closely than the later Mahayana schools do.

13. Ibid.

14. Pinnock, "Toward an Evangelical Theology of Religions," 366.

15. Some Mahayana schools—e.g., Nichiren Shoshu—do claim Sakyamuni for their teachings. Nichiren, for example, relied on the Lotus Sutra which, though not from Sakyamuni himself, claims to have been written by him.

16. Buddhist cosmology contains many heavens. The traditional abode of Buddhas is Tushido heaven, where Sakyamuni himself was supposed to have ascended during his lifetime in order to preach the *dharma* to his mother, Mahamaya. Sakyamuni descended after this and departed for *nirvana* permanently a while later.

17. Pinnock, *Wideness*, 101.

18. Ibid.

19. Ibid., 100.

20. Rudolf Otto, *India's Religion of Grace and Christianity Compared and Contrasted* (New York: Macmillan, 1930).

21. Pinnock, *Wideness*, 88.

22. There are forms of Hinduism called *Shaktism* or *Tantrism* that do indeed promote sexual actions as a part of their ritual. In these forms spiritual power is supposed to be found through emulation of Shiva and the goddess (his *shakti*), usually represented as Kali or Durga in these contexts.

23. Pinnock, *Wideness*, 100.

24. Qur'an 5:116-120.

25. Qur'an 4:157.

26. Pinnock, *Wideness*, 110.

27. Ibid.

28. Ibid.

29. Ibid., 112.

30. Ibid., 158; "Toward an Evangelical Theology of Religions," 365.

SEVEN

FORUM DISCUSSION ON INCLUSIVISM

PAUL R. HOUSE, TIMOTHY GEORGE, CARL F. H. HENRY, D. A. CARSON, SCOTT HAFEMANN, C. BEN MITCHELL

House (moderator): Historically, why have Christian missionaries believed salvation does not come through other religions?

Timothy George: In 1792 William Carey, an English shoemaker turned Baptist pastor, published a little treatise entitled *An Inquiry Into the Obligations of Christians to Use Means for the Conversion of the Heathens.* Using the best statistics available to him at the time, Carey surveyed the religious state of the world and concluded that "a very considerable part of mankind is still involved in all the darkness of heathenism." Against certain hyper-Calvinistic Christians, he argued that the Great Commission was still in effect and that the missionary mandate of Jesus required believers "to use every lawful method to spread the knowledge of His Name" to all peoples everywhere. For forty-one years Carey himself labored in India, proclaiming to Muslims, Hindus, Buddhists, and all others a "free salvation for poor and perishing sinners."

Carey is still honored as "The Father of Modern Missions," but his understanding of the exclusive claims of Christ has been denigrated by many modern theologians. Today we wince at words such as *heathen* and *sinners* when applied to those who do not consciously profess faith in Jesus Christ. Is there really a culture-permeable Gospel without the knowledge of which men and women are irretrievably lost? What about those who have never heard the name of Jesus? Is Jesus indeed "the only way" or merely one of several possible pathways to God? Both religious pluralism and Christian inclusivism seek to answer these questions in ways that soften the offense of the message Carey and generations of missionaries who followed in his wake believed they had been commissioned to proclaim: Personal faith in Jesus Christ is the only way of salvation for all people everywhere, and those who die without this saving knowledge face eternal separation from God.

Religious pluralism holds that the divine transcendent reality has many different "faces" revealed in the various religious traditions among humankind. Thus what is called "salvation" in Christianity is more or less equivalent to *nirvana* in Buddhism, submission to Allah in Islam, or following the way of Torah in Judaism. In this view, the aim of missions and evangelism should not be conversion, but rather (as the famous Hocking Report of 1932 put it) "the emergence of the various religions out of their isolation into a world fellowship in which each will find its appropriate place." However, far from engendering greater respect for the various world religions, the pluralist perspective is marked by profound disrespect because it relativizes and disregards the distinctive claims made by the adherents of these religious traditions. For example, Islam regards the Qur'an not merely as one religious writing among many, but as the definitive revelation of Allah. Likewise, Buddhism does not desire eternal bliss in the Kingdom of God, but rather the annihilation of the self and the transcendence of existence altogether. Had the early Christians been guided by the pluralist paradigm, they could certainly have escaped persecution at the hands of the Romans, who were happy for "followers of the Way" to worship Jesus alongside the imperial deity, as one Lord among many. This the Christians could not do. Their faith was rooted in the Old Testament declaration, "Hear, O Israel, the Lord our God is one," and the New Testament confession, "Jesus Christ is Lord."

Christian inclusivists, whether of the Roman Catholic or revisionist evangelical variety, agree with biblical particularists that Jesus Christ is the one mediator between God and humanity. However, out of concern for the "fairness" of God and the "wider hope" of universal salvation, they teach that many of the unevangelized may be saved through God's general revelation. According to some (though not all) proponents of this view, the major world religions contain sufficient truth to bring their adherents to a saving knowledge of God, apart from the special revelation of Jesus Christ and the Scriptures.

From the standpoint of biblical theology, however, this theory trivializes the tragic consequences of the Fall and thus exalts too highly the possibilities of common grace. The specific message of Jesus Christ, his cross and resurrection, is not an extra "add-on" to what is already present to the human psyche through creation and culture. Rather, it is an absolutely decisive factor in bringing lost sinners into right relationship with God. See not only John 14:6 and Acts 4:12, but also John 3:18 and 1 John 5:12.

This does not mean, of course, that there is no value or truth in non-Christian religions, but rather that such systems are unable to lead anyone to salvation—because of their own falsity as well as human fallenness. Thus Carey said of those who asked him about the Hindu *Shastras* and other holy books of India, "I told them that their books were like a loaf of bread, in which was a considerable quantity of good flour, but also a little very malignant poison, which made the whole so poisonous that whoever should eat of it would die." According to Paul in Romans 1—3, general revelation does serve a crucial purpose: it renders us inexcusable before God and thus accountable for the light we have received both through creation and in our conscience.

Should we then dogmatically declare that no one could be saved apart from the preaching of the Gospel through human missionaries and evangelists? Biblical particularists who believe in the sovereignty of God will be cautious in making such a blanket claim. God is God and can work by extraordinary as well as ordinary means to accomplish his purpose. Thus the Second London Confession of 1689 speaks of the salvation of babies who die in infancy, as well as that of "other elect persons, who are incapable of being outwardly called by the ministry of the Word." The risen Christ himself appeared to Saul of Tarsus, and the apostle raises the possibility of angelic proclamation. But he also says that Satan himself can sometimes appear as an angel of light and warns that the message proclaimed by angels may be another gospel (2 Cor. 11:14; Gal. 1:8). If such special communications of the Gospel are extended in the gracious providence of God, and there is nothing in Scripture to indicate that this is so, then we can be sure that their content will be identical with that of the apostolic witness—that is, salvation by grace alone, received by faith alone, on the basis of Christ's finished work on the cross alone. In the meantime, what John Calvin said about predestination should also guide us in our discussion of *salux extra muros ecclesiae*: "We should not investigate what the Lord has left hidden in secret, nor neglect what he has brought out into the open, so that we may not be convicted of excessive curiosity on the one hand, or of excessive ingratitude on the other" (*Institutes*, 3.21.4).

House: Many inclusivists argue that Christ's death mediates salvation even through other religions. Is this viewpoint biblically and theologically valid?

Carl F. H. Henry: Notions of universal salvation have been promoted by critics of the doctrine of eternal punishment of the wicked. Many deplore the doctrine of hell as unchristian, and especially as incompatible with God's love. Yet Jesus is quoted by the Gospels as saying more about hell than about heaven.

For more than a century champions of salvific inclusivism have shared in this repudiation on one ground or another. In 1878 the English churchman Frederic W. Farrar published five sermons titled *Eternal Hope*, which affirmed that while some unbelievers who resist Christ even in the life to come may fall under endless divine judgment, full salvation awaits the great majority.

Modernists and mediating evangelicals have championed the doctrine of universal salvation. So severe is the judgment that Jesus passes on the unrepentant wicked that one can understand Farrar's enduring hope for the salvation of all. But scriptural passages that speak of universal reconciliation include in their biblical context an exhortation for repentance and regeneration.

It is all too easy, as some profess to do, to find traces of the divine in all world history and to postulate everywhere a latent or unconscious Christianity. A generation ago the Hindu theologian Raymond Pannikar wrote of *The Unknown Christ of Hinduism* (1965) and contended that in all religions devout believers confess what is implicitly a christological faith. The religion of the Bible is then considered a foundation shared by all religions.

Somewhat the same misunderstanding underlies the view expressed by the Catholic theologian Karl Rahner, who regards the ethico-religious consciousness of all humans as a basis on which the Gospel rests. Yet nowhere does the apostle Paul commend such a view. As *Today's English Version* puts it, "Salvation is to be found through him [Jesus] alone; for there is no one else in all the world, whose name God has given to men, by whom we can be saved" (Acts 4:12). An exclusivity is here affirmed: Christ is *the* truth, not simply one among many. Precluded is the notion that God reveals himself in all religions, among which Christianity is chronologically somewhat a tardy phenomenon.

This need not imply that the Christian missionary outreach is obliged to condemn the nonbiblical religions as a preliminary phase of its public task and to displace and replace them. Such a program would only undermine the existing social structures, worldviews, and cultural customs through which the existing religions seek to fend off chaos, without providing an alternative. This is not to welcome the various alternatives to revealed religion as acceptable equivalents. It is rather to remind us that the evangelical task is to exalt Christ and to proclaim the good news of biblical revelation and redemption, and not simply to discredit existing options.

The Christian revelation is not to be assimilated or subordinated to religion-in-general or to the rival nonbiblical faiths. The Great Commission provides no call to legitimize the nonbiblical options as if the so-called great religions of the world offer equivalent values. Christ's incarnation is not to be found in the nonbiblical religions, either by way of promise or fulfillment. The competing and conflicting world cultures do not offer access to Christ. Properly understood, they are in fact challenged and confronted by revelation, rather than providing a preliminary disclosure of grace that supposedly permeates all human life, outside as well as inside the Church.

House: Does the Johannine corpus leave room for salvation through means other than specific faith in Christ?

D. A. Carson: In some ways this question is remarkably perverse.
I understand why it must be asked, of course; not for a moment am I suggesting there is perversity in the editor who put the question to me. It has to be asked because today there are increasingly strident voices that argue that although all salvation comes through Jesus Christ, it does not follow that there must be personal, self-conscious faith for salvation to take place. God in his grace, it is argued, may save some people by the merits of his Son without their ever having heard of his Son. So is it not legitimate to ask whether the books of the Johannine corpus leave room for salvation "through means other than specific faith in Christ"?

So yes, the question may be asked. Indeed, in today's climate it *must* be asked. Still, in some ways it is perverse. It is a little like the questions teenagers sometimes ask: "Is there anything in the Bible to stop me from doing X?" "What's wrong with Y?" Once again, the questions must be asked, and answered. But at best, such questions are remarkably immature. They try to get the Bible to answer things that, strictly speaking, are not quite on the Bible's agenda. Worse, they focus on something just slightly skewed. As compared with the teens' questions, surely the Bible's focus is on how to please God, what are our most important priorities, and the like—not what we can get away with. Similarly, there can be little doubt that the Bible's focus is on the plan of salvation God has provided. Men and women can be reconciled to their Maker through the death of the Son he sent into the world. Men and women must repent and put their faith in him. The Gospel must be preached everywhere, and it will draw people together from every tribe and language and people and nation. Strictly speaking, it does not focus an enormous amount of attention on the question as to whether some might be saved even if they do not consciously trust Christ, or if so, how many such a group might comprise. So I am being asked if the Bible, in one of its corpora, allows space for such a view. This is a bit like trying to disprove a negative proposition. Moreover, this particular vision of the "anonymous Christian" (the expression is Karl Rahner's) is on the face of it remarkably insulting to devout believers of other faiths. Most devout Hindus or Muslims whom I know would not like to be informed they are really "anonymous Christians," any more than devout Christians want to be told they are "anonymous Buddhists."

Certainly the Johannine corpus includes many passages that insist on some kind of exclusion. One thinks, for instance, of Thomas's question and Jesus' answer. Thomas protests, "Lord, we don't know where you are going, so how can we know the way?" Jesus answers, "I am the way and the truth and the life. No one comes to the Father except through me" (John 14:5-6). But the critic might well respond that this sort of text does not really address the crucial question. For both sides of this particular debate agree that people gain salvation solely through Jesus Christ: no one comes to the Father except through him. But does this passage, they ask, necessarily exclude those who may be saved by him who have nevertheless not self-consciously reposed their faith in him, because they have never had the privilege of hearing about him?

At one level, of course, the critics are right: *formally*, John 14:6 does not address that question. Nevertheless, the Gospel of John so repeatedly insists that *faith in Jesus* is the condition of salvation that the drift of this book is all in one direction. God gave his Son so that "whoever *believes* in him shall not perish but have eternal life" (3:16). Again, "I tell you the truth, whoever hears my word and believes him who sent me has eternal life and will not be condemned; he has crossed over from death to life" (5:24). And this is the fruit of God's loving the world and sending his Son into the world (3:16-17). In other words, the mission of the Son's being sent into the world is to result in people believing in him and experiencing eternal life. The Son's mission is never cast as providing eternal life for certain people whether they have believed in him or not. If the Gospel of John does not *formally* exclude such a possibility, it is only because it does not set out to address that particular question. Its direction does not encourage speculation along that front.

First John is more focused yet. As in the fourth Gospel, there is an emphasis on the cross as the place where sin was dealt with, and therefore as the ground on which people approach God (2:2; 4:10). Potentially, that ground is sufficient for the whole world (2:2). At the same time, 1 John is patently clear that the whole world is not saved. When this epistle describes who is "in" and who is "out," it deploys a number of criteria, what Robert Law famously called "the tests of life." Law's category has its problems, but these need not concern us. Law detected three "tests": Genuine Christians (1) love other Christians, (2) do what Christ says, and (3) believe the truth, in particular the truth about who Jesus is.

It is this latter category that is most applicable to the topic at hand, precisely because it is worded in several ways. In 1 John 2:23 we are told, "No one who denies the Son has the Father; whoever acknowledges the Son has the Father also." The critic may respond, "Yes, but this text does not specifically deal with the person who does not *deny* the Son, yet who has not specifically *acknowledged* the Son either. That person may not even have heard of the Son." Formally, of course, that is correct, though on the face of it, it flies in the face of the tenor of the book. Moreover, 1 John 4:2-3 is even stronger: "Every spirit that acknowledges that Jesus Christ has come in the flesh is from God, but every spirit that does *not acknowledge* Jesus is not from God." Formally, this excludes those who *do not acknowledge* who Jesus is. Doubtless someone may argue that this is merely a rhetorical way of saying that such people *deny* who Jesus is. But if the critic is allowed to appeal to the larger rhetoric of the document, so may I—and I insist that the rhetoric of the document aligns who is "in" with certain faith-content and certain performance-in-life, even while insisting that the *ground* of acceptance before God is the Atonement. The only reason one wants to appeal to the most pedantic reading is because that is the kind of pedantry the critics deploy to avoid what the text says in, say, John 14:6. If we respond with the same level of pedantry, citing 1 John 4:2-3, the text is against them.

The same sort of polarization between who is "in" and who is "out" is found in the Apocalypse, though there, of course, the imagery is very different. In the massive vision of Revelation 4—5 no one is found who is worthy to approach the throne of God and open the seals of the scroll in his right hand (5:3). In the symbolism of the vision, this means that no one was found worthy to bring to pass all God's purposes for blessing and judgment. John weeps at the news, until an interpreting elder reassures him: The Lion of the tribe of Judah, who is also the Lamb, who emerges from the center of the throne of God, has prevailed, and he alone brings to pass God's purposes. As the book progresses, a massive dualism controls the dramatic apocalyptic symbolism. Either one bears the mark of the beast and is thereby spared the beast's wrath but faces the wrath of the Lamb, or one bears the mark of the Lamb and is thereby spared the Lamb's wrath but faces the wrath of the beast (Rev. 13—14). Implicitly the question becomes, whose wrath do you want to face? Everyone bears one mark or the other.

Attempts by some writers to define "the eternal gospel" in Revelation 14:6 as a generic appeal to the God of creation or the like, without reference to the Lamb and his death, which are so central to the unfolding drama of this book, are desperate expedients deployed to support a lost cause. Specifically, this appeal argues that the content of "the eternal gospel" in 14:6 is simply to "Fear God and give him glory" (14:7). But by this stage in the church's history, *gospel* is a word so bound up with the good news of Jesus that this is an extraordinarily ahistorical reading—the more so in a book in which the Lamb, both slaughtered and reigning, is the One who alone has brought about God's purposes for redemption and judgment. It is better by far to understand 14:7 and its exhortation to "fear God" to be the warning added to (but not identified with) "the eternal gospel" (14:6) that has already been explained.

So, does the Johannine corpus "leave room for salvation through means other than specific faith in Christ"? Certainly not on its most obvious reading.

House: What are the main challenges being raised against the exclusivity of the Gospel as presented by Paul?

Scott Hafemann: Due to our extreme isolation and homogeneity in the past, most Christians in the West have only recently been confronted with the problem of pluralism. These days encountering sincere adherents of other faiths has caused many to rethink whether the exclusive claims of the Gospel can be maintained. But this uncertainty is more a reflection of the sudden shock caused by our own cross-cultural myopia and provincialism than it is a discovery that the Bible actually teaches universalism. Indeed, the pluralism of the modern world is no more dramatic than that faced by Israel or Paul. In Paul's day every Roman was born into a nexus of personal religious affiliations and family household cults. Add to this milieu the Roman imperial cult, the Greco-Roman pantheon of deities descending from Jupiter, and the mystery religions venerating gods from Greece, Anatolia, Egypt, Persia, and Syria, and our situation looks tame in comparison. In Corinth, for example, remains have been found of official temples and shrines to the emperor, the Greek deities Apollo, Athena, Aphrodite, Asclepius, Tyche, Dionysus, Zeus, Neptune, Demeter and Kore, Palaimon, and Sisyphus, as well as to the Egyptian gods Isis and Sarapis. To assert the one God of Israel and Jesus as his Messiah, *the* Son of God, was just as startling and exclusive then as it is now (cf. 1 Cor. 8:5-6; Phil. 2:9-11).

Yet Paul plainly teaches the reality of eternal judgment for those who do not embrace Christ (cf. 2 Thess. 1:8-9; 2:8-12; Gal. 6:7-8; Phil. 3:18-19; 1 Cor. 6:9-10; 16:22; Rom. 1:18—2:12; etc.). He holds no hope for those who remain in idolatry and its lifestyles, for he attributes the practice to demons (cf. Rom. 1:25,·28-32; 1 Cor. 6:9-10, 12-20; 8:4; 10:14-22; 12:2; Gal. 4:8; 1 Thess. 1:9; 4:5; Eph. 2:12; Col. 2:8, 15; etc.). Of course, many today simply reject these declarations as patently false or reinterpret them in view of some abstracted theological principle (such as a universal "election" in *the* elect one, Christ). These challenges are clear-cut, for they are related to questions of the authority of Scripture and theological method.

More challenging are the arguments of those who argue for a universalism within Paul's own thought. Those who take this tack usually point to the parallels in Romans 5:15-18 (cf. 2 Cor. 5:19; 1 Tim. 4:10; Titus 2:11) between the consequences of Adam's sin and Christ's act of righteousness (see esp. 5:18). They argue that while some people are justified by faith already in this life, Paul believes that the rest of humanity will be justified at the final judgment, when Christ's final, cosmic act of deliverance will bring eternal life to all creation (cf. Rom. 8:21-25).

But it is clear from many passages that the terms "all" (Greek *pas*) and "world" (*kosmos*) do not always mean "every single human being." The former is often limited by context (cf. Rom. 8:32; 12:17-18; 14:2; 16:19). The latter often refers to the realm of rebellion under this evil age (1 Cor. 6:2; 7:31, 33; 2 Cor. 4:4 [KJV, RSV, etc.]; Rom. 12:2; Gal. 1:4 [KJV, etc.]; 6:14; Eph. 2:2; 6:12; Col. 2:8; 2 Tim. 4:10), the inhabited earth generally or part of it (Rom. 1:8; 10:18; Col. 1:6; 1 Cor. 4:9 [KJV, RSV, etc.]; 1 Tim. 1:15; 6:7), or the diversity of those within the world as made up of Jews and Gentiles (Rom. 11:12, 15). Context is king; we must determine the specific meaning of these terms in their own respective contexts. Thus, in his recent, excellent commentary, Douglas Moo rightly observes that in Romans 5:15,

> "The many" refers simply to a great number; how inclusive that number might be can be determined only by context. In the protasis of this verse, "the many" clearly includes all people; for Paul has already said that "all died" with reference to the sin of Adam (v. 12). But in the apodosis ("how much more . . .") "the many" must be qualified by Paul's insistence in v. 17 that only those who "receive" the gift benefit from Christ's act. Here it refers to "a great number" of people (but not all of them) or to "all who respond to the gift of grace."[1]

Romans 5:17 reminds us—lest we have forgotten Romans 1-4!—that righteousness and life are for those who *respond* to God's grace in Christ and that they are *only* for those who respond. What appears at first sight to be a universalism on both sides of the Adam/Christ parallel is here, then, importantly qualified.[2]

Hence Paul's point in 5:18 is not so much that the groups affected by Christ and Adam respectively are coextensive, but that Christ affects those who are his just as certainly as Adam does those who are his. When we ask who belongs to, or is "in," Adam and Christ respectively, Paul makes his answer clear: Every person, without exception, is "in Adam" (cf. vv. 12d-14); but only those who "receive" the gift (v. 17; those who "believe," according to Rom. 1:16—5:11) are "in Christ."[3]

Those who try to argue exegetically that Paul taught an ultimate universalism will have difficulty convincing anyone who is not predisposed to that view.

The importance of one's predisposition can be seen most

poignantly in the corollary question of the status of the Jews within salvation history. We may concede that Paul believed that Gentile pagans need Jesus. But do the Jews need to know Jesus as the Christ in order to belong to God's eschatological people? In the shadow of modern Zionism, the Holocaust, the reestablishment of the state of Israel, and the influence of dispensational theology, this question is filled with the intense emotion of an apparent anti-Semitism.

For almost forty years Krister Stendahl, long-time professor of New Testament at Harvard Divinity School and former Bishop of Stockholm, has argued that Paul's doctrine of justification by faith alone served the very narrow purpose of defending the rights of Gentile converts to full participation in God's promises to Israel—i.e., to be "honorary Jews," without having to keep the Law.[4] Conversely, Stendahl argues that Paul's purpose in Romans 9—11 is to counter Gentile pride in the face of Jewish rejection of Jesus and to affirm "a God-willed coexistence between Judaism and Christianity in which the missionary urge to convert Israel is held in check."[5] God has a mysterious plan of salvation for Israel *outside* of Christ, just as he has deemed Gentiles to be saved *in* Christ. In short, there are two covenants—Sinai for the Jews and Jesus for the Gentiles. Stendahl's view has been immensely influential and has since been widened out to embrace other religions as valid for Gentiles as well.[6]

The answer to Stendahl's thesis resides in a detailed exegesis of Romans 11:25-36 itself, which forms the heart of his argument, against the backdrop of a reevaluation of Stendahl's understanding of Paul's "conversion" and the role of justification in Paul's thought. In the space permitted here, let me call attention to two glaring facts and the fundamental issue that grounds them.

First, Paul feels great anguish over his fellow Jews' rejection of Jesus as the Messiah, since they above all are the ones to whom the covenant blessings and promises have been given. He would even give himself over to God's eternal curse if this could save them (Rom. 9:2-3)! Second, Paul's concern that Israel's rejection of Jesus seems to call into question the character and faithfulness of God *himself* (Rom. 9:4-6) only makes sense if Paul regarded those among his "kinsmen by race" (RSV) who are rejecting Jesus to be outside of God's covenant people. It is this feeling of personal anguish and this fundamental theological question that drive Paul's argument in Romans 9—11.

The central issue underlying both issues is whether God's faithfulness to himself and to his promised redemptive, saving activity can be maintained in spite of Israel's rejection of Jesus. This would be no problem at all if Paul thought that there was salvation for the Jews (or for anyone else for that matter) outside of Christ. Nor would Paul be concerned with Israel's future as an ethnic people in 11:1 if her present rejection of Christ did not have salvific implications! Furthermore, faith (in Jesus Christ) is explicitly referred to as the way to salvation for both Jews and Gentiles in 11:20 and 11:23. Paul's God-centered doxology in 11:33-36 is not an attempt to downplay the centrality of Jesus (*contra* Stendahl) but is intended to show that all, both Jews and Gentiles, will one day be worshiping the same Father for the same reason—namely, his sovereign, electing mercy in Christ (cf. 11:35 with 9:16). The parallel between Romans 9:30-33 and 11:5-7 indicates that Paul's doctrine of justification by faith alone through grace is to be applied equally to both Gentiles and Jews.

Of course, Gentiles and Jews alike stand before God only by faith in response to God's mercy and sovereign grace (Rom. 11:17-24). Those who preach to others should do so with humility and fear (Rom. 11:20). Paul's missionary activity is not the expression of a colonial imperialism designed to conquer and exploit others for one's own aggrandizement. It is the heartfelt cry of one convinced that the Gospel was God's one and final word of reconciliation for all, both Jews and Gentiles (Rom. 1:16-17; 2 Cor. 5:14-21).

House: How sound is the inclusivists' claim that God's love necessitates their view?

C. Ben Mitchell: The Johannine assertion that "God is love" is one of the greatest affirmations in the Bible. That the divine nature is suffused with love as an attribute is at once both a comfort and a promise. At the same time, universalism of a Christian variety is prone to "agapetitus" of a peculiarly maudlin, American style. Philosophically, the argument looks something like this: (1) If God's nature is truly love and his relation to his creatures fundamentally one of love, then he desires the eternal salvation of all his creatures. (2) If God is truly sovereign, then he is capable of bringing about his most earnest desire, the salvation of all persons. (3) Temporally speaking, not all persons have responded to Christ in faith. (4) Therefore, either (a) God is not sovereign, (b) God is not love, or (c) in due course and by means currently beyond our grasp, God will indeed bring all persons to salvation.

Of course, inclusivists alter premise (3) to remove its Christo-centrism. Faith in Christ was never a necessary condition of salvation, an inclusivist might say. Sincerity, belief in a divine being, or some other less particularistic condition is usually added. The point is, inclusivism is nothing new. It has been around for centuries. What is new is that it is being proposed by evangelicals who at the same time espouse the inerrancy of the Bible.

Regardless of its type, inclusivism suffers from one or more philo-sophical problems (not to mention a dubious hermeneutic). First, the kind of love that animates the inclusivist god is more akin to senti-mentalism than God's holy affection. If love means God abandons all of his other attributes, then love itself is deified. The love of God does not dictate that he abandon his justice or holiness. In fact, the glory of the Gospel is that God is both just and the justifier of the ungodly. God does not allow unregenerate sinners to do as they will, worship what they wish, live as they please, and still go free. In the divine scheme of things, sin demands punishment. The rebellion of self-wor-ship requires wrath. Yet, the God of wrath is no less God than the God of mercy. He is the same God. Were God never to have offered salva-tion to any sinner, his love would still survive unblemished. The real-ity and richness of God's love is not measured in the number of persons saved, but in the magnificence of the attribute itself. Inclusivists insist that love makes demands on God. He *must* respond to the human predicament *because* of love. Nevertheless, God would not be diminished one bit in his justice or glory were he to consign every person who ever lived to eternal torment. If, however, one begins with the premise that God must love in such a way that no one is condemned, love is defined by the creature rather than the Creator.

Similarly, contrary to some contemporary theodicists, what God does is what we must define as "the good." That is to say, the fact that God has decided to create a place of damnation and chooses to reserve it for those who reject him does not violate his love—unless we have already defined *love* in such a way as to preclude the existence, not to mention the use, of such a place. Our definition of love must fit the facts. And the facts, as Jesus knew them, are that there is a place where the worm does not die and to which those who do not trust Christ savingly will be consigned. By definition, such a reality is consistent with the love of God. To argue otherwise is to load the word *love* with baggage it will not hold.

Finally, this all means that the love of God must be understood not as an isolated term to be defined philosophically. Rather, it must be understood in light of revelation. We do not, therefore, presume a definition of love and then bring Scripture into line with that definition. We define the idea according to revelation. And those who, under the inspiration of the Holy Spirit, penned the Scriptures were well aware of its sometimes counterintuitive turn. For instance, the apostle Paul sets up the following debate:

> Just as it is written, "Jacob I loved, but Esau I hated." What shall we say then? There is no injustice with God, is there? May it never be! For He says to Moses, "I will have mercy on whom I have mercy, and I will have compassion on whom I have compassion." So then it does not depend on the man who wills or the man who runs, but on God who has mercy. For the Scripture says to Pharaoh, "For this very purpose I raised you up, to demonstrate My power in you, and that My name might be proclaimed throughout the whole earth." So then He has mercy on whom He desires, and He hardens whom He desires. You will say to me then, "Why does He still find fault? For who resists His will?" On the contrary, who are you, O man, who answers back to God? The thing molded will not say to the molder, "Why did you make me like this," will it? Or does not the potter have a right over the clay, to make from the same lump one vessel for honorable use, and another for common use? What if God, although willing to demonstrate His wrath and to make His power known, endured with much patience vessels of wrath prepared for destruction? And He did so in order that He might make known the riches of

His glory upon vessels of mercy, which He prepared beforehand for glory, even us, whom He also called, not from among Jews only, but also from among Gentiles.

—Rom. 9:13-24, NASB

Paul's very line of argument presupposes a view of divine love similar to that of inclusivism. He nevertheless affirms God's love in its particularity. So God can show mercy to whom he wills, and not be accused of any injustice or any diminished affection.

The reality of God's distinguishing love, his absolute justice, the exclusivity of Christ, and the doctrine of eternal punishment are all hard pills to swallow. Inclusivists hope to rescue God from accusations of injustice by positing a postmodern deity with a kind of love that borders on romanticism. Instead, let us proclaim, without compromise, the God who loves sinners so much that he sent his only begotten Son, so that whoever believes in him will not perish but will have everlasting life.

CHAPTER 7

1.   Douglas J. Moo, *The Epistle to the Romans* (Grand Rapids, Mich.: Eerdmans, 1996), 336-337.
2.   Ibid., 340.
3.   Ibid., 343.
4.   See his *Paul Among Jews and Gentiles and Other Essays* (Philadelphia: Fortress Press, 1976), esp. 2-9, 130.
5.   Ibid., 4.
6.   See Stendahl, "Christ's Lordship and Religious Pluralism," in *Meanings: The Bible as Document and as Guide* (Philadelphia: Fortress Press, 1984), 233-244.

PART THREE

HOW SHALL
THE LOST HEAR
THE GOSPEL?

INTRODUCTION

PAUL R. HOUSE

Over twenty-five years ago Dean Kelley offered reasons *Why Conservative Churches Are Growing* (Harper & Row, 1972). He argued that congregations that held a high view of Scripture, that were making a concerted effort to reach persons they considered lost, and that expressed high expectations for its members were thriving. In contrast, more liberal churches were not growing because they did not emphasize those ideals. Instead, the liberal churches were stressing society's "felt needs," the desirability of the church's being involved in social action, the necessity of having loose membership standards lest people be "turned off," and a critical approach to the Bible. Ironically, by trying to reach the masses through these means, they failed to convince the very people they sought to influence of the importance of the Church and its mission. More and more people simply considered liberal churches to be weaker, less compelling versions of the churches their parents and grandparents attended. Thus they had no desire to attend such churches, much less go on mission fields to proclaim the ideas they heard there.

More recently, Dean R. Hoge, Benton Johnson, and Donald A. Luidens have confirmed Kelley's research in their *Vanishing Boundaries: The Religion of Mainline Protestant Baby Boomers* (Westminster/John Knox, 1994). They agree that many mainline churches have so relaxed their definition of Christianity and church membership that many congregations consist of baptized unbelievers. The way back to numerical health in a relativistic age, they write, is for churches to recapture moral authority without returning to conservative notions of the Bible, the Church, or the Church's authority. Perhaps in this way the baby boomers who have left or ignored the mainline churches will once again participate in worship of and service for the Lord. Though they do not advocate the proper answer for the mainline denominations, they have analyzed much of the problem accurately.

Many conservative pastors and denominational leaders have cited such studies to prove that conservatism has triumphed over its liberal competitors. They seem to think that simply claiming a high view of Scripture and preaching about evangelism will keep conservative churches from going the way of the liberal denominations. They also seem to believe that having large numbers of members and missionaries proves their vibrant spirituality.

Though biblical authority, committed evangelism, and numerical growth are all desirable components of a healthy church, conservatives had better learn from the mainline experience, not just soothe themselves with the notion that they are immune to what has harmed other groups. Indeed, unless biblical theology and missiology are wed, conservative churches will eventually be rendered ineffective, though for different reasons than the mainline churches. Without a biblical approach to conversion and church membership, mission work at home and abroad will falter. On the other hand, faithful theology combined with faithful service will lead to renewal.

CONVERSION AND CONSERVATIVE CHURCHES

The problem with conservative churches is not that they lack members. The problem is that many of those members are not converted. Millions of members of evangelical churches are absent from worship services each Sunday and are equally absent from Christian living during the rest of the week. Biblical illiteracy and unethical conduct by Christians seem to be on the rise. Many people who attend are indifferent to the truths of Christianity, and others are divisive, even mean-spirited.

Clearly, many persons have not embraced the fact that Christians must be committed to Christ and his teachings. They may have mentally assented to certain gospel facts. They may have hoped that joining a church would help solve life's problems. They may have been told that repeating a prayer amounted to a saving experience. They may have walked forward at an evangelistic meeting. But by any biblical measurement they were never converted. There was no trans-forming conviction of sin, no repentance, no commitment to Christ's lordship, no love for those who love Christ. Such theology is not worth exporting to mission fields.

Gratefully, many people wake up to the fact that they were never saved. For instance, statistics compiled by the North American Mission Board of the Southern Baptist Convention reveal that as many as half of all the adults baptized in Southern Baptist churches are rebaptisms of persons already baptized by Southern Baptist pastors. Another 40 percent of adults baptized are Christians from other denominations who had never been immersed. Only 10 percent of all adults baptized by Southern Baptists churches are making first-time professions of faith. Though it is wonderful that many persons are converted after a false start, these statistics cause one to wonder what Southern Baptist churches are teaching about salvation. One also has to wonder if things are all that different in many other denominations.

Conservative churches must beware of adapting their theology to gain numbers. They ought to recall that as liberals modified their views on conversion and commitment they took in large numbers of new members for a time. In the heyday of modernism crowds of peo-ple rejoiced in the relaxing of doctrine and the way in which those churches adapted to current cultural opinions. In time, however, peo-ple of substance came to question the value of a church without bib-lical authority and biblical definitions of discipleship. They either stayed away from church altogether or sought churches with solid convictions. The day may come when persons seeking New Testament Christianity will avoid conservative churches that baptize the lost in the name of evangelism and church growth.

COSTLY GRACE AND COMING REVIVAL

Sixty years ago, in *The Cost of Discipleship*, Dietrich Bonhoeffer warned against "cheap grace," which he defined as "grace we bestow on our-selves." He argued that "grace" disconnected from real conversion that leads to costly discipleship is not grace at all. It is simply nonbeliev-ers letting themselves off the hook. His context was quite different from ours, but his diagnosis is applicable to today's conservative churches and their missions and evangelism efforts.

Conservative churches will stop growing if they do not awaken. Mouthing traditional platitudes will not suffice. A return to the theology of the Bible we rightly call infallible and inerrant is needed. Biblical definitions of evangelism, conversion, baptism, and discipleship must be recovered. Worship of numbers must cease. Courage to be God's remnant must emerge.

If spiritual awakening does not occur, the Lord will call out a remnant, just as he always does. The tragedy will be that churches that knew better did not act better. They simply became as attached to conservative cultural mores as liberal churches were to liberal cultural traditions. They worshiped numbers, influence, power, and ease instead of the living God. Thus they lost the opportunity to participate in the evangelization of the lost.

If awakening does come, and there are many dedicated believers praying and working to that end, it will probably come slowly, painfully, and gloriously. The gates of hell will not prevail against the Church, a promise we have received from the highest possible authority. The question is whether we will be a constructive part of that revival or whether our children and grandchildren will be writing books about how conservative churches stopped growing, their mission forces declined, and their spiritual strength evaporated.

EIGHT

THE GOSPEL TRUTH

A Sermon on Ephesians 2:1-10

TIMOTHY A. MCCOY

When you are confronted with a decision, how important is it to know the truth? As you are weighing competing options, how vital is it to have the facts? As you stand at a crossroads attempting to chart a successful course, how critical is it to have accurate information?

I suppose if the decision is of little consequence, if all the options have similar outcomes, and if all paths lead to the same destination, then it may not be so important to know the truth.

But when the consequences are weighty, when the outcomes are not equal but are eternal, and when the destinations are as different as heaven and hell, then every one of us will surely want to know the truth . . . the gospel truth!

Fortunately, when it comes to the core issue of our lives—how we may be rightly related to the living God—the Bible gives us completely reliable and accurate information, it clearly and explicitly lays out the facts we need to know, and it candidly communicates the truth that sets us free.

One of the places in the Bible where the truth of the Christian Gospel is set forth in brief but beautiful fashion is in the first ten verses of the second chapter of the apostle Paul's letter to the church at Ephesus. In what one writer has called "a veritable mine of spiritual truth,"[1] the first three verses tell us the truth about ourselves, verses

4 through 7 tell us the truth about God, and the final three verses tell us the truth about salvation.

THE TRUTH ABOUT OURSELVES

First, the Bible teaches us the truth about ourselves—who we are apart from Christ. And to tell you the truth, the news is not good. The facts are startling and sobering.

Apart from Jesus Christ, the Bible says, we are dead—"dead in your trespasses and sins" (v. 1). Our spiritual condition is that of a corpse. Spiritually speaking, we are lifeless, helpless, and hopeless. We are alienated from God, cut off from his presence, and disconnected from his power. Because we are genuinely dead spiritually, we are both unable and unwilling to do anything about our calamitous condition.

I must confess that I have not always conveyed this truth accurately. In fact, I once narrated an illustration that described our condition apart from Christ as follows: "A man was at sea, his ship sank, and he was left bobbing on the waves far from shore with his energy dissipating rapidly. Indeed, he went under once, he went under twice, and he was just about to go under for the third time when miraculously a rescue ship appeared. A life preserver was thrown to him, and just before he went under for the last time he clutched the life preserver and was saved."

As I applied the illustration I would say, "The life preserver was grace—that's God's part. But the drowning man had to grasp it by faith—that's man's part. Together, God's grace and man's faith combine to produce salvation."

It sounds like a great illustration, does it not? Perhaps you have heard it or even used it! The only problem is that it is wrong. It does not accurately convey what the Bible says about our condition apart from Christ.

Notice that the Bible does not say that our condition is life-threatening and that we will soon die. Rather, the Bible says that before we were made alive in Christ, we were actually, really, and genuinely "dead in . . . transgressions and sins" (v. 1).

In terms of the illustration, we have not only gone under once, then twice, but we have gone down for the third and final time. Now we are lying at the bottom of the sea of sin . . . completely lifeless, utterly helpless, and absolutely unable to do anything to effect our own rescue. We are spiritually dead!

Unfortunately, the truth about us does not get any better. The Bible says that this spiritual death is a universal condition. All of us are dead in sin. Notice the beginning of verse 3, where Paul says, "All of us also lived among them at one time." Here he specifically includes himself and his people, the Jews, with the recipients of his letter, the Gentiles (cf. v. 11) as being among those who were spiritually dead.

In the book of Romans Paul states the universality of our sinful condition even more directly by asserting that "Jews and Gentiles alike are all under sin" (3:9). Further, he declares that "'there is no one righteous, not even one; there is no one who understands, no one who seeks God. All have turned away, they have together become worthless; there is no one who does good, not even one'" (3:10-12).

There are no exceptions and no exemptions. Apart from Christ, every person on the planet is dead in sin. As Curtis Vaughn has written: "It is as though the whole world were one vast graveyard and every gravestone had the same inscription: 'Dead through sin.'"[2]

The Bible then concludes this brief but devastating description of who we are apart from Christ by stating flatly: "we were by nature objects of wrath" (v. 3). The truth is that our sinfulness is part of our very nature. We do not become sinners because we sin. Rather, it is because we are "by nature" sinners that we sin.

Again the book of Romans is perhaps the best commentary. "Therefore," Paul writes, "just as sin entered the world through one man, and death through sin . . . in this way death came to all men" (5:12). And again he says, "the result of one trespass was condemnation for all men" (5:18). And again, "through the disobedience of the one man the many were made sinners" (5:19).

Michael Horton has it right in his excellent book entitled *Putting Amazing Back into Grace* when he states: "Like the victims of a contaminated blood transfusion, we all have inherited Adam's guilt and corruption. . . . Adam included us all in his decision, and that decision was fatal for the entire race."[3]

This truth may be difficult to accept, but it is not at all difficult to observe. Two simple questions will make the matter obvious. Question 1: How many of you are parents? Question 2: How many of you parents had to teach your children to disobey? Of course, you did not. None of us did. They, and we, were inclined to it naturally.

As the founders of The Southern Baptist Theological Seminary affirmed in *The Abstract of Principles* that have guided that institution since its inception, all of Adam's "posterity inherit a nature corrupt and wholly opposed to God and His law, are under condemnation, and as soon as they are capable of moral action, become actual transgressors."[4]

The final truth about us is that because we are sinners—both by nature and by choice—we are "objects of wrath." Literally, the text says that we are "children of wrath." Every child of Adam's race comes to this world as an enemy of God, is under his condemnation, and is a recipient of his wrath—a divine hostility that is the necessary response of a righteous God to all that is evil.

The truth is that apart from Christ ours is a desperate plight. Sin, death, and wrath are the common experiences of us all. We are spiritually destitute and are justly condemned by a holy God.

While our condition apart from Christ should certainly not be overemphasized, that is hardly the temptation of our day. Rather, it is especially imperative today that we enunciate this truth distinctly. For it is only against the backdrop of this bleak, dark truth about us that we can properly see the brilliance and breathtaking beauty of the truth about God.

THE TRUTH ABOUT GOD

One of the best ways for us to succinctly but accurately unfold the truth about God that is packed into this text is to pose a series of questions. The answers will then emerge one after the other as we walk through verses 4 through 7 together.

The first question is: *Who is God?* The answer, found in verse 4, is that he is a God who has "great love for us" and is "rich in mercy."

The juxtaposition of these twin affirmations of God's love and God's mercy with God's wrath in verse 3 is certainly no happenstance.

In the space of two verses the Bible has again welded together in our thinking two great dimensions of God's character that are often made to be enemies when in reality they are not. The God who is holy is also loving. The God who is righteous is also merciful. The God who reveals his wrath "from heaven against all the godlessness and wickedness of men" (Rom. 1:18) also "wants all men to be saved and to come to a knowledge of the truth" (1 Tim. 2:4). Or as Paul puts it so magnificently in Romans chapter 3, God is "just and the one who justifies the man who has faith in Jesus" (v. 26).

The second question we should ask is: *What does God do?* The threefold answer is that he "made us alive with Christ" (v. 5), "raised us up with Christ" (v. 6), and "seated us with him in the heavenly realms" (v. 6). Notice at the end of verse 6 that all of this occurs "in Christ Jesus."

It is vital to observe that these three verbs—"made alive," "raised," and "seated"—are all in the aorist tense and together "express what God has already done for His children in Christ."[5]

Again as Curtis Vaughn has written: "We accept the truth that the quickening and the resurrection are spiritual realities from the very moment of conversion. But it staggers the imagination to be told that the enthronement with Christ is already an accomplished fact. Paul is presenting the matter from God's point of view, and in the mind of God our position in Christ is fixed and certain."[6]

This awesome truth is not unlike what Paul wrote to the Roman believers when he reminded them that "those God foreknew he also predestined. . . . And those he predestined, he also called; those he called, he also justified; those he justified, he also glorified" (Rom. 8:29-30). What we know in our spiritual experience as believers now (calling and justification) is bound inextricably to God's choice in eternity past (predestination) and his promise of glory with Christ in eternity future (glorification). Absolutely awesome!

Furthermore, the pattern for what we experience *with* Christ has already been established by what happened *to* Christ. Look carefully at Ephesians 1:19-20, where we learn that God has already demonstrated "incomparably great power" in Christ when "he raised him from the dead and seated him at his right hand in the heavenly realms."

Notice in verse 18 of chapter 1 that God's intention is that the eyes of our heart may be enlightened in order that we may know that same "incomparably great power" as we are made alive in Christ, raised with him, and enthroned with him!

The third question we should ask of our text is: *When did God do this?* The answer, clearly stated in verse 5, is "when we were dead in transgressions." While we were utterly helpless, dead at the bottom of the sea of sin, God, only because of his great love and mercy, did for us what we could never have done for ourselves. He made us alive in the Lord Jesus.

C. H. Spurgeon summarized the entire event well when he wrote:

> Understand, that the doctrine of the Holy Scriptures is, that man by nature, since the fall, is dead; he is a corrupt and ruined thing; in a spiritual sense, utterly and entirely dead. And if any of us shall come to spiritual life, it must be by the quickening of God's Spirit, vouchsafed to us sovereignly through the good will of God the Father, not for any merits of our own, but entirely of his own abounding and infinite grace.[7]

The fourth and final question is: *Why? Why does God do all this?* The remarkable answer found in verse 7 says that God does all this "in order that in the coming ages he might show the incomparable riches of his grace, expressed in his kindness to us in Christ Jesus." Put another way, God's intention is that all whom he makes alive in Christ, all whom he saves by grace, will be exhibits, displays, or trophies of his grace.

Have you ever been in a friend's home and been invited into his trophy room? Perhaps he is a golfer, apparently a pretty good one at that, and he is eager to show you the trophy for the club championship, the trophy for the city championship, the award for the low handicap at the club, and an assortment of other trophies, medals, and honors he has won.

So what is really going on here? What does he want you to do?

How does he want you to respond? Does he want you to examine the trophies and then exclaim, "Wow, what exquisite trophies these are! Look at the size of that marble base. Did you notice the detailed craftsmanship on that eagle? Look at the beauty of the engraving. These really are magnificent trophies."

Oh, no. That's not the purpose. The intent is for you to adequately examine the trophies and then turn to your friend and say, "Wow, what an extraordinarily gifted golfer you must be!"

In much the same way, God's desire for those who see us—trophies of his grace—is not so they will say to us, "Wow, what an extraordinary person you are." Oh, no. God's intent is that they see our lives, then turn to *him* and say, "Wow, what an awesome God you are!"

In other words, the ultimate end of our salvation is not for us, but for God. Our being made alive, raised, and seated with Christ is ultimately intended to bring honor and glory to God! As Paul says three different times in Ephesians chapter 1, all that God does for us in Christ is "to the praise of his glorious grace"(v. 6; cf. vv. 12, 14). Do not miss the point: Even in our salvation the final focus is not on us but on God.

This truth is especially critical today to help ensure that we keep our world-and-life-view as believers thoroughly and consistently God-centered. For we not only live in a *world* dead to God and centered on self, but we also are part of a generation of *believers* who seem especially tempted to embrace a subtle yet insidious kind of "evangelical humanism." This perspective professes to follow Christ and yet allows, and sometimes even encourages, the focus and attention of Christian living to be on self. To quote Michael Horton again: "Never before, not even in the medieval church, have Christians been so obsessed with themselves. Never before have people entertained such grandiose notions about humans and such puny views of God."[8]

We must make sure that an exalted self is not at the center of our thinking or living. Instead, we should remember who is at the center of the circle in Revelation chapter 5 and begin even now to lift our voices with the choir of the ages whose refrain will forever and always be, "To him who sits on the throne and to the Lamb be praise and honor and glory and power, for ever and ever!"

Now, you may have noticed that as we have unfolded the truth about God in these four verses there is one key phrase that we have neglected. The phrase is at the end of verse 5 where Paul seems to almost shout, "it is by grace you have been saved." Our omission has not been inadvertent, but intentional. For even though Paul cannot resist interjecting this truth in verse 5, he does not explain it fully until the last three verses of our text. Having told us the truth about us and the truth about God, Paul is now ready to tell us the truth about salvation.

THE TRUTH ABOUT SALVATION

Nowhere in all of the Bible is the essence and character of our salvation stated more clearly than in verses 8 through 10 of our text. It is, as F. F. Bruce has observed, "one of the great evangelical summaries of the New Testament."[9]

The preview we were given in verse 5 is now repeated, expanded, and expounded: "For it is by grace you have been saved, through faith—and this not from yourselves, it is the gift of God—not by works, so that no one can boast. For we are God's workmanship, created in Christ Jesus to do good works, which God prepared in advance for us to do" (vv. 8-10).

Notice first that the Bible says *salvation is by grace.* From start to finish, it is God's work entirely. We have done nothing to earn it, nothing to merit it, nothing to deserve it. It is wholly and completely "the gift of God."

Our salvation was initiated by God, it was accomplished by God, and it will be completed by God. The Father chose us "before the creation of the world" (1:4), redeemed us through the blood of Jesus Christ (cf. 1:7; 2:13), called us by the power of the Holy Spirit, and "will keep [us] strong to the end, so that [we] will be blameless on the day of our Lord Jesus Christ" (1 Cor. 1:8). In every sense, we are "God's workmanship." Salvation is all of grace!

Next the Bible says that *salvation is through faith.* God's great gift must be received, and the way we receive it is through faith—a trusting, believing, self-surrendering response that is itself part of "the gift of God."

"But wait," someone says, "I thought grace was God's part, and faith was our part." But what does the Bible say? To what does the phrase "and this not from yourselves, it is the gift of God" refer? Does it refer specifically to faith or more generally to salvation? Grammatical considerations ("this" is neuter in Greek, while "faith" is feminine) suggest the latter. Yet, as F. F. Bruce, comments, "It is true, in either case, that we could never exercise saving faith did not the Holy Spirit 'persuade and enable us to embrace Jesus Christ, freely offered to us in the gospel.'"[10]

So the Bible says that the entire process of our salvation, which includes both grace and faith, does not originate with us ("not from yourselves") but is completely "the gift of God."

As John Stott has insightfully observed, "We must never think of salvation as a kind of transaction between God and us in which he contributes grace and we contribute faith. For we were dead and had to be quickened before we could believe. No, Christ's apostles clearly teach elsewhere that saving faith too is God's gracious gift."[11]

To be sure, without faith it is impossible to please God (Heb. 11:6). Only those who believe in the Son have eternal life (cf. John 3:16-18, 36), and only through faith are we justified (Rom. 5:1).

But we must never conceive of saving faith as something we initiate, do, or accomplish so that it becomes our work. For the Bible is absolutely clear that our salvation is "not by works, so that no one can boast." As one of the great Reformers has written, faith simply "brings a man empty to God, that he may be filled with the blessings of Christ."[12]

So what is saving faith? How shall we define it? Hear again the *Abstract of Principles.* "Wrought in the heart by the Holy Spirit," saving faith is "the belief, on God's authority, of whatsoever is revealed in His Word concerning Christ; accepting and resting upon Him alone for justification and eternal life."[13]

Analyzed further, we see that saving faith includes three elements. The first is knowledge, acquaintance with the Gospel as presented in the Bible. The second is agreement, assent that the Gospel is true. The third is trust, "personal dependence on the grace of Father, Son, and Spirit for salvation, with thankful cessation of all attempts to save oneself by establishing one's own righteousness."[14] Salvation is through faith alone!

Next we should note that the Bible says that *salvation is in Christ.* We are, verse 10 says, "created in Christ Jesus." This is, in fact, the third time in five verses that Paul has underscored the fact that everything God does for us in salvation is "in Christ" (cf. vv. 6-7).

When we were dead in sin, we were "in Adam." But the life God gives us, indeed "every spiritual blessing" we receive from him, is "in Christ" (cf. 1:3). Therefore, the critical distinction for us all is whether we are "in Adam" or "in Christ."

Finally, the Bible says that *salvation is unto good works.* Though our salvation is not gained "by works" (v. 9), the evidence of its authenticity is that we "do good works, which God prepared in advance for us to do" (v. 10). As J. I. Packer has pungently put it, "The truth is that, though we are justified by faith alone, the faith that justifies is never alone."[15] It always produces a transformed life, moral fruit, "good works," the absence of which indicates that it is not really saving faith. Or, as James says, "faith by itself, if it is not accompanied by action, is dead" (2:17).

So what is the truth about salvation? The truth is that salvation is by grace, through faith, in Christ, and unto good works!

With power and persuasion, the ten verses of Scripture that we have examined have told us the essence of the gospel truth—the truth about ourselves, the truth about God, and the truth about salvation. In this truth there is awesome liberating power. In fact, the Bible says in Ephesians 1:13 that it is through hearing and believing "the word of truth" that we are "included in Christ."

Have you believed and received the truth? If not, acknowledge your helpless condition. Receive God's awesome gift of grace. Trust the Lord Jesus today. Cast yourself upon Christ and Christ alone. For Jesus' promise made long ago remains true today. "Whoever comes to me," he declared, "I will never drive away" (John 6:37).

If you have already been transformed by the gospel truth, then rejoice again that God has enabled you to know the truth, and that the truth has made you free (cf. John 8:32). Celebrate anew the excellency of his great grace, and live every moment "to the praise of his glory"!

CHAPTER 8

1. Curtis Vaughn, *Ephesians: A Study Guide Commentary* (Grand Rapids, Mich.: Zondervan, 1977), 54.

2. Ibid., 44.

3. Michael Scott Horton, *Putting Amazing Back into Grace: Who Does What in Salvation* (Grand Rapids, Mich.: Baker, 1991), 58.

4. *Abstract of Principles*, The Southern Baptist Theological Seminary, Article IV.

5. F. F. Bruce, *The Epistle to the Ephesians* (Old Tappan, N.J.: Fleming H. Revell, 1961), 50.

6. Vaughn, *Ephesians: A Study Guide Commentary*, 49-50.

7. Charles Haddon Spurgeon, "Spiritual Resurrection," *The New Park Street Pulpit*, Vol. III (1857; rpt. Pasadena, Tex.: Pilgrim Publications, 1975), 161-168.

8. Horton, *Putting Amazing Back into Grace*, 17.

9. Bruce, *The Epistle to the Ephesians*, 51.

10. Ibid.

11. Horton, *Putting Amazing Back into Grace*, 158.

12. Vaughn, *Ephesians: A Study Guide Commentary*, 52.

13. *Abstract of Principles*, Article X.

14. J. I. Packer, *Concise Theology: A Guide to Historic Christian Beliefs* (Wheaton, Ill.: Tyndale House, 1993), 159-160.

15. Ibid., 160.

NINE

NO OTHER GOSPEL

GEORGE MARTIN

Tell me the old, old story
Of unseen things above,
Of Jesus and His glory,
Of Jesus and His love.

So go the opening lines of the great old hymn so familiar to many.
Then, filling out the story and its meaning, lyricist Katherine Hankey
continues:

Tell me the story slowly,
That I may take it in—
That wonderful redemption,
God's remedy for sin.
Tell me the story often,
For I forget so soon;
The early dew of morning
Has passed away at noon.

The gospel message is about redemption, the remedy for sin.
These truths are easily forgotten, and thus we need constantly to be
reminded—"Tell me the story often, for I forget so soon." The question arises, though, as to whether the core of that old, old story that
is loved so passionately—that Jesus came to die as God's remedy for
sin—is a story with universal application.

REACHING PEOPLE FOR JESUS

The following scenarios indicate that not all professing Christians agree on the answer to the question just posed. Envision a discussion about possible strategies for reaching animists[1] with the Gospel.[2] The discussion ranges far afield, touching on the best use of financial and human resources, the linguistic and cultural barriers involved in evangelizing animists, and many other pertinent matters.

At one point in the discussion the following statements are made. "We should not present Jesus Christ to the animists as the savior of sinners. After all, their concept of sin is not the same as ours. Nor do they, in the same sense as we, understand themselves to need a savior. The great concern of the animists is to be delivered from the malevolent spirits, which they believe inhabit the world around them. Thus we need to present Jesus to them not as the savior of sinners but as the Great Spirit who can protect them and enrich their lives."

Imagine a different dialogue, at another place and time, among a number of people who are keenly interested in missions. Thinking about the difficulty of communicating the Gospel across cultures, the statement is made, "Western missionaries press on with the concept of 'justification' even among people for whom that is not a concern. Often they are more concerned about the quality of life and other issues. We need to remember that Jesus did not only speak about justification but also about abundant life. We must focus on the teaching about abundant life in the places where that is the major concern."

The question then arises, are the above missiological/evangelistic approaches sufficient? In other words, is it enough simply to "get people to Jesus," no matter which Jesus that might be—i.e., the Jesus who can keep me safe from physical harm, the Jesus who can make me feel fulfilled in life, etc.? Stated differently: Is it sufficient for the missionary to present Jesus as the one who can meet the individual's felt need at the time (whatever that felt need might be), or is the gospel message definite in nature—that is, does it address a particular need of which the hearer must be made aware? Must the hearer acknowledge certain, particular truths? Must he respond in a specific manner?

REACHING PEOPLE IN EVERY CULTURE

If missionaries of the cross are not careful, they can ignore or forget the particularistic content of the Gospel. The gospel message is then transformed and translated to meet whatever is the perceived need of the moment. This changing of the Gospel might take the form of cultural redefinition. For example, one often encounters the concept of "regional theologies," that is, the suggestion that there exists an "African theology" for Africans, an "Asian theology" for Asians, a "western theology" that addresses the needs of white Europeans and North Americans, and so forth. Thus David Bosch writes:

> Western theology is today suspect in many parts of the world. It is often regarded as irrelevant, speculative, and the product of ivory tower institutions. In many parts of the world it is being replaced by Third-World theologies: liberation theology, black theology, contextual theology, minjung theology, African theology, Asian theology, and the like.[3]

The idea here is that peoples in other parts of the world have developed and possess theologies that are different from the theology of the western churches.

Of course, any particular theology encompasses a great many concepts and applications—theology proper (the study of God), anthropology, ethics, etc. Consideration of all that is touched by the Christian religion must recognize that legitimate culture-specific questions arise: What worship style should be followed by the congregation? What constitutes discreet clothing? What are acceptable family structures? How exactly should the organized churches relate to the government of the country in which they exist? Clearly, the answers to these questions and many others will vary from culture to culture.

In other words, the Christian religion does not demand that every believer in every culture conform to the same mold. The earliest church council came to this conclusion. Acts 15 recounts that certain Jewish men were teaching the Gentiles that in order to be truly Christian they must become Jewish in all matters. In the letter sent

to the Gentiles in Antioch, however, the apostles and elders
instructed them:

> For it seemed good to the Holy Spirit and to us to lay upon you no
> greater burden than these essentials: that you abstain from things
> sacrificed to idols and from blood and from things strangled and
> from fornication; if you keep yourselves free from such things, you
> will do well.[4]

Cultural issues, however, are not this chapter's most pressing concern. The concern here is different, one that is much more fundamental to the Christian task. To restate the matter, I believe it is
legitimate to speak of doing theology in various contexts—e.g., in an
Asian context, in a Latin American context, etc. Also, it is obvious that
theology done in the context of one culture results in different
emphases and different questions being asked than when theology is
done in another culture. Still, the core content of the Gospel never
changes.[5] As the opening illustrations and the experiences of many
missionaries indicate, some proceed in the missionary task with a
sense that the core values of the Gospel are negotiable from one culture to another. In culture A one must preach an "A gospel" that
focuses on abundant life. In culture B one should preach a "B gospel"
that emphasizes deliverance from malevolent spirits. In culture C one
offers a "C gospel" that stresses liberation from political oppression.
And so on.

Certainly the concept of *culture* is important to the work of the
missionary. As a matter of fact, the faculty of the Billy Graham School
of Missions, Evangelism, and Church Growth considers a right understanding and approach to different cultures so vital to missionary
work that its faculty offers, among others, courses entitled "Cross-
Cultural Communication" and "The Gospel Across Cultures."
Teachers in these courses implicitly affirm several important matters.
First, they acknowledge the need for missionaries to be culturally sensitive. Second, they understand the necessity of stating the Gospel in
a manner that can be understood and accepted by individuals in cultures different from that of the missionary. Third, they acknowledge
the importance of meeting perceived needs. After all, perceived needs

often are real needs. A malnourished child's empty belly will cause him to perceive that he is hungry. That hunger is not merely a figment of his imagination. He really is hungry and might even be starving. Jesus had much to say about such needs. He has commanded believers to feed the hungry. The thirsty must be given water. The fearful and anxious must hear of the one whose name is "Wonderful Counselor" (Isa. 9:6). In other words, people everywhere face similar problems, and the answers to these problems are found in Jesus Christ. An obedient church must minister Christ's love. Thus in every culture people must be directed to him by a loving church.

DIRECTING PEOPLE TO A PARTICULAR JESUS

Having acknowledged the cross-cultural nature of the missionary task, it is important to repeat the question this chapter addresses: Is there any aspect of the missionary message that is truly universal?[6] Asked differently, does the missionary bear a core message that transcends cultural barriers and that never changes in the process of being carried from one people to another? In examining the task of preaching the Gospel in a pluralistic culture, Don Carson argues that the rudiments of the historic Gospel must be declared repeatedly. He concludes, "There is intellectual content in this heralded gospel, content that must be grasped, proclaimed and taught, grasped afresh, proclaimed afresh, in an ongoing cycle."[7] A danger exists, however, that in the name of cultural sensitivity and contextualization, the missionary will be tempted to change this rudimentary truth or will do so unwittingly.[8]

Some argue that in certain circumstances Jesus should be presented not as one who justifies, but as one who brings abundant life. They see this as a positive illustration of making the Christian Gospel relevant to the hearer. Such a presentation, however, is not so much a case of making the Gospel relevant as it is a matter of changing its very message and meaning.

It is one thing to maintain and present the core content of the message in different language and forms, and with illustrations that make the message understandable to the hearer. It is something altogether different to change the core content in order to make it palatable and acceptable to the hearer. Byang H. Kato asserts that the missionary task is "to make Christianity culturally relevant without destroying its ever-abiding message."[9]

Many evangelicals quickly discern the danger of substituting liberation theology, which promotes liberation from political and economic oppression, for the biblical message, which offers liberation from sin and its consequences. The presentation of Jesus as the giver of abundant life or as the supreme Spirit, separated from the message that he saves from sin, is less problematic for many. The distinction, however, is only a matter of degree; in reality, the message has still been changed. To guard against the danger of a changed Gospel, it is absolutely essential to reaffirm that the gospel message is about redemption and the remedy for sin.[10] As David Hesselgrave points out, "the great themes to be specially emphasized are sin, righteousness, and judgment; and . . . this Good News of God's provision for sinners is to flow out of, and lead into, the whole counsel of God."[11] Hesselgrave argues correctly that there is a core content of the Gospel that never changes. The apostle Paul was adamant about the need to guard the content of the Gospel when he appealed to the Galatians:

> But even though we, or an angel from heaven, should preach to you
> a gospel contrary to that which we have preached to you, let him
> be accursed. As we have said before, so I say again now, if any man
> is preaching to you a gospel contrary to that which you received,
> let him be accursed.[12]

Thus, to return to a concept introduced above, one may speak rightly of regional or cultural theologies in the loosest of senses. By this I mean that every culture has its own specific problems and concerns and that certain emphases of the preacher will vary from one culture to another. In the secular, humanistic societies of the West the missionary likely will emphasize, among other matters, the dangers of materialism and rationalism. In the animistic cultures found on the Indonesian island of Kalimantan the missionary rightly will emphasize the power of Jesus Christ over the entirety of creation.

Though in each culture the missionary must address culture-specific concerns, he or she must never accept the validity of "regional gospels." There is one Gospel, and it is universal and applicable to all cultures. The Gospel is universally applicable because the one great need of all human beings is the same: they all need to be reconciled with the Creator.

One might suppose that the universal nature of the Gospel would never be questioned by professing Christians. Conclusions reached by Per Frostin, however, demonstrate that such a supposition is mistaken. In a report to the Seventh Nordic Systematic Theology Congress in Copenhagen, Frostin argues:

> The assertion of *the contextuality of theology* implies a rejection of all claims of universal validity raised by any theology. Hence, this assertion is a critical principle of great significance, implying that *all* theologies, also those with universal claims, actually are stamped by their contexts.[13]

No doubt Frostin is correct in his conclusion that all theologies are stamped by their contexts. But it is not true that the universal claims of the Gospel are culture-specific. To the contrary, the great themes of the Gospel—God's holiness, man's sinfulness, and redemption from sin in Jesus Christ—are constant and universal in terms of geography, time, and culture. If the core content of the Gospel changes, ostensibly better to answer the needs of a particular culture, then the result is a terribly corrupted Gospel or no gospel at all.

For example, John Mbiti and Byang Kato write that

> ecclesiology is not well developed in Africa because many African theologians are persuaded that a more important need of African Christianity is selfhood and identity after long foreign domination.[14]

Thus, in the name of recovering their native identity, some "include both dead ancestors and the as-yet-unborn in the 'Great Family' of the church in a way that does violence to both biblical ecclesiology and the Christian tradition."[15] Obviously, such teaching makes dangerous inroads against the biblical Gospel. To include in the

"'Great Family' of the church" dead ancestors[16] and future descendants is to pervert the clear biblical teaching that one enters the family of God only through a faith response to the risen Christ. If Mbiti's and Kato's evaluation of this particular trend in African theology is accurate, we must conclude that concern with national identity and traditions has evolved into a perversion of the gospel message.

Yet another example of a change in the gospel message is the rise of various prophetic movements in South Africa. Mark Shaw writes about Isaiah Shembe, one of the most famous and controversial of the Zionist prophets of South Africa. According to Shaw, in the Zionist theology,

> Shembe is more than a prophet; he is the Christ. He referred to himself as the "Promised One" and in the official theology of the church he rose from the dead in 1935 and wrote hymns for the church confirming his messianic status.[17]

To his followers and others who have analyzed the movement, Shembe's rise is the quintessential example of a truly indigenous African theology and gospel. However, if Bengt Sundkler is correct in his evaluation that in the Zionist movement "there is no room for the Son in the creed and life of the believers . . . His place [having been] usurped by another,"[18] we have moved beyond the mere regionalization of theology and the Gospel to something much more sinister.[19]

At the risk of being repetitive, I affirm once more the need for the missionary to understand the culture in which he or she ministers, as well as the need to do everything possible in order to make the gospel message understandable and attractive to those to whom he or she goes. New believers are not bound to the cultural activities favored by those who brought them the Gospel. For instance, Shaw also describes the work of Mojola Agbebi in Lagos, Nigeria. Disagreeing with the Baptist missionary who was leading the work in that place, "Agbebi africanized his name and rejected European dress."[20] Then, according to Adrian Hastings's notes, Shaw states that Agbebi rejected "hymnbooks, harmoniums, dedications, pew constructions, surpliced choir, the white man's names, the white man's dress, so many non-essentials, so many props and crutches affecting the religious manhood of the Christian Africans."[21]

There is nothing wrong with Agbebi's actions. After all, all these other things (hymnbooks, harmoniums, etc.) are cultural trappings and preferences that in no way affect the integrity of the Gospel. The missionary must always be ready to jettison such baggage when it serves as an obstacle to the Gospel. On the other hand, missionaries must be careful not to jettison or compromise the Gospel itself. Sinners in every culture must be brought not just to any Jesus, but to the Jesus who saves from sin.

CONCLUSIONS AND APPLICATIONS

Several conclusions and applications follow from the truth of the Christian Gospel and its universal application. First, as illustrated in a recent prayer request from a Southern Baptist couple serving in a cross-cultural setting,[22] the goal of the missionary is to make the Gospel understandable. The missionary couple wrote: "Please pray for us as we begin to work among the people of _____. Pray especially that the Lord will enable us to present the Gospel in a way that is understandable to these people so that they might become followers of Christ." In the simple request for prayer from these missionaries lies the primary goal for the cross-cultural witness of the Gospel. These missionaries have dedicated themselves to making the Gospel understandable for people in a different cultural background. While doing so, they labor with the hope that the message will be accepted.

A related concern is the need for a comprehensive presentation of the Gospel that relates its message to all of life. The missionary must resist mere decisionalist approaches that present a series of questions that elicit a nodding "Yes." Matthew 28:19-20 commands Christians to make disciples, to baptize, and to teach. In other words, the missionary must be competent in birthing new converts and bringing them to full maturity in Christ.[23]

More specifically, the missionary must emphasize the forgiveness of sin and the justification of the sinner through the person and work of Jesus Christ. Where Jesus is not named, and where his redemptive work of reconciliation is not known, there is no salvation. I attended a worship service in Indonesia where a woman was asked to give a testimony about her salvation. She told how she had been ill for a number of years and had visited the local shaman,[24] who was unable to help her. She then turned to Islam, but that was of no help. She had tried this, and she had tried that. She had been in and out of various hospitals. One day a friend encouraged her to "try Jesus." She did, and according to her testimony, he healed her. There before us she expressed thanksgiving for this healing.

Reflection on this testimony reveals the absence of one vital element. The woman was asked to give a testimony about how Jesus had saved her. One might assume that she would tell how Christ had saved her from sin and its consequences. One could also have anticipated that she would talk about her resultant fellowship with God and her service to him. But at no time did the woman mention these matters and her experience of them.

We must adhere to the fundamental truth that Jesus Christ came into this world to save his people from their sins.[25] If we do not keep to this most basic of Christian teachings in our preaching, mission work, and personal experience, then we have fundamentally altered the religion of the New Testament.

We must distinguish between points of contact and the core message. The missionary entering new cultures will discover many new and strange things. Some of these things will not be comprehended. On the other hand, some concepts, actions, attitudes, and beliefs will be familiar. These points of contact between cultures can be employed as "door openers" or, to use Don Richardson's terminology, "eye openers."[26] The goal is to establish "a beachhead for the truth in the understanding."[27]

The apostle Paul was always looking for "door openers" and effective approaches for preaching the Gospel. Thus he testified: "I have become all things to all men, that I may by all means save some."[28] Paul adhered to this principle when preaching to the citizens of Athens. He found a point of contact—their acknowledgment of the existence of God who rules providentially over his creation—and used that shared belief to preach Christ's resurrection.

Two things must be noted about Paul's approach. First, he found a point of contact. Second, he then moved beyond it to the pivotal issue. In other words, he used the "eye opener" to establish common ground and then proclaimed the core message of the Gospel.

The same methodology can be discovered in the ministry of Jesus. He began with people where they were. In the temple during Passover, Jesus used the temple motif to refer to his own death and resurrection (John 2:13-22). To the Samaritan woman, Christ said, "Give Me a drink" (John 4:7, NASB). Then, building upon the common experience he shared with the woman, he spoke of sin and directed her to himself, the Messiah. He capitalized on the hunger of the multitude to preach about the bread of life (John 6). Many other such illustrations from the ministry of Jesus could be given.

So it must be with every missionary. The missionary to a people suffering oppression under a tyrannical regime must identify with the people and seek to encourage them and help them. But this missionary must then tell them how Jesus saves from the most dangerous tyranny of all, that of sin. The missionary to an animistic culture is always looking for door openers but must move beyond the initial point of contact to declare and explain the essentials of the Gospel.

And what are the essentials? Again, the gospel message is about redemption, the remedy for sin. To use J. I. Packer's outline, the Gospel is a message about God and his holiness, man and his sinfulness, the person and work of Jesus Christ, and a summons to repentance and faith.[29] If these truths are not declared, then no matter what else might have been preached, it was not the Gospel. "Eye openers" are good. They are useful and even necessary as one ventures to preach the Gospel in other cultures. But "eye openers" are not the Gospel.

Additionally, missionaries must realize they can learn much from people in other cultures. Important aspects of the biblical revelation, which one may have missed, are often brought to light when viewed through a different cultural lens. So even those who affirm the concept *of sola scriptura* and insist on theology and theologizing based on revelation can acknowledge that personal experiences sometimes assist in understanding revelation.

As Americans, my family and I had grown accustomed to enjoying Christmas in "the American way," that is, spending the day alone as a family, for the most part away from other members of our society and even from our church family. For us, Christmas day was a time of family fellowship, relaxing in our home, and enjoying the day.

Our lives began drastically to change, however, when we went as missionaries to Indonesia. We arrived in Indonesia in November, and toward the end of December we were invited by a local congregation to spend Christmas day with them. Still tired, unsure of ourselves, and intimidated, we declined this gracious invitation. In Djakarta the following year, however, we accepted the invitation from a congregation in that city. Spending Christmas day with the Djakarta congregation meant that we awakened at 5:00 in the morning so we could be at the church by 6:00 to enjoy breakfast with our church family. Throughout the day we worshiped and enjoyed wonderful fellowship together with Christ. We returned home in the dark after having spent a long Christmas day with Indonesian brothers and sisters. We were tired, but from that experience we came to understand better the biblical teaching regarding the nature of the Church.

We did not substitute a newly experienced cultural concept for a biblical concept. Rather, the new cultural experience shed much light on an old biblical concept and helped us to understand better our place in the family of God. Perhaps this is what A. R. Tippet means when he affirms "that it was his experience as a missionary to the Fiji people rather than his study of western theology or his experience in western churches that taught him most of what he understands to be a sound doctrine of the church."[30] Charles Kraft explains, "A western cultural perspective, focused as it is on individuality, seems peculiarly blind to . . . the human need for well-integrated groupness."[31] In a similar vein, Kraft himself relates that he gained a heightened understanding of and respect for the Old Testament (even the genealogies) as a result of his experience in Africa.[32]

Finally, Christians must face the fact that they are living in an increasingly diversified and pluralistic world, and they must wrestle with the implications of this reality. Charles Van Engen claims, "Christians and non-Christians, pluralists, inclusivists, and exclusivists are beginning to share one thing in common. We are all being radically impacted by the largest redistribution of people the globe has ever seen."[33]

It is increasingly likely, even in the United States, that one's next-door neighbor will be a Hindu, a Buddhist, a Moslem, or an adherent of any number of other religions and cults. The issue of making the Gospel understandable to those of other cultures and religions is no longer only the concern of the missionary in a distant land. Virtually all believers will likely have opportunities to perform the ministry of reconciliation to those who are culturally and religiously different from them.

As the Church embraces these opportunities, it would do well to consider the words of John Hick, who admits:

For if Jesus was literally God incarnate, the Second Person of the Holy Trinity living a human life, so that the Christian religion was founded by God-on-earth in person, it is then very hard to escape from the traditional view that all mankind must be converted to the Christian faith.[34]

This is this very conclusion that I cannot escape!

CHAPTER 9

1. *Animism* refers to the beliefs and practices of a people who attempt to appease or control, by various rituals, sacrifices, and/or taboos, the supernatural spirits that can influence the individual either positively or negatively.

2. A recent discussion of this subject can be found in Gailyn Van Rheenen, *Communicating Christ in Animistic Contexts* (Grand Rapids, Mich.: Baker, 1991). For an earlier discussion, see Alan R. Tippett, "The Evangelization of Animists," in *Let the Earth Hear His Voice*, ed. J. D. Douglas (Minneapolis: World Wide Publications, 1975), 844-855.

3. David J. Bosch, *Transforming Mission: Paradigm Shifts in Theology of Mission* (Maryknoll, N.Y.: Orbis Books, 1996), 4.

4. Acts 15:28-29, NASB. Even these restrictions were loosened by Paul. See 1 Cor. 8:4-13.

5. John Mbiti, rather than employing the terms *theology* in a general sense and *the Gospel* in a narrower sense, makes a distinction between *Christianity* and *the Gospel*. The former, he wrote, "results from the encounter of the Gospel with any given local society" and thus is always influenced by the local culture. The latter, however, is "God-given, eternal and does not change." "Christianity and Traditional Religions in Africa," *International Review of Mission* 59 (October 1970), 438.

6. Charles Kraft employs the phrase "supracultural truth" to identify this concept. *Christianity in Culture: A Study in Dynamic Biblical Theologizing in Cross-Cultural Perspective* (Maryknoll, N.Y.: Orbis Books, 1979), 124-125, etc.

7. Donald A. Carson, *The Gagging of God: Christianity Confronts Pluralism* (Grand Rapids, Mich.: Zondervan, 1996), 506.

8. Nor is this danger restricted to the international mission field. The danger can be illustrated many times over in churches in the United States.

9. Byang H. Kato, "The Gospel, Cultural Context and Religious Syncretism," in *Let the Earth Hear His Voice*, 1217.

10. See the opening paragraphs.

11. David J. Hesselgrave, *Planting Churches Cross-Culturally: A Guide for Home and Foreign Missions* (Grand Rapids, Mich.: Baker, 1980), 205.

12. Gal. 1:8-9, NASB. In his first letter to the church at Corinth, Paul articulates the unchanging facts of this Gospel and emphasizes that it is by this Gospel that we are saved.

13. Per Frostin, "The Hermeneutics of the Poor—The Epistemological 'Break' in Third World Theologies," *Studia Theologica* 39 (1985), 135.

14. John S. Mbiti and Byang H. Kato, "Africa," *Contextualization: Meanings, Methods, and Models*, eds. David J. Hesselgrave and Edward Rommen (Grand Rapids, Mich.: Baker, 1989), 97.

15. Ibid.

16. Apparently these dead ancestors include those who did not make any sort of faith response to Jesus.

17. Mark Shaw, *The Kingdom of God in Africa* (Grand Rapids, Mich.: Baker, 1996), 247.

18. Bengt Sundkler, *Bantu Prophets in South Africa*, 2nd ed. (London: Oxford University Press, 1961), 283.

19. For a recent evaluation of some of the African indigenous churches by one of their own leaders, see Solomon Zvanaka, "African Independent Churches in Context," *Missiology* 25 (January 1997), 69-75.

20. Shaw, *The Kingdom of God in Africa*, 243.

21. Ibid.

22. The names of the missionaries and the country in which they serve are not reported because of the sensitive nature of their work.

23. Paul Hiebert explains, "Ultimately, the relationship of gospel and culture is not a problem to be solved, but the process of discipling all peoples—individuals and communities—in all things (Matthew 28:19)." "Gospel and Culture: The WCC Project" *Missiology* 25 (April 1997), 206.

24. A person set apart as especially attuned to the spirit world, believed to possess supernatural powers, and called upon to deal with it on behalf of others.

25. Matt. 1:21.

26. An illustration of this type of "eye opener" is the Peace Child ideal in the Sawi cultures. See Don Richardson, *Peace Child* (Glendale, Calif.: Regal, 1974).

27. Don Richardson, "Finding the Eye Opener," in *Perspectives on the World Christian Movement* (Pasadena, Calif.: William Carey Library, 1992).

28. 1 Cor. 9:22, NASB.

29. J. I. Packer, *Evangelism and the Sovereignty of God* (Downers Grove, Ill.: InterVarsity Press, 1961).

30. A. R. Tippett, a private conversation reported by Charles Kraft in *Christianity in Culture*, 298.

31. Kraft, *Christianity in Culture*, 298.

32. Ibid.

33. Charles Van Engen, *Mission on the Way: Issues in Mission Theology* (Grand Rapids, Mich.: Baker, 1996), 179.

34. John Hick, *God Has Many Names* (Philadelphia: Westminster, 1982), 19. Hick does not hold to the traditional view.

TEN

THE GREAT COMMISSION TO REACH A NEW GENERATION

THOM RAINER

Between the years 1977 and 1994 a tremendous upsurge in live births in America caught most demographers by surprise. Birth rates had declined precipitously during the "baby bust" of 1964 to 1976, and few people expected such a dramatic reversal of this trend. Indeed, this new baby boom was almost as large as the well-documented baby boom of 1946 to 1964.

This generation has been unnamed for the most part. In isolated articles some writers have referred to them as "the next boom," "the echoboomers," "the new boom," "the vava boom" (because so many of the mothers of this generation had their first child later in life, usually in their thirties), and "the millennial generation."

I have named this generation "the bridgers" for two reasons.[1] First and foremost, these 72 million *bridge* two centuries and two millennia. Though their birth dates will have twentieth-century markings, their generation will be most influential during their adulthood in the twenty-first century.

A second reason for using the bridger nomenclature is one of hope and promise. While we are living in a time of upheaval and uncertainty, we are also paradoxically living in a time of unprecedented awakenings, prayer movements, and awareness of God. Indeed, the bridger generation is already being cited as a "religious" generation, though "religious" and "Christian" are hardly synonymous. But is it possible that this group of 72 million may be the bridge between the secular and the sacred?

In the twenty-first century the bridgers will shape the attitudes, values, economics, and lifestyles of America. They will be the dominant adult population group for at least the first half of the twenty-first century. In 1995 the bridgers accounted for 27.5 percent of the total United States population.[2] Though the boomer generation was slightly larger, it is the bridgers who will be moving into positions of power and influence in the twenty-first century.

THEIR RELIGIOUS WORLD

Perhaps more than any twentieth-century generation, the bridgers are a religious group. But "religious" is about as specific as one can get in describing their beliefs. The bridgers as a generation believe in almost any expression of a higher being or higher power. They resist any claim that one faith system is superior or exclusive. The Church has an incredible challenge in sharing an exclusive Gospel with a generation that resists absolutes of any type.

Much publicity has been given to America's preoccupation with New Age religions. But the primary "competition" for the bridgers' allegiance may come from a growing religious force in America—Muslims. A 1991 poll of twelve- to seventeen-year-olds by the George H. Gallup International Institute confirmed the increasing influence of Muslims in America. Almost three-fourths of the respondents said they receive too little information at school about Muslims.[3] They were actually asking for religious instruction in public schools, but the instruction they desired was not Christian.

The Church in America has intentionally attempted to reach two earlier generations, the boomers and the busters. In terms of generational penetration, the efforts have largely been a failure. What can we learn from these earlier efforts as we try to reach the bridgers?

THE CHURCH:
LEARNING FROM PAST FAILURES

In both the boomer and the buster generations, the Church did experience a season of success in reaching a large number from each group. But the success was ephemeral. The quick surge of church growth from these generations was almost equally matched by a quick exodus over three to seven years. Two primary factors explain this phenomenon in simplest terms.

The Eagerness to Accommodate

Church leaders of the seventies through the nineties were told that they and their churches were hopelessly out of date and out of touch. The forms and liturgies of worship, the ancient hymns, and fifties-style buildings were irrelevant to the unchurched generations, it was said. Many of the critics were right. The evangelical church had its figurative head in the sand and did not understand the culture it was trying to reach. Change was necessary.

But in the course of making necessary changes, some churches went overboard. For these churches, changes in style shifted to changes in substance. The user-friendly exuberance meant low expectations and subtle encouragement of biblical illiteracy. So the boomers and busters entered the church looking for something different. They were initially attracted by the relevancy of the worship, the ability to remain anonymous, and the hope of the Christian faith. But they quietly left the church when they discovered it to be amazingly similar to the world they knew. They were looking for something different; what they found was often more worldly than heavenly. They were looking for a challenge; what they found was the lowest of expectations.

Waiting for Adulthood

A second major mistake made by many churches attempting to reach the boomers and busters is that they waited until these generations reached adulthood. Yet the most receptive time of a person's life to be reached for the Gospel is when he or she is a child or teenager. Eighty-one percent of all persons who accept Christ become Christians before they turn twenty years old.[4]

THE CHALLENGE: AN AMORAL GENERATION

Many of the problems in the boomer generation were related to immoral behavior. They had behavioral patterns that were contrary to their parents' teachings. Many of them did wrong, but at least they knew that the behaviors were wrong.

The busters who followed were largely like the boomer predecessors. Most who engaged in wrongful behavior did so with a clear understanding of right and wrong. Some simply made immoral decisions rather than moral decisions.

In an ironic way, we can celebrate the concept of immorality among the boomers and the busters. At least the majority in the generation could define moral or immoral behavior, even if they chose immorality. At least they knew right from wrong. The bridgers know no such boundaries. For the first time in American history, an entire generation will grow up without certain moral values. Look at some of these attitudes in a survey of older bridgers:[5]

• *Statement*: What is right for one person in a given situation might not be right for another person in a similar situation.

Agree: 91%   Disagree: 8%   Uncertain: 1%

• *Statement*: When it comes to matters of morals and ethics, truth means different things to different people; no one can be absolutely positive that they know the truth.

Agree: 80%   Disagree: 19%   Uncertain: 1%

• *Statement*: Lying is sometimes necessary.

Agree: 57%   Disagree: 42%   Uncertain: 1%

• *Statement*: The main purpose of life is enjoyment and personal fulfillment.

Agree: 64%   Disagree: 36%   Uncertain: 0%

The bridger generation clearly has no certainty of right and wrong. The reasons behind the growth of an amoral generation can best be understood in light of the development of the moral standard of previous generations.

The builders, born before 1946, continue to accept the basic

Judeo-Christian principles they were taught as children in order to discern right from wrong. They believe that the Bible is a moral guide for life. The builders' children, boomers and older busters, withdrew in large numbers from church and other Christian activities. Without the influence of the Church, they began to engage in large numbers in activities clearly defined as immoral by their parents. They did have the absolute standards of their parents' morality, but they accepted them in theory rather than in practice.

But the bridger generation has neither a moral standard, such as the Bible, nor a moral example in their parents. Their understanding of right and wrong is fuzzy at best. An entire amoral generation will soon enter adulthood.

We could point to numerous examples of the consequences of amorality. For now let us look at the bridgers and their sexual activity. Recent data from the U.S. Centers for Disease Control indicates that 40 percent of ninth graders have had sex; 48 percent of tenth graders, 57 percent of eleventh graders, and 72 percent of high school seniors have had sexual intercourse.[6]

These discouraging numbers become even more dismal when one examines the age at which kids become sexually active. High school boys who are sexually active report that they lost their virginity at an average age of 13.2, while sexually active girls averaged an age of 14.6 years.[7] One doctor reported treating girls at age eight and nine years old for severe vaginal injuries resulting from sexual experimentation.[8] And most early attempts at intercourse are typically preceded by other sexual activity such as fondling and oral sex.[9]

As a rule, these bridgers cannot give a clear reason why they should not be involved in such behavior. Amorality among these children will soon reap disastrous consequences.

A GREATER CHALLENGE:
A PLURALISTIC GENERATION

The PBS series *Genesis* premiered in October 1996 with a celebrated promotion called "The Resurgence of Faith." The host, Bill Moyers, asked this question prior to the beginning of the series: "Can a plu-

ralistic America avoid the bitter fruits of religion—intolerance, igno-
rance and murderous fanaticism—that have occurred throughout history when faith is used as a wedge to drive people apart?"[10] Then
Moyers asked the question that is fast becoming the question of the
bridger generation: "How can I hold *my* truth to be the truth when so
many others see truth so differently?"[11]

Such is the world of faith in which bridgers have been raised. It
is a world that finally has room for God but refuses to define God in
precise terms. Pam Janis further explains this perspective of God by
stating, "The God of pop culture is not necessarily a Judeo-Christian
God. He (or she) can be any form of love and power."[12]

The bridger generation has adopted this view of God. Even many
bridgers in evangelical churches refuse to confine their understanding
of God to the One who has been revealed in the person of Jesus Christ.
When we speak of the bridgers' religion, we cannot speak of their faith.
For the vast majority we can describe it best as the *faiths* of the bridgers.

History may remember the bridger generation as the most religious group America has ever known. Their generation is being raised
in a time when the Gallup Organization reports that religion is playing a more important role in the lives of Americans.[13] Public confidence in both organized religion and the clergy has been renewed,
despite the moral failures of many church leaders.[14] Church atten-
dance has held steady for most age groups but is increasing among the
bridger generation.[15] Moyers writes: "We shouldn't be surprised by all
this stirring. It's a confusing time, marked by social and moral ambivalence and, for many, economic insecurity. People yearn for spiritual
certainty and collective self-confidence."[16]

But Moyers's ideas about "spiritual certainty" are anything but certain. He celebrates "the resurgence of religion in America, and the
arrival on our shores of so many believers of different faiths."[17] For
him the different views do not bring confusion but hope. The bridgers
seem to be catching that same pluralistic fever. It does not matter what
you believe as long as you believe something.

The bridgers are the first generation of Americans to be raised
without the cultural presumption that they would become Christians
or explore Christianity. Barna notes that they "take the best from each

faith group they're exposed to and combine those valued elements into a comfortable, customized religious smorgasbord."[18] They may even call themselves "Christians," but the term is used generically. Barna found their belief system "is a combination of Christianity, pragmatism, Far Eastern traditions and utilitarianism."[19]

Such descriptions do not mean that bridgers are not religious. To the contrary, they are more religious than the boomers ever were. But we cannot make religion synonymous with Christianity. The former have some general type of belief in God that may have many expressions. The latter believe only in God as revealed in the person of Jesus Christ. The former are "tolerant" and open to many faiths. The latter are "narrow-minded" and see only one way to God.

Where did the bridgers learn their lessons about faith? For the most part, their boomer parents created an environment of moral relativism and a world void of absolutes. An exclusive God without whom there is no other way to salvation and heaven simply does not fit into this "I'm okay, you're okay" climate.

THE URGENCY OF THE MOMENT

The vast majority of bridgers today have not accepted Christ. In a recent and informal survey of 211 bridgers, only 4 percent responded that they were born-again Christians who had trusted in Christ alone for salvation.[20] In comparison with other generations, two-thirds of builders indicated they were Christians, as well as one-third of boomers and 15 percent of busters.[21] According to present trends, we are about to lose eternally the second largest generation in America's history.

In a survey of approximately 1,300 Christians of various backgrounds and regions, our research team asked them at what age they had accepted Christ. The responses were amazing:[22]

Age At Which You Became a Christian

Before age	6	6%
Ages	6-9	24%
Ages	10-12	26%
Ages	13-14	15%
Ages	15-19	10%
Ages	20 and over	19%

Over 80 percent of the respondents indicated they had become Christians before they turned twenty years old. And 71 percent said they had accepted Christ before the age of fifteen. George Barna's research seems to affirm our surveys. He comments that "one of the most significant discoveries from our research among all age groups of the population has been that most people make their lifelong, faith-shaping choices when they are young."[23]

Our survey was focused on all of the teen years; so the question asked about specific ages up to nineteen. Barna researched the specific ages up to age eighteen and found that "if a person is ever going to become a Christian, the chances are that he or she will do so before reaching the age of 18."[24] Whereas 81 percent of our respondents became Christians before age nineteen, Barna found that "three quarters of all people who have consciously, intentionally, and personally chosen to embrace Jesus Christ as their Savior did so before their eighteenth birthday."[25]

My research and Barna's research are very close in their conclusions. Over three-fourths of persons become Christians before they turn twenty years old. Not many churches, unfortunately, are paying much attention to this reality.

THE CHURCH RESPONDS

While Christians can understand the eternal importance of the Church for the bridgers, it is interesting that the secular world is reaching that same conclusion, though for different reasons. "The link between religious participation and avoidance of drug abuse, alcoholism, crime, and other social pathologies is grist for new research,"[26] write U. S. News & World Report correspondents Joseph P. Shapiro and Andrea R. Wright. Brookings Institute political scientist John DiIulio comments, "It's remarkable how much good empirical evidence there is that religious belief can make a positive difference."[27] Shapiro and Wright cite a "survey by John Gartner of Loyola College of Maryland and David Larson of Duke University Medical Center [which] found over thirty studies that show a correlation between religious participation and avoidance of crime and substance abuse."[28]

Other statistics show the positive influence of church on all persons, particularly the bridgers:

> The two most reliable predictors of teenage drug avoidance [are] optimism about the future and regular church attendance.[29]
>
> The divorce rate for regular churchgoers is 18 percent; for those who attend services less than once a year, 24 percent.[30]
>
> Frequent churchgoers are about 50 percent less likely to report psychological problems and 71 percent less likely to be alcoholics.[31]

The Church is indeed a real and present hope for the bridgers. We already have evidence of Great Commission churches that are reaching and impacting this generation. Though the characteristics are not exhaustive, let us look at some traits of bridger-reaching churches.

A Community of Unconditional Love

The Church cannot be a replacement for the nuclear family, but it can offer love and community that is like a family. Many of the bridgers have been rejected by their parents and peers. For them there is a powerful blessing in the knowledge that God accepts them in their sinfulness, that through Christ they will not face rejection from God.

But these young people must first see the love of Christ in the lives of the believers in the churches. For many believers such a challenge will be difficult. The bridgers are different from them. They come from a different culture with a different vocabulary. They are not opposed to the culture of the Church; they are simply ignorant of it. For too many years too many churches have accepted only those who are like them. Bridger-reaching churches must not fit that description.

Adult/Bridger Mentoring

Less than three-fourths of the bridgers have two parents at home.[32] But in many of the two-parent homes, only one will be a biological parent. More bridgers live with never-married mothers than any previous generation.[33] Even in those homes where both biological parents are present, the likelihood is that both parents work. Parents are spending less and less time with their kids. One study found that working mothers spend an average of eleven minutes a day in meaningful time with their children on weekdays and only thirty minutes a day on weekends. Working fathers did worse, averaging eight minutes a day with their kids on weekdays and fourteen minutes a day on weekends.[34]

The children and youth of the bridger generation are starved for adult attention and interaction. That need will not be met by a handful of adults standing before a large group of bridgers. They long for the one-on-one attention they are not receiving at home.

In two different studies of effective evangelistic churches across our nation, I noted a keen awareness of the need to reach young people before they reached adulthood. In many of the more effective churches, one-on-one mentoring and discipling was taking place between adults and youth. Indeed, in those churches that were reaching bridgers, this approach seemed to be among the most effective.[35]

Intentionally Evangelistic

My research team at The Southern Baptist Theological Seminary has studied over 1,000 churches that are reaching people for Christ. One consistent theme emanates from all of their ministries, activities, and programs: intentionality in evangelism. Churches can have a plethora of programs for bridgers, but without an explicit effort to reach them for Christ, the evangelistic results will be anemic. Evangelism is not a passive activity. Throughout Scripture the emphases of evangelistic ministries are "go" and "tell." Bridger-reaching churches of the twenty-first century will be intentional in their evangelistic efforts.

High Expectations

Church leaders shared with us on numerous occasions their weariness of low expectations that resulted in weak commitment. A Michigan pastor said, "I've been in churches all my life where church membership means no more than a group of people yelling 'Amen' after someone walks the aisle. That is nothing like the New Testament pattern of total commitment and discipleship. We have weak churches with apathetic members because we place no biblical expectations on them!"[36]

Many churches have discovered that low expectations and the search for the greatest level of seeker comfort have backfired. Instead of filling churches with new members who are committed Christians, they have been left with persons who have a consumer mentality, typified by an attitude of "What has the church done for me lately?"

Many of the bridgers are in schools that have "dumbed down" their educational standards so everyone can pass. Many bridgers have parents who impose little or no discipline. They are hungry for a place that demonstrates unconditional love along with clear expectations. They are responding well to churches that demonstrate a belief that these kids are capable of meeting vigorous demands. They are just waiting for someone to tell them they are smart enough to achieve something great. They will thrive in a church that teaches them they can do anything in Christ's power, but they will avoid or leave quickly those churches that have no expectations of them. That low-expectation world is the one they are trying to leave.

Biblical Preaching

In our study of 576 churches, we found an amazing correlation not only in preaching and evangelistic effectiveness, but also in preaching and reaching the bridgers.[37] Those pastors who gave a high priority to the preaching of God's Word led their churches to see lives changed in all age groups, and the bridgers were no exception.

The pastors we interviewed had a high view of Scripture. They believed not only in the truthfulness of the totality of God's Word, but they also believed that it had the power to change lives. Thus they preached with a sense of expectancy and urgency.

If we are to have any hope of reaching America's second largest generation for Christ, we must provide them with teaching from God's own Word. Many of the mainline denominations have lost young people because the kids fail to see what is unique about the faith of their parents. C. Peter Wagner notes, "Studies of the denominations that have been losing members have shown that one factor across the board has been their inability to persuade their children to join their parents' churches."[38] It seems that children have not learned the essentials of their faith and how it makes a difference in this world, and preaching has been diluted, minimized, and proclaimed without authority.

Prayer Ministries

Another correlative factor in churches that reach bridgers is an emphasis on corporate prayer ministries. These churches not only emphasize prayer in each believer's life—they stress that the church must pray *together!*

Many of these churches are including bridgers in the prayer ministry. I visited seven churches in our evangelistic churches research project that had more young people than adults involved in their prayer ministries. Bridgers indeed respond better when asked to do ministry.

In our fascination with demographic trends, innovative methodologies, and culturally-sensitive ministries, we must not forget that only a sovereign God can send a revival to reach the bridgers. If past historical and biblical patterns can be projected into the future, prayer will be used by God to precipitate these revivals.

Teaching the Parents

The proportion of the bridger generation in the Church today is less than all previous generations. We can therefore surmise that many of the members in our churches have bridger children who are not involved in the Church.

We have the opportunity to teach the adults in our churches to have a positive influence on their bridger children. As a consequence, many bridgers may choose to come to church; others who are attending may choose to stay.

What can we adults learn that can make a difference in the lives of our bridger children? When 100,000 children between the ages of eight and fourteen were asked what they wanted most in their parents, they listed these ten qualities:

1. Parents who do not argue in front of them.
2. Parents who treat each member of the family the same.
3. Parents who are honest.

4. Parents who welcome their friends to the home.

5. Parents who are tolerant of others.

6. Parents who build a team spirit with their children.

7. Parents who answer their questions.

8. Parents who are consistent.

9. Parents who concentrate on their good points instead of their weaknesses.

10. Parents who give punishment when needed, but not in front of others, especially their friends.[39]

Godly Youth Leadership

Among the key leadership positions in churches today should be those who teach our children and our youth. We should commit our resources of time and money for those leaders to be able to reach the bridger generation. Barna is rather blunt about churches' failure to support youth leaders with adequate funding when he writes:

> Churches spend the vast majority of their evangelistic dollars (more than 70 percent of it, by some of our preliminary research) trying to penetrate the adult market. After decades and decades of such toil, we can confidently announce the results: such efforts bear little fruit. On the other hand, the amount of money and effort we pour into reaching kids with the gospel pays off rather handsomely. The fact demands that we ask why we don't concentrate evangelistic efforts on youth.[40]

The churches that reach the bridgers in the twenty-first century will emphasize that some of the key positions of leadership, whether paid or volunteer, will be positions of youth and children's leadership. The churches should seek the most godly and dedicated persons to lead these ministries and support them enthusiastically with money, time, and prayers.

Effective Bible Study

Churches are losing young people because these young people have not learned the essentials and distinctives of their faith. Like their adult predecessors, the bridgers are woefully ignorant of the Bible.

How can we expect to impact the lives of the bridger generation unless they understand the book that is our guide and direct word from God?

Dean R. Hoge, Benton Johnson, and Donald Luidens, three sociologists of mainline religion, came to this honest and compelling conclusion about mainline churches: "Our findings show that belief is the single best predictor of church participation, but it is orthodox Christian belief, and not the trends of lay liberalism, that impels people to be involved in the church."[41]

Further, the sociologists stress that these beliefs *must* be communicated to the next generations: "Unless the *youth* are firmly socialized into its tenets and standards, the strength of the religious community will eventually ebb away."[42] Sunday school has been among the key methodologies of the past two centuries to train adults *and* youth in the depths of the Bible. C. Peter Wagner agrees, writing, "Some may say, 'But Sunday School is not part of our tradition.' This may be true, but if it is not, some functional substitute must be found."[43]

Exclusivity

Bridger-reaching churches of the twenty-first century will be bold and uncompromising in their stand that Christ is the only way of salvation. Many bridgers will resist that rigidity, calling it narrow-minded and intolerant. But no bridger will be truly reached for Christ unless he or she comes through the Savior, believing him to be the only way of salvation. Watch for this issue to be one of the most debated theological issues of the early twenty-first century.

Involved Youth

Finally, a notable characteristic of bridger-reaching churches will be the involvement of the youth in ministry. These churches will not be satisfied to fill the pews with bridgers; they will make every effort to involve each young person in ministry.

THEREFORE GO: THE COMMISSION TO REACH THE BRIDGER GENERATION NOW

The command of the Great Commission in Matthew 28:19 is to reach *all peoples*. Missiologists often suggest that this mandate particularly refers to people groups, those with similar cultural traits. Though the bridger generation is by no means a monolithic cultural group, many of the 72 million do share common characteristics. And perhaps the most common trait is their rejection of the exclusivistic claims of Christ.

Our research is fallible. We may reach considerably more than the predicted 4 percent of the bridger generation, but we may reach less. Every day that passes, however, is one less day to reach the second largest generation in America's history. If previous patterns prove true, the ability to reach the bridgers will become more difficult the older they get.

We who are believers in Jesus Christ cannot be complacent. Eternal matters are at stake. Our children currently may be receptive to the Gospel of Jesus Christ, but that moment of openness may soon pass.

We serve a risen Savior who has given us the hope of eternity. However, the large majority of bridgers do not yet have that hope. While the Great Commission was directed at billions of people beyond the bridger generation, it was certainly directed at these young people as well. The consequences of the churches' response are eternal. The urgency is great. We cannot wait.

CHAPTER 10

1. See Thom S. Rainer, *The Bridger Generation* (Nashville: Broadman & Holman, 1997) for a thorough investigation of this generation.
2. Bureau of the Census, *Projections of the United States by Age, Sex, Race, and Hispanic Origin: 1992 to 2050*. The chart on page 199 was also derived from this publication.
3. Susan Mitchell, "The Next Baby Boom," *American Demographics*, 17/10 (October 1995), 23.
4. This phenomenon of receptivity at an early age became apparent in my research for *The Bridger Generation*. See chapter 10, "The Church Responds: Now, Not Later."
5. George Barna, *Generation Next* (Ventura, Calif.: Regal, 1995), 32.
6. Cited in Walt Mueller, *Understanding Today's Youth Culture* (Wheaton, Ill.: Tyndale, 1994), 213.
7. Ibid.
8. Ibid.
9. Ibid.
10. Bill Moyers, "America's Religious Mosaic," *USA Weekend*, October 11-13, 1996, 5.
11. Ibid.
12. Ibid.
13. Ibid.
14. Ibid.

15. Ibid.
16. Ibid.
17. Ibid.
18. Barna, *Generation Next*, 74.
19. Ibid.
20. This survey was conducted in three states over a seven-month period in 1995 and 1996 by the Billy Graham School of Missions, Evangelism and Church Growth at The Southern Baptist Theological Seminary.
21. Ibid.
22. This survey was conducted in seventeen states over a fifteen-month period in 1995 and 1996 by the Billy Graham School of Missions, Evangelism and Church Growth at The Southern Baptist Theological Seminary.
23. Barna, *Generation Next*, 77.
24. Ibid.
25. Ibid.
26. Joseph P. Shapiro and Andrea R. Wright, "Can Churches Save America?" *U. S. News & World Report*, September 9, 1996, 50.
27. Ibid.
28. Ibid.
29. Ibid.
30. Ibid.
31. Ibid.
32. Mitchell, "The Next Baby Boom," 24.
33. Ibid.
34. David Elkind, *Miseducation* (New York: Knopf, 1987), 24. Cited in Walt Mueller, *Understanding Today's Youth Culture*, 41.
35. See Thom S. Rainer, *Effective Evangelistic Churches* (Nashville: Broadman & Holman, 1996) and Thom S. Rainer, *High Expectation Churches* (Nashville: Broadman & Holman, 1999).
36. Rainer, *Effective Evangelistic Churches*, 174.
37. Ibid.; see especially chapter 3.
38. C. Peter Wagner, *The Healthy Church* (Ventura, Calif.: Regal, 1996), 146.
39. "Parental Behavior," *Coral Ridge Encounter*, April 1990, 41.
40. Barna, *Generation Next*, 77.
41. Dean R. Hoge, Benton Johnson, and Donald A. Luidens, *Vanishing Boundaries: The Religion of Mainline Protestant Baby Boomers* (Louisville: Westminster/John Knox, 1994), 185.
42. Ibid., 183.
43. Wagner, *The Healthy Church*, 147.

ELEVEN

"THE PROPER SUBJECT OF THEOLOGY"

Giving Voice to the Doctrine of Salvation in a New Century

GREGORY A. THORNBURY

This volume has demonstrated that doctrinal compromise marks virtually every area of the current evangelical theological landscape, from the de-emphasis of the classical understanding of the doctrine of God to current missiological practice. These severe challenges confronting the doctrine of salvation stem from more fundamental problems within the doctrinal systems of certain academic theologians, popular pastors, and teachers. Specifically, the reorientation of the doctrines of God and anthropology in recent evangelical scholarship has paved the way for the now infamous Openness of God movement as well as other "post-conservative" forms of evangelical theology.

Moving into a new century and a new millennium, the evangelical church needs a reaffirmation of the traditional thesis concerning the doctrine of salvation, as well as a new emphasis on the biblical portrait of God and his relationship with human beings. What is required is nothing less than a revisitation of the theological assertions that have provided evangelicalism with powerful conviction in the past. Thus I would like to offer a thesis statement that will hopefully help evangelicals refocus their theological commitment to the doctrine of salvation. For the articulation of this thesis I turn to the work of

Luther, whose ability for theological clarity and discernment has given evangelicals clear direction since the Reformation. Luther never tired of stating that the truth of the Gospel rests on prior commitments to the doctrines of God and of humanity. If the Church goes wrong on either of these critical truths, Luther averred, the Gospel will be lost.

In his commentary on Psalm 51, Luther warned of the dangers that result when theologians skew or add to the primary message of the Gospel. Luther wrote, "The proper subject of theology is man the guilty and ruined sinner and God the justifier and savior of sinful men. Whatever is sought or debated beyond this subject in theology is error and poison."[1] Luther exhorted theologians to avoid at all costs the temptation of going beyond "the proper subject of theology" by reorienting the doctrines of God and humanity. Theological disputation that either robs God of his glory or exalts human beings too highly will inevitably produce disastrous results. It is poison, Luther said, that if ingested will prove fatal to the Church and her ministry.

Luther's warning provides a needed corrective for contemporary evangelical theologians. With regard to the doctrine of salvation, Luther's directive on the proper subject of theology rebukes us and, if heeded, will guide us safely through the theological crises that threaten evangelical theology at this critical period in the life and witness of the Church. If anything characterizes evangelicalism today, it is debate, and usually contentious debate. The current impasse on issues such as epistemology, the use and meaning of theological language, and the doctrine of God (among other topics) serves as evidence that evangelicalism currently lacks any theological coherence. As David Wells opines:

> By the end of the 1970s . . . evangelicalism was losing its momentum. As the theological boundaries of evangelicalism expanded, as the theological core began to disintegrate, the ground for unity had to shift from a common confession of theological unity, to a common acceptance of diversity. In the process, evangelicalism was transformed into little more than a fraternity organization.[2]

The many faces of contemporary evangelicalism make Wells's pessimism understandable. Nevertheless, the problem for evangelicalism today arises not so much from disputed issues on the theological periphery but from the lack of consensus on the core of the Gospel and its supporting doctrinal affirmations. In fact, Gary Dorrien doubts whether "there exists any golden thread that links all of the groups that call themselves evangelical. Though *evangelical* means 'message of good news,' there is no precisely defined belief about this message that evangelicals distinctly emphasize or agree on."[3] No one could fail to miss the incredible irony of evangelicals who refuse to agree upon the Evangel.

Luther would argue that this lack of central agreement on the meaning of the Gospel demonstrates precisely the influence of the errors and poisons he feared. That evangelicals cannot unite around a common understanding of the meaning and content of the doctrine of salvation should cause every one of us to reflect upon which errors and poisons have gained ascendancy in *our* thinking. Luther's thesis on the proper subject of theology strikes at the problem on two fronts. First, it asserts that the doctrine of salvation will never be right unless its supporting doctrines of God and humanity are right. Second, Luther's thesis posits that theological method strays into perilous territory when it gets too far from the axioms of the doctrine of salvation—God's gracious rescue of ruined sinners. On the former point, evangelicals have increasingly betrayed themselves by assuming too much power for human beings and too little power for God himself. On the latter point, evangelicals have lost ground by focusing too much on peripheral issues that, according to Luther's understanding, not only occasionally transgress the boundaries of "the proper subject of theology," but also show a determination to settle permanently into new territories of theological discourse. Once evangelical theology develops a routine of addressing peripheral issues, the Gospel begins to serve only as a convenient point of reference.

GOING BEYOND
"THE PROPER SUBJECT OF THEOLOGY"

Recently Roger Olson envisioned the future of evangelical theology as "a 'big tent' with definite but sometimes uncertain boundaries and a strong center stage."[4] Olson contends that there will always be fringe groups who stand either just on the outside of or just under the big tent of evangelicalism. Mainstream groups will occupy the center of activity. Although Olson's comparison of evangelicalism to a circus event unfortunately appears to be an appropriate analogy, his understanding of what constitutes "center stage" in evangelicalism suffers from a lack of specificity.[5] Olson defines salvation as "the forgiving and transforming grace of God through Jesus Christ in the experience called conversion."[6] While Olson expresses vital truths about the Gospel, his minimalist account reveals an uneasiness with claiming too much with regard to a distinctly evangelical doctrine of salvation. In Olson's account of the future of evangelical theology, his understanding of the evangelical mainstream appears to lack the particularities needed to generate continuing interest in the "center stage." Instead, the greatest amount of attention goes to the sideshows on the periphery of Olson's big tent. Theological discussions that hardly qualify as issues of critical concern for evangelicals often receive the most attention, the most press, and the most energy.

Evangelical theologians from across the theological spectrum, both left and right, deserve blame for the current situation. The de-emphasis on the doctrine of salvation and its supporting doctrines has produced an environment among evangelicals that has generated more sentimentality than discernment and more pundits than theologians. As a result, evangelicalism excels in those topics that Luther would warn go beyond the proper subject of theology. On the leftward side of evangelicalism, the revision of the traditional doctrines of God and humanity have fostered a very different understanding of salvation than the one that has served the Church so well since the Protestant Reformation. On the right, the concern for specificity has led in some cases, whether intentional or not, to unhealthy forms of dogmatism and legalism that may obscure the grandeur of the grace of God in salvation. I do not intend to say that evangelicals cannot spend their time profitably in cultural critique or in detailed and complex theological formulation. However, we must continually examine our work to insure that positive doctrinal work with regard to redemptive history characterizes our approach to theological method.

The "Risky" Theology of the Openness of God Movement

As I have indicated, evangelicalism currently suffers on two fronts with regard to the doctrine of salvation. On the first, the battle is waged at the level of doctrinal definition regarding the doctrines of God and humanity. Leading the charge, as this book has detailed, are the proponents of the Openness of God agenda, including figures such as Clark Pinnock, John Sanders, Richard Rice, and David Basinger. Although we need not rehearse the architecture of thought employed by the Openness of God movement, there is no doubt that the "Evangelical Megashift" envisioned by Robert Brow in *Christianity Today* in 1990 has now achieved partial establishment status in many evangelical seminaries, periodicals, and publishing houses.[7] The seminal doctrinal work of Clark Pinnock in the last decade has inspired a legion of followers in the evangelical scholarly community. To their credit, and to the dismay of their opponents, the adherents of this theology of a limited God have developed their thesis in the form of major books and articles and have popularized their understanding of "creative love theism."[8]

The clearest recent example of the continued growth of the limited God hypothesis comes in the form of John Sanders's significant theology of providence, *The God Who Risks*. One of the original authors of the Openness of God movement, Sanders has produced a thoughtful and substantive volume detailing the features of a doctrine of providence in light of a God who is a contingent being. As the title of the work indicates, Sanders holds that God takes risks in his relations with the world. Unable unilaterally to effect his will, Sanders's God is "conditioned by his creatures."[9] Because God restricts himself in such a way that he can "take risks," Sanders argues that some events in the history of human affairs "go contrary to what God intends and may not turn out completely as God desires."[10] As a result, God manages the universe to the best of his abilities but finds himself thwarted and frustrated by human stubbornness and self-will. In this picture, God's relationship to human beings often resembles that of a forlorn lover whose advances are spurned by a capricious love interest. "Consequently," Sanders argues, "love is precarious, because the intentions of the lover may not be satisfied. Love may be received properly or may be rejected entirely."[11]

Not accidentally, therefore, Sanders compares the biblical picture of God as king to our use of *king* in popular culture. Sanders writes, "When we assert that Elvis is the king of rock 'n' roll, we make a comparison between kingship and Elvis's relation to other rock 'n' roll singers. When we assert that God is the king of the earth, we also make a comparison between kingship and God's relation to the world."[12] Like many other modern theologians, Sanders avers that biblical imagery functions metaphorically, not literally. On this account, when we say that God is king, we do not mean that God *actually* rules over and controls the world in a determinate and sovereign sense. Sanders contends that God exercises kingship only relatively speaking. Evidently for Sanders, God, like Elvis, is simply the greatest king among lesser kings. In other words, God exists as king by comparison. God has no equal. But his kingly rule does not, and cannot, always have its way in the affairs of other sovereign kingdoms—the kingdom of the individual human will.

Sanders's understanding of God's sovereignty contrasts *de jure* with *de facto* sovereignty. While God may be sovereign by right (*de jure*), God is not in actual fact (*de facto*) sovereign over the affairs of the world. Increasing numbers of professed evangelicals embrace this distinction. As Stanley J. Grenz recently observed, "Applied to God, we may say that at every moment God is completely sovereign *de jure* but not necessarily *de facto*." Grenz concludes, "Insofar as we are not what God intends for us to be nor do what God intends that we do, God is not now *de facto* sovereign."[13] Put differently, according to this outlook, God is sovereign in theory, but not in practice.

By necessity, this limitation of God's sovereignty significantly alters the doctrine of salvation. In Sanders's theology of risk, God limits his power with regard to the rule of his creatures. Subsequently, Sanders reconceptualizes the meaning and scope of salvation. First, Sanders ameliorates the biblical picture of the wrath of God in order to present sin not so much as the willful and depraved violation of God's perfect law, but in relational terms as estrangement. Sanders argues, "I understand sin to primarily be alienation, or a broken relationship, rather than a state of being or guilt."[14] Sanders argues that the problem human beings face in their relationship to God does not stem from a guilty status and the ruinous effects of a life lived in rebellion against a holy and good God.[15] In place of the model offered by historic theological orthodoxy, Sanders proposes that sin refers to God's lack of ability to trust us. We are "out of sorts" with God. Because of the mistrust between God and human beings, Jesus stepped forward, placed his trust in God, and put an end to the "cold war" between God and his creation.

For Sanders, the atonement amounts to Jesus' proving to us that we can trust God again. Jesus "suffers for us in order to restore us to a trusting relationship with God. . . . He trusts the Father—despite the agony and uncertainty—obediently doing what he and the Father had agreed on."[16] Sanders continues, "Who will trust in God? Jesus will! Jesus shows that we can trust the Father even unto death. Jesus' filial relationship with the Father gave him the confidence to follow through with his mission."[17] By offering this model, Sanders merely updates the moral example theory of the Atonement.

Reminding ourselves of Luther's thesis stated earlier, Sanders's "theology of risk" violates both of the fundamental axioms of the doctrine of salvation. First, Sanders denies that human beings by nature are in fact guilty and ruined sinners. Sanders clearly advocates that the sinner's obstacle is not guilt or depravity but a lack of trust. Such an understanding shows a thorough optimism about the human dilemma. But such a position clearly denies the biblical picture of the desperate nature of men and women apart from the work of God through Christ. Scripture does not shrink from the proposition that a violation of God's Law results in a guilty or condemned status. The book of Leviticus clearly indicates that any violation of the Law, whether intentional or unintentional, eventuates in a guilty verdict from God himself. In the book of Romans, after Paul paints the fatal portrait of the human condition in 3:9-18, no questions remain regarding our standing before God. "Now we know that whatever the law says, it says to those who are under the law, so that every mouth may be stopped, and all the world may become guilty before God" (Romans 3:19, NKJV). As Paul says elsewhere, all those outside of Christ are "objects of wrath" (Eph. 2:3). Contrary to Sanders's hopeful reinterpretation, guilt remains the human problem before a holy

God. God's act in Christ through the cross is not so much an attempt to get alienated humans to trust God again, but a sovereign, certain, salvific accomplishment by God on behalf of sinners. Only this standpoint coincides with the biblical doctrine of salvation.

Potential Dangers from Certain Sectors of Reformed Evangelicalism

Earlier I mentioned two fronts on which battles surrounding the doctrine of salvation are currently being fought. On the second of these fronts are skirmishes from within the camp of classical theological orthodoxy, particularly in the Reformed tradition. The current problem stems from some theologians in the Calvinist tradition who want to ensure that a great deal of specificity is included in even a basic articulation of the doctrine of salvation. They feel that evangelicalism has grown so broad that only a return to a precise understanding of Reformed theology will remedy evangelicalism's ills. In a recent address Michael Horton stated:

> If we are really convinced of the justice in the Reformation's critique of medieval Rome, we can no longer . . . regard Arminianism within Protestant circles as any more acceptable. It is not only Rome, but the Wesleyan system, especially as it is mediated through Charles Finney, Pentecostalism, and the revivalist tradition, that must be rejected to the extent that each fails to sufficiently honor God's grace.[18]

Although many Reformed theologians agree with Horton's imprecations concerning the doctrinal excesses of certain strains of the Wesleyan tradition, other adherents of Reformation theology have cautioned against the temptation to equate all of the particularities of the Reformed doctrines of grace with an affirmation of the basic gospel message. In a response to the "Cambridge Declaration" (a document drafted by a group of evangelicals), Timothy George offered the following warning about potential problems with the spirit of the document:

> The Cambridge Declaration does a good job of affirming the essentials of Reformation theology, but its critique of several

contemporary ideas and trends is imbalanced, too broad-brushed, and at points, seemingly more exclusionary than enlightening. A more judicious and more precise statement reflecting the considered wisdom of classic theological manifestos in the past would better serve the cause of theological renewal today. Most of those who attended the . . . meeting in Cambridge were from conservative Presbyterian denominations, along with a sprinkling of Baptists, Lutherans, and other assorted evangelicals. Members of the Wesleyan, Anabaptist, and Pentecostal wings of the evangelical family were conspicuous by their absence.[19]

George continues:

It is proper for those of us who are Reformed evangelicals to declare allegiance to the doctrines of grace set forth in Augustinian theology and the great Reformation confessions. However, many of the issues addressed in the Cambridge Declaration concern other evangelicals, too: the evaporation of scriptural normativity, the loss of God-centered worship, and compromise over the sole sufficiency of Jesus Christ as the only way of salvation to all peoples everywhere. We should not draw the evangelical circle too tightly lest, like Jesus' cliquish disciples we exclude those who are earnestly doing the Lord's work because they "are not one of us."[20]

George emphasizes an important point. Although Reformed evangelicals need not shrink from their contention that the leading features of Reformed theology offer the most complete understanding of the biblical witness, they must avoid the temptation of theological hubris and of excluding true brothers and sisters in Christ. Often advocates of Reformed theology may unintentionally offend others with whom they disagree by implying that Reformed thinking alone offers solutions to the problems faced by the evangelical church today. For example, in a recent editorial on the current state of evangelicalism, Douglas Wilson, an articulate voice among Reformed evangelicals today, lamented the "looming death of a noble movement." Reflecting on what he sees as the inevitable demise of evangelicalism as an interdenominational witness to the Gospel, Wilson wrote, "Can nothing be done [to save evangelicalism]? The history of the church indicates not. However, this history also shows us that those who survive the demise of this movement will have to land somewhere. And their only real choice is between those who will be former evangelicals, and those who will be Reformed evangelicals."[21]

Is Wilson's assertion correct? Must evangelicalism inevitably gravitate to either a thoroughgoing Reformed theology or unmitigated theological oblivion? Probably not. Certainly we need not deny that modern evangelicalism faces the genuine threat of theological compromise in order to affirm that the Gospel may be truly embraced by those who do not assent completely to all of the canons of Dort.

The great temptation for those of us who affirm Reformed theology is to assume that one does not believe "the Gospel" until he or she is able to articulate the particularities of the exact nature of imputation or the precise extent of the Atonement. But as Mark Dever, pastor of Capitol Hill Baptist Church in Washington, D.C., has wisely noted, "It should be my earnest desire to see everyone in my charge in heaven, not in Geneva."[22] This spirit must characterize all of our reflections on the doctrine of salvation in the new century. When dealing with our brothers and sisters in Christ with whom we passionately disagree, we must exhibit a spirit of grace. As Jonathan Edwards reminded us, one's practice may not always square with one's articulation of doctrine. In his "Discourse on Justification by Faith Alone," Edwards concluded his thoughts by reflecting on how much disparity there may be between one's theological understanding and one's piety. Edwards queried:

> How far a wonderful and mysterious agency of God's Spirit may so influence some men's hearts, that their practice in this regard [belief in justification by faith alone] may be contrary to their own principles, so that they shall not trust in their own righteousness, though they profess that men are justified by their own righteousness—or how far they may believe the doctrine of justification by men's own righteousness in general, and yet not believe it in a particular application of it to themselves—or how far that error which they may have been led

into by education, or cunning sophistry or others, may yet be contrary to the prevailing disposition of their hearts, and contrary to their practice—or how far some may seem to maintain a doctrine contrary to this gospel doctrine of justification, that really do not, but only express themselves differently from others; or seem to oppose it through their misunderstanding of our expressions, or we of theirs, when indeed our real sentiments are the same in the main—or may seem to differ more than they do, by using terms that are without a precisely fixed and determinate meaning—or to be wide in their sentiments from this doctrine, for want of a distinct understanding of it; whose hearts, at the same time, entirely agree with it, and if once it was clearly explained to their understandings, would immediately close with it, and embrace it:—how far these things may be, I will not determine; but am fully persuaded that great allowances are to be made on these and such like accounts, in innumerable instances; though it is manifest from what has been said, that the teaching and propagating contrary doctrines and schemes, is of a pernicious and fatal tendency.[23]

Edwards's statement wisely navigates through the dangerous sea of polemical theology. On the one hand Edwards affirms that a gracious spirit should mark the theologian. One may simultaneously demonstrate bad theology but good piety. On the other hand, Edwards stands firm on the necessity of theological precision and the deleterious effects of persistent and recalcitrant theological error. We must avoid the temptation, Edwards contends, to say nothing convictional at all. After all, the passage cited from Edwards above followed a vigorous and passionate defense of the doctrine of justification by faith alone. Edwards never once wavers on the importance of truth and contending earnestly for the faith once for all delivered to the saints. But Edwards cautions us to err on the side of grace and encourages us that "great allowances are to be made on these and such like accounts, in innumerable instances."[24]

The encouraging news is that more recently some Reformed Christians have demonstrated rhetorical sensitivity to other evangelicals with whom they disagree. Thus they combine theological conviction and polemical wisdom. In a recent edition of *modern*

Reformation magazine Michael Horton observes that all theological argumentation should have as its aim the unity of the Church, though without compromising the truth. Horton writes:

> It was Jesus' prayer (in John 17), after all, that his body would be one. He came to divide us from the world, but to unite us to himself—and he is not divided. But as soon as we ask the next questions—So who is Jesus? What did he accomplish?—we find those claiming to be his followers beginning to divide. So how can we seek unity without sacrificing truth? We must recall that creeds and confessions, though they do indeed aim to distinguish orthodoxy from heterodoxy, also aim to boldly proclaim the truth around which God's people can unite. The *shema*, or confession of faith, of Deut. 6 ("Hear, O Israel: The LORD our God is one LORD") was a rallying cry by which the monotheistic Jews distinguished themselves from the nations. There was unity in this truth.[25]

Evangelicals should constantly monitor themselves to ensure that their elenctic theology stems from both proper conviction and piety. Certainly we must vigorously defend those propositions that stand at the heart of the Christian truth-claim and Gospel. But we must also guard against an undue harshness toward other brothers and sisters in Christ. Evangelicalism needs to embark upon a new era of irenic polemics in which its theologians emphasize points of agreement and contend for points of disagreement convictionally *and* judiciously. We would do well to remind ourselves, as J. I. Packer stated in his introduction to Owen's *Death of Death*, that

> Calvinism in itself is essentially expository, pastoral, and constructive. It can define its position in terms of Scripture without any reference to Arminianism, and it does not need to forever be fighting real or imaginary Arminians in order to keep itself alive. Calvinism has no interest in negatives, as such; when Calvinists fight, they fight for positive evangelical values.[26]

Where error arises, we ought to rebuke it expositorily, pastorally, and constructively. Our motto should be that of Herman Witsius, the great Dutch Reformed pastor of the seventeenth century: "Unanimity in things necessary; liberty in things not necessary; in all things prudence and charity."[27]

THE PROPER SUBJECT OF THEOLOGY:
A FUTURE FOR THE DOCTRINE OF SALVATION

I return once again to my thesis statement borrowed from Luther: "The proper subject of theology is man the guilty and ruined sinner and God the justifier and savior of sinful men. Whatever is sought or debated beyond this subject in theology is error and poison."[28] Luther's words remind us that evangelicals must never waver on the cardinal doctrines that form a biblical understanding of the Gospel. First of all, we cannot compromise the biblical doctrine of God who is sovereign and omnipotent, the one who is just and yet the one who justifies sinners by giving them new hearts, by giving them faith, thereby making them alive in Christ. As Carl F. H. Henry reminded us earlier in this volume, we serve the majestic "living God of the Bible." This is not the embattled God of much recent crisis-oriented theology, but rather the almighty Lord God "who works out everything in conformity with the purpose of his will" (Eph. 1:11).

We affirm that God in every way acts as the "justifier and savior of sinful men." For evangelicals, this requires a rigorous adherence to the doctrine of justification by faith alone. We confess that salvation, from beginning to end, is the work of God alone on behalf of a radically sinful and rebellious humanity. For the affirmation of the doctrine of justification by faith, we must also assert the doctrine of God, which supports the grandeur of justification. God is the one who, by the power of his will, acts unilaterally on the dead and unaffected human being and gives him or her a living heart (Jer. 31:33). The overwhelming picture of God then, throughout Scripture, is a remarkably consistent one of the person and work of God toward sinners. D. A. Carson describes it this way: "The ways of speaking about God in the Bible are extraordinarily diverse. What is striking about them, from the perspective of reflection upon salvation, is how almost every one of these ways of talking about God brings with it an

obverse description of human beings that exposes our lostness."[29]
The biblical portrait of salvation, then, centers around an antithesis
between the greatness of God and the desperate condition of
humanity.

In the future, evangelicals must continue to present the biblical
picture of the antithesis between humanity and God. This antithesis
provides a faithful representation of the doctrine of salvation. The con-
comitant affirmation of the confession of a biblical view of God and
humanity is the unashamed assertion that Christianity stands as the
only hope of salvation for the world in the new millennium. As Alister
McGrath warns:

> We must challenge the lazy assumption, common to the super-
> ficial discussion of such issues that has become characteristic
> of Western liberalism, that "all religions are the same" and the
> conclusion drawn from this—that all religions are saying more
> or less the same thing. Evangelicals must insist that the *unique-
> ness* of the Christian conception of the basis, nature and mode
> of procurement of salvation be recognized as a matter of
> integrity.[30]

To this I would add the implication of the *finality* of the Christian
revelational truth-claim in Jesus Christ that confesses that "salvation
is found in no one else, for there is no other name under heaven given
to men by which we must be saved" (Acts 4:12).

In sum, evangelicals must maintain those theological commitments that make them evangelicals. We must join ourselves to the
overwhelming consensus of our predecessors in the faith. With
respect to the doctrine of salvation, we must pursue a positive course
of doctrinal assertion that posits the "proper subject of theology," as
Luther so wisely put it. Heeding the warning of the author of Hebrews,
we cannot "ignore such a great salvation" (2:3). And finally, we must
declare the wonder of the God of our salvation as so beautifully
described in the hymn written by John Newton:

> *Great God of wonders! All Thy ways*
> *are matchless, God-like, and divine;*

But the fair glories of Thy grace more
God-like and unrivaled shine,
More God-like and unrivaled shine.
Who is a pard'ning God like Thee?
Or who has grace so rich and free?

In wonder lost, with trembling joy,
we take the pardon of our God;
Pardon for crimes of deepest dye, a
pardon bought with Jesus' blood,
A pardon bought with Jesus' blood.
Who is a pard'ning God like Thee?
Or who has grace so rich and free?

O may this strange, this matchless grace,
this God-like miracle of love
Fill the whole earth with grateful praise,
and all the angelic choirs above.
Who is a pard'ning God like Thee?
Or who has grace so rich and free?
Or who has grace so rich and free?[31]

CHAPTER 11

1. Martin Luther, *Werke*. Kritische Gesamtausgabe ("Weimarer Ausgabe") (Weimar: Bohlau, 1883), 40/2, 328: "*Nam Theologiae proprium subjectum est homo peccati reus ac perditus et Deus iustificans ac salvator hominis peccatoris. Quicquid extra hoc subjectum in Theologia quaeritur aut disputatur, est error et venenum.*" A word of thanks is due to Mark Seifrid for directing me to this passage in Luther.

2. David F. Wells, *God in the Wasteland* (Grand Rapids, Mich.: Eerdmans, 1994), 25.

3. Gary Dorrien, *The Remaking of Evangelical Theology* (Louisville: Westminster/John Knox Press, 1998), 8.

4. Roger Olson, "The Future of Evangelical Theology," *Christianity Today*, February 9, 1998, 40.

5. Ibid. Olson characterizes the heart of evangelical theology in this way:

I believe that evangelicalism does indeed exist, though what holds it together is sometimes hard to discern (much like the work of the Holy Spirit who animates the movement). I want to argue that evangelicalism is primarily a theological movement that has the following four minimum characteristics:
—It looks to the Bible as the supreme norm of truth for Christian belief and practice— the biblical message enshrined in its narratives and its interpretations of those narratives;
—It holds a supernatural world-view that is centered in a transcendent, personal God who interacts with, and intervenes in, creation;
—It focuses on the forgiving and transforming grace of God through Jesus Christ in the experience called conversion as the center of authentic Christian experience;

—And it believes that the primary task of Christian theology is to serve the church's mission of bringing God's grace to the whole world through proclamation and service.

6. Ibid.

7. Robert Brow, "The Evangelical Megashift," *Christianity Today*, February 19, 1990.

8. For more detail regarding the proposal of "creative love theism," see R. Albert Mohler, Jr.'s chapter (Chapter 2, "The Eclipse of God at Century's End) in this book.

9. John Sanders, *The God Who Risks: A Theology of Providence* (Downers Grove, Ill.: InterVarsity Press, 1998), 10.

10. Ibid., 11.

11. Ibid., 177.

12. Ibid., 15.

13. Stanley J. Grenz, *Theology for the Community of God* (Nashville: Broadman & Holman, 1994), 142.

14. Sanders, *The God Who Risks*, 105.

15. With respect to sin, Sanders follows closely the "family" or relational model offered by Robert Brow and Clark Pinnock in *Unbounded Love* (Downers Grove, Ill.: InterVarsity Press, 1991).

16. Sanders, *The God Who Risks*, 105.

17. Ibid.

18. Michael Horton, quoted in Joe Maxwell, "God and Man at Cambridge," *World*, May 11-18, 1996; database on-line (http://www.worldmag.com/world/issue/05-11-96/cover_1.asp).

19. Timothy George, "Promoting Renewal, Not Tribalism," *Christianity Today*, June 17, 1996, 14.

20. Ibid.

21. Douglas Wilson, "Requiem for Modern Evangelicalism," *Credenda Agenda* 8, No. 1, 10.

22. Mark Dever, "The Synod of Dort in History," The Southern Baptist Founder's Conference, 1996, cassette.

23. Jonathan Edwards, *The Works of Jonathan Edwards*, Vol. 1, ed. Edward Hickman (reprint, Edinburgh: The Banner of Truth Trust, 1995), 654.

24. Ibid.

25. Michael Horton, "In This Issue," *modern Reformation* 7, No. 8, 2. Horton goes on to develop this theme in a full-length article in the same issue entitled, "What Are the Prospects for the Greater Unity of the Body of Christ in Our Time?"

26. J. I. Packer, *A Quest for Godliness* (Wheaton, Ill.: Crossway Books, 1990), 129.

27. Michael W. Honeycutt, "Introduction," in *Witsius on the Character of a True Theologian*, ed. J. Ligon Duncan III (Greenville, S.C.: Reformed Academic Press, 1994), 14.

28. Luther, WA 40/2, 328.

29. D. A. Carson, "Reflections on Salvation and Justification in the New Testament," *Journal of the Evangelical Theological Society* 40, No. 4 (December 1997), 584.

30. Alister McGrath, "New Dimensions in Salvation," in *New Dimensions in Evangelical Theology*, ed. David S. Dockery (Downers Grove, Ill.: InterVarsity Press, 1998), 329.

31. John Newton, "Great God of Wonders," in *Psalms, Hymns, and Spiritual Songs* (Cape Coral, Fla.: Founders Press, 1994).

AFTERWORD

The Need for Vigilance and Vision

PAUL R. HOUSE

Books always take some time to come to press. This fact of publishing life is especially true of a collection of essays such as this one. By the time that these pieces had been written, included in the first two years of *The Southern Baptist Journal of Theology* or penned for this volume, edited, prepared for printing, and placed in readers' hands, three years had elapsed. Thus, it is reasonable to wonder if the issue that led to the book's writing remains important. After all, some perceived problems pass quickly from the scene, never to trouble us again. Sadly, these articles are as needed today as they were three years ago, if not more so. In fact, theological vigilance and theological vision will be needed for some time to come, perhaps until the Lord returns.

THE NEED FOR THEOLOGICAL VIGILANCE

There are at least four reasons why theological vigilance is needed for orthodox views of the doctrines of God and salvation to flourish in the contemporary setting. First, as Don Carson points out in *SBJT* 1/1, there have been attempts to undermine the doctrine of God since the Garden of Eden. The tempter sought to convince Eve not only that God's word was not true, but that God's character was also suspect. He claimed that God simply did not have Eve's best interests at heart. Indeed he argued that the Lord was afraid that Eve would become his equal. From that time on those who deviated and deviate from God's revealed Word have offered revisionist views of God's nature. Thus Christian scholars, pastors, and laypersons must always be alert for unbiblical definitions of God. The newer definitions of the Lord's character simply warn us that we will never reach a time when sound theology will go unchallenged.

Second, the overall Christian scene indicates that unbiblical notions of God and salvation are a growing threat to the church. In the fall of 1999 I began teaching at Trinity Episcopal School for Ministry, the only overtly evangelical seminary associated with the Episcopal Church USA (ECUSA). This new experience has reminded me that while we should be grateful for the evangelical wings of the mainline denominations, these wings are as of yet largely remnant movements within those denominations. In general, the notions that God does not change because he does not need to change and that salvation comes only by grace through explicit, knowing faith in Christ are not majority opinions among many mainline denominational leaders and scholars. Growing numbers of laypersons have adopted their leaders' views. Even where these truths are held, their adherents are forced to fight on so many theological and ethical fronts that exhaustion among the faithful is a real problem.

Without question, some ground has been gained over the past decades. Still, there is no indication that the many varieties of process theology are on the wane, that biblical theology has won the day, that historic creeds and confessions are believed, not just recited, or that evangelism and missions are sufficiently stressed in mainline denominations. Until that time comes, we need to continue to teach and contend for the truths about God and salvation found in Scripture, summarized in the creeds, and lived out by stalwart believers through the ages. Until then we need to continue to act on the theological vision of the best of our evangelical heritage.

Third, there is no evidence that the evangelical movement itself is immune to the erosion of biblical views of God and salvation. Signing an inerrancy statement does not guarantee that one will not find freewill theism or Openness of God theology attractive, even compelling. Proponents of these approaches are neither evil nor secretive. They make their views known, and they are quite often thoughtful, creative speakers and writers. Given the correspondence between their views and parts of the prevailing culture, the prickly style of many traditional theologians, and the perception that traditional theories do not deal adequately with such subjects as evil and suffering, many hearers and readers are convinced by their arguments.

College and seminary students are particularly good candidates to become new adherents of these positions, for they have been raised in a culture that affirms unbounded openness, tolerance, and acceptance of all apparently reasonable ideas regardless of their adherence to traditional beliefs. The same could be said for laypersons with low levels of theological expertise. Therefore, it is vital that Christian colleges integrate the faith once delivered to the saints into all academic disciplines. It is important for evangelical seminaries to address the new views of the nature of God and salvation. Pastors must be more willing to engage the current culture and nontraditional scholars' opinions. Otherwise, we can logically expect the culture's views on these matters or those of individuals who are orthodox on all matters but these to win the day.

Fourth, the need for world evangelization has not abated, and the opinions this volume opposes remain hindrances to that enterprise. On the one hand, those who offer new ways of conceiving of God are right to stress the need to avoid alienating adherents of other religions. They are also correct to caution evangelicals against arrogance. On the other hand, it is possible to be irenic and humble, yet remain traditionally orthodox in one's views of God and salvation.

What the church needs now is an infusion of new missionaries who are theologically orthodox, knowledgeable about the beliefs of non-Christian people, committed to serving Christ regardless of personal cost, flexible in their approach to the missions task, and able to work effectively with all evangelical missionaries. It is impossible for such a cadre of ministers to rally around the notion of God's limited omniscience or the possibility of salvation in other religions. Why? Not just because such beliefs are unfamiliar to many evangelicals, but because they are quite simply impossible to square with biblical theology. The future of evangelical missions lies in obedience to the risen Christ's great commission, not in adapting evangelical theology to current non-evangelical theology.

SUGGESTIONS FOR THEOLOGICAL VISION

As Gregory A. Thornbury's article in this volume indicates, it is not enough simply to critique process theology, universalism, freewill theism, or Openness of God approaches. Orthodox evangelicals must address the issues that caused thoughtful proponents of the ideas this volume critiques to write in the first place. We have not solved the problems associated with world evangelization, evil and suffering, God's character, or human responsibility by disagreeing with others. We must be more creative, more pastoral, more insightful, more diligent, and more scholarly. We must find appropriate ways to relate the truth about God and salvation to today's world.

How will these goals be reached? Certain things are clearly needed. First, a new emphasis on unitary biblical theology must emerge if novel ideas about God are to be refuted. The whole of Scripture must be consulted in any discussion of the doctrine of God, or the result will be a truncated version of the living God of the Bible. Evangelicals' lack of facility in Old Testament theology is especially noticeable in this regard, which is unfortunate, since it is no easier to formulate a thorough doctrine of God from the Old Testament alone than it is to arrive at a thorough doctrine of Christ solely from the New Testament.

Second, there must be more significant cooperative interaction between biblical theologians and systematic theologians. In the current academic situation it is impossible for one scholar to keep pace with all the literature in one field, much less in two or more. Thus collaborative efforts should become a mainstay in theological research. There are several potential positive results of such projects, but I will mention just two. Biblical theology can help fill in gaps in systematic treatments of such subjects as creation, the nature of God the Father, and the nature of Scripture. Similarly, systematic theology can help biblical theology grasp the wholeness of revelation. It can aid in the effort to state how the canon reflects the unity of the God who inspired it.

Third, pastoral theology must integrate theology, ethics, and evangelism, not simply adopt the latest methods drawn from secular models. The early church was most useful when it preached the meaning of Christ through the lens of the whole of Scripture. It was most powerful when it maintained integrity with God and other human beings. It was most evangelistic when it understood that adherents of other religions, whether Jewish or Greek or Roman, faced eternal judgment without Christ.

Clearly, the early church did not keep theology, ethics, pastoral care, or evangelism separate. Rather, they offered a balanced ministry to a hurting world. They did not seek ways to conceive of how the world might be able to reach heaven without a specific, self-conscious commitment to Jesus Christ. Instead, they preached the risen Lord as the one who could reconcile them to God. They did not simply use the most up-to-date marketing techniques. No, they lived the Gospel, shared the Gospel, and carried the Gospel, always with a willingness to suffer for the Gospel.

Fourth, laypersons must become better informed on theological issues and more willing to think and act for Jesus' sake. Today's theological battles are not simply played out in ivory towers and in university presses. They are borne on Internet wings to the ends of the earth. They are advocated as often on television as they are in liberal churches. Thus, it is time to call laypersons to active Christian thinking. Gratefully, there are faithful churches, Christian colleges, evangelical presses, and parachurch groups trying to answer this call. Indeed, some of them were sounding and answering this call long before I was born! Still, they need reinforcement. They need help to keep the body of Christ from ceasing to matter long before it ceases to exist.

CONCLUSION

Sometimes students or laypeople ask me if I am optimistic about the future of the church. Of course, I am optimistic because I believe Christ will come again to judge the living and the dead. I am optimistic because of God's great promises. I am also optimistic when I see remnant believers and remnant groups standing for the Lord. The battle is not over yet, and there are many who have not quit. These facts do not lessen the terrible challenges we face, but they do help on dark days when the church seems to take a terrific pounding.

Beyond these basic reassurances, at least one other trend heartens me. That is the tremendous growth in worldwide Christianity. For example, I am told that in Nigeria there are sixteen million Anglicans, which is more than in England, Canada, and the United States combined. Churches of various denominations in Singapore, China, and other parts of Asia are flourishing, often despite persecution. The same could be said of churches in other places. Not surprisingly, most of these growing fellowships are orthodox in their theology. They are certain that God is inherently perfect, fully omniscient, wonderfully omnipotent, and greater than our understanding. They preach Christ crucified as the only means of freedom from religious bondage of all sorts.

And they are growing weary of western liberalism. The day is swiftly coming when they will call the West into account. Stated bluntly, the day may be approaching when they will graciously save us from ourselves. Just as westerners once brought the Gospel to their lands, so they will soon insist that westerners confess the truths we once proclaimed boldly to them. This prospect should humble us but should also be welcomed by evangelicals, who of all people should love the truth more than national pride.

So I am optimistic about what the future *may* hold. As the future unfolds, I pray that scholars, pastors, and laypersons will step forward with theological and evangelistic vigor. I hope that we will never doubt the power of the Gospel stated in evangelical and orthodox terms to convince minds and transform hearts. I believe this can be a new moment for expressing the truth accurately and attractively even as we refuse to depart from old doctrinal paths. In other words, I think theological vigilance and theological vision can lead to church renewal.

SCRIPTURE INDEX

Genesis

1:26	20, 23
2:7	20, 23
8:21	33
9:6	32
14:17-24	113
18:25	99
20:1-18	114

Exodus

3:14	20
8:10	19
15:11	19, 29
18:1-12	114
18:11	29
20:2ff.	21
20:3	27
20:3-5	24
20:4	32
32:32	37

Leviticus

1:1—27:34	215 (whole book)

Numbers

23—24	114
23:19	16
27:16	37

Deuteronomy

4:19	34
4:23ff.	24
4:35	19, 21
5:7	27
5:7-9	24
6	220
6:13-15	24
7:9	21
29:19	33
30:15-20	37
32:12	24
32:39	37
32:46-47	37

1 Samuel

12:21	24

1 Kings

18:21	21, 27
18:37	21

2 Kings

18:33ff.	29, 30
19:15	19
19:16	19

1 Chronicles

17:20	19
29:18	33

Job

2:10	19
12:10	37

Psalms

14:1	19
23:4, 6	38
31:6	24
36:9	20
53:2	19
69:28	37
72:18ff.	29
73:23ff.	38
82:1	26
86:8	19, 29
89:8	19
90	16
93:3	29
96:4	29
102:25ff.	23
106:19ff.	30

Proverbs

6:18	33
8:22-31	67-68

Isaiah

4:3	37
6	95
6:3	24
9:6	183
44:6	29
44:8	29

44:9-20	30
45:18-23	21
52:13—53:12	65

Jeremiah

2:11	24
2:13	20
2:19	30
2:24	30
5:7	24
5:12	19
10:2	34
10:14	19, 24
16:19	24
16:19ff.	29, 30
17:13	20
23:17	33
31:33	221

Ezekiel

8:16ff.	34
17:16	19
33:11	19

Daniel

11:36	26

Malachi

2:10	26
3:16	37

Matthew

1:23	71
2:1-12	114
4:4	23
5:13-16	71
6:24	37
8:22	38
10:28	102
24:14	104
25:37	123
25:46	96
28:19	206
28:19-20	187

Mark

1:27	38
10:18	40

Luke

1:51	33
6:36	40
12:15	23
12:19	37
12:20	37
15:24	38
16:26	96

John

1:1-4	67
1:1-18	62, 72
1:3	20
1:5	126
1:9	123-124
1:14	63, 64, 65
1:18	63, 68
2:13-22	189
3:16	23, 40, 63, 151
3:16-17	151
3:16-18	175
3:18	63, 99-100, 147
3:33	40
3:36	40, 175
4:7	189
5:24	151
5:24-25	38
5:26	19, 20
6	189
6:37	176
8:32	177
11:25ff.	38
12:32	90
13:3-17	65
14:5-6	151
14:6	16, 20, 123, 147, 151, 152
15:26	37
16:4-9ff.	37
17	220
17:11	40
17:25	40

Acts

3:15	20
3:21	91
4:12	16, 72, 81, 100, 147, 149, 222
4:19	37

5:29	37	9:3	93
7:40ff.	36	9:4-6	156
10	113	9:13-24	159-160
14	113	9:30-33	157
14:15	19	10:9	60
15	121, 181	10:13-15	104
15:28-29	182, 191	10:18	155
17	113	11:1	157
17:27	124	11	93
		11:5-7	157

Romans

		11:12	155
1	130, 141	11:15	155
1—3	147	11:17-24	157
1—4	155	11:20	157
1:8	155	11:23	157
1:16-17	157	11:25-36	156
1:16—5:11	155	11:33-36	157
1:18	171	12	69
1:18—2:12	154	12:2	155
1:21	34	12:17-18	155
1:21ff.	31	14:2	155
1:22	32	16:19	155
1:23	37	16:27	40
1:25	37, 154		

1 Corinthians

1:28-32	154		
2:7	124	1:8	174
2:15	124	1:21	31
3:9	169	4:9	155
3:9-18	215	6:2	155
3:10-12	169	6:9-10	154
3:19	215	6:12-20	154
3:26	171	7:31	155
5:1	175	7:33	155
5	93	8:4	36, 154
5:12	155, 169	8:4ff.	30
5:12-14	155	8:5	30
5:15	155	8:5-6	154
5:15-18	154	8:6	31
5:17	155	9:22	192
5:18	154, 155, 169	10:7	36
5:19	169	10:14-22	154
8:21-25	154	10:18-22	31
8:28	40	10:19	36
8:29-30	171	10:19ff.	30
8:29ff.	40	11:1	67
8:32	155	12	69
8:38-39	29	12:2	154
9—11	156, 157	12:3	59
9:2-3	156	12:10	37

15:26-28	91
15:56	38
16:22	154

2 Corinthians

1:19	37
4:4	155
5	93
5:10	96
5:14-21	157
5:19	90, 94, 154
5:20	94
6:9	39
6:16	37
11:14	148

Galatians

1:4	155
1:8	148
1:8-9	192
4:8	37, 154
4:8ff.	37
6:7	96
6:7-8	154
6:14	155

Ephesians

1:3	176
1:4	174
1:6	173
1:7	174
1:10	91
1:11	221
1:12	173
1:13	176
1:14	173
1:18	172
1:19-20	171
2:1	38, 168
2:1-3	167
2:1-10	167-177
2:2	37, 155
2:3	169, 171, 215
2:4	170
2:4-7	168, 170
2:5	171, 172, 174
2:5ff.	39
2:6	171
2:6-7	176

2:7	172
2:8-10	174
2:9	176
2:9-11	168
2:10	176
2:11	169
2:12	154
2:13	174
4	69
6:12	155

Philippians

1:21	20
1:23	38
2	67
2:2	65
2:3	65, 66
2:4	65
2:5	65
2:6	65, 66
2:6-11	65-67, 72
2:7	66
2:9	67
2:9-11	67, 91, 154
2:11	59
3:18-19	154
3:19	37

Colossians

1:6	155
1:13	68
1:15-17	68
1:15-20	67-69, 72
1:16ff.	31
1:18-20	68
1:21-23	68
2:8	154, 155
2:13	38
2:15	154
3:4	20

1 Timothy

1:15	155
1:17	40
2:4	90, 171
4:10	61, 154
6:7	155
6:12	38
6:16	40

6:19   38

2 Timothy

4:10   155

1 Thessalonians

1:9   37, 154
4:5   154

2 Thessalonians

1:8-9   154
2:8-12   154

Hebrews

1:1-3   69-70, 72
1   69
1:2   70
1:2-4   67
1:3   70
2:3   222
2:9   90
9:27   96
11:6   123, 175
13:8   59, 72

James

2:17   176
2:19   26
4:15   37

Titus

2:11   90, 154

1 Peter

3:19   94
4   69

2 Peter

3:9   90

1 John

1:2   20
1:5   40, 139
2:2   90, 151
2:23   152
4:1-3   37
4:2-3   152
4:4-6   37
4:8   40
4:9   63
4:10   151
4:14   61
4:16   40
5:12   147
5:21   36

Jude

3   62
25   40

Revelation

4   95
4—5   152
5   173
5:3   152
5:9   61
13—14   153
14:6   153
14:7   153
16:7   99
19:16   59

NAME INDEX

Adeyemo, Tokunboh, 97
Agbebi, Mojola, 186, 187
Altizer, Thomas J. J., 35
Anselm, 71
Anthanasius, 71
Aristotle, 28
Armstrong, Karen, 45-46
Augustine, 34, 53, 62, 87

Baab, Otto, 32
Barna, George, 61, 85, 198-199, 200, 205
Barrett, C. K., 63
Barth, Karl, 20, 88-89, 90
Basinger, David, 16, 52, 213
Bauckham, Richard, 84, 87-88
Baxter, Richard, 101, 102
Bettis, Joseph, 96
Blue, Ronald, 84
Boer, Henry, 55
Bonhoeffer, Dietrich, 72, 165
Bosch, David, 181
Braaten, Carl, 89, 90
Bromiley, G. W., 89
Brooks, Phillips, 101
Brow, Robert, 51-52, 213
Brown, Harold O. J., 95
Bruce, F. F., 67, 174, 175

Caird, G. B., 34
Calvin, John, 148
Carey, William, 145, 147
Carson, D. A. (Don), 63, 183, 221, 225
Carter, Jimmy, 86
Celsus, 55
Chesterton, G. K., 100
Cicero, 66
Climenhaga, Arthur, 95
Corduan, Winfried, 78
Cox, Harvey, 25

Denck, John, 87
Dever, Mark, 218
Dorrien, Gary, 211
Dunn, James D. G., 59, 64, 66
Duthie, Charles, 92, 93

Edwards, David, 92, 100
Edwards, Jonathan, 100, 120, 218-219
Erickson, Millard, 16, 62, 66, 67
Erigena, John Scotus, 87

Farley, Edward, 46
Farrar, F. (Frederic) W., 87, 148
Ferré, Nels, 88, 91-92
Feuerbach, 30
Finney, Charles, 216
Ford, Leighton, 86
Frederick, Carl, 32
Freud, Sigmund, 45
Fromm, Erich, 31-32
Frostin, Per, 185

Gartner, John, 200
Glasson, T. F., 90, 95
Geivett, Doug, 78
George, Timothy, 216-217
Goethe, Johann Wolfgang von, 72
Gregory of Nyssa, 87
Grenz, Stanley J., 214

Hackett, H. B., 121
Hamilton, Kenneth, 26-29, 32-36
Hankey, Katherine, 179
Hasker, William, 52
Hastings, Adrian, 186
Hawthorne, Gerald, 65
Hendricks, William, 67
Henry, Carl F. H., 15, 65, 221
Heraclitus, 21
Hesselgrave, David, 184

Hick, John, 131, 191
Hodge, Charles, 123
Hoge, Dean R., 163, 206
Horton, Michael, 169, 173, 216, 220
Hunter, James Davison, 51, 85, 97

Janis, Pam, 198
Jenson, Robert, 50
Johnson, Benton, 163, 206
Jones, Herbert, 96

Kane, J. Herbert, 103
Kaiser, Walter C., Jr., 16
Kantzer, Kenneth, 98, 99
Kato, Byang H., 184, 185, 186
Kelley, Dean, 163
Kermode, Frank, 43
Kraft, Charles, 121, 190
Kreeft, Peter, 124
Kuhn, Harold, 96
Kuhn, Karl Georg, 41

Ladd, George Eldon, 15
Lane, William, 69, 70
Larson, David, 200
Law, Robert, 152
Lewis, C. S., 121, 125
Lindsell, Harold, 94
Luidens, Donald A., 163, 206
Luther, Martin, 210, 211, 212, 215,
    221, 222

MacIntyre, Alasdair, 49
Martin, Walter, 96
Marshall, I. Howard, 71
Marx, Karl, 45
Maurice, F. D., 87
Mbiti, John, 185, 186
McGrath, Alister, 16, 72, 120, 222
Melanchthon, Philip, 70
Menninger, Karl, 100
Mohler, R. Albert, Jr., 61
Moo, Douglas, 155
Moyers, Bill, 197-198

Newton, John, 222
Nietzsche, Friedrich, 43, 45

Ogden, Schubert, 22
Olson, Roger, 211-212
Otto, Rudolf, 137
Origen, 55, 86-87, 92

Packer, J. I., 16, 50, 88, 98, 176, 189,
    220
Pannenberg, Wolfhart, 69
Pannikar, Raymond, 149
Pelikan, Jaroslav, 62
Pinnock, Clark, 16, 52-57, 77, 78,
    129, 136, 138, 140-141, 213
Plato, 28
Pusey, E. B., 87

Quell, Gottfried, 26

Rahner, Karl, 149, 150
Ramm, Bernard, 62, 86
Robinson, John A. T., 46, 88, 92, 96
Rice, Richard, 16, 52, 77, 213
Richardson, Don, 125, 188

Sanders, John, 16, 52, 77, 113, 124,
    213-215
Sartre, Jean-Paul, 32
Schaeffer, Francis, 69
Schleiermacher, F. E. D., 87, 98
Shapiro, Joseph P., 200
Shaw, Mark, 186
Shembe, Isaiah, 186
Socrates, 72
Sproul, R. C., 46
Spurgeon, C. H., 102, 172
Stauffer, Ethelbert, 37
Stendahl, Krister, 156, 157
Stott, John R. W., 16, 100, 104, 123,
    124, 175
Strong, A. H., 121
Sundkler, Bengt, 186

Tacelli, Ronald, 124
Thielicke, Helmut, 29-31
Thornbury, Gregory A., 228
Tillich, Paul, 98
Tippet, A. R., 190
Toplady, Augustus M., 101
Torrance, T. F., 97
Tozer, A. W., 46-47
Tract Written by an Atheist, 103

Van Engen, Charles, 190
Vaughn, Curtis, 169, 171
Vitz, Paul C., 31, 32

Wagner, C. Peter, 203, 206
Warfield, B. B., 57, 63-64

Warren, Max, 111
Wells, David, 15, 210
Wesley, 121
Wilson, Douglas, 217-218
Wilson, H. B., 87
Wiseman, Donald J., 34
Witherington, Ben, 67
Witsius, Herman, 220
Wright, Andrea R., 200
Wright, N. T., 70, 84, 91, 93, 95

Zwemer, Samuel, 139